"Dr. Vakharia gives an easy-to-follow explanation of harm reduction and shows that we can do so much more to keep our communities safe and healthy. She defines the concepts, terms, and philosophy of harm reduction in a digestible way – a rare feat for such a complex topic. Weaving in her real-life experience as a product of DARE drug prevention, then a substance use treatment counselor, and, later, a harm reduction provider, the reader witnesses her transformation and is transformed too. Dr. Vakharia shows that there are multiple paths to helping our loved ones; we must be open to the possibilities."

Kassandra Frederique, *Executive Director,*
Drug Policy Alliance, USA

"The best way to protect young people from getting into trouble with drugs, and to save lives and help communities that are already devastated by drugs, is to bridge the gap between ignorance and fear of drugs and their use spiraling out of control. Dr. Sheila Vakharia brings together her own life as a youth in the era of DARE drug education scare tactics, her experience as a counselor in drug treatment, and her mastery of drug policy to clearly argue that harm reduction bridges that gap. In this very readable and intelligent book, she lays out the ways that harm reduction can help individuals, families, and communities be knowledgeable and healthy in our relationship with intoxicating substances."

Jeannie Little, LCSW, *Co-Founder, Harm Reduction*
Therapy Center, USA

"A smart, compassionate and highly readable introduction to a better way of understanding and managing drugs and drug-related problems. Sheila Vakharia has written a one-of-a-kind book that meets the reader where they are and doesn't just leave them there. She brings them to harm reduction."

Maia Szalavitz, New York Times *Contributing Opinion Writer*
and award-winning neuroscience journalist, USA

The Harm Reduction Gap

This long-awaited book teaches how harm reduction can be a safety net for people with substance use disorders that our current addiction treatment rejects, abandons, and leaves behind.

Harm reduction is an approach to helping people who engage in high-risk activities to develop the skills and strategies to keep them and their communities safe. This can include the provision of sterile equipment, low-threshold and low-barrier care, and the acceptance of non-abstinence goals in treatment. In this novel guide, Dr. Vakharia discusses the shortcomings of the dominant "Just Say No" drug prevention messages and abstinence-only treatment approaches, introduces harm reduction strategies and technologies borne from people who use drugs themselves, and suggests various policy options available as alternatives to the current policies that criminalize drugs, drug-using equipment, and the settings in which people use drugs. The final chapter calls on the reader to destigmatize drug use and support efforts to reform our drug policies.

By highlighting the large gap in our current approach to substance use – the harm reduction gap – this book is the first step for those interested in learning more about the limitations of our current approach to drug use and how to support local efforts to ensure people who use drugs and their communities can stay safe.

Sheila P. Vakharia, PhD, MSW, is a nationally recognized harm reduction expert with over 15 years of combined experience in addiction treatment, harm reduction, higher education, research, and drug policy reform. She currently works at the Drug Policy Alliance, a national advocacy organization fighting to end the war on drugs.

The Harm Reduction Gap

Helping Individuals Left Behind by
Conventional Drug Prevention and
Abstinence-only Addiction Treatment

Sheila P. Vakharia

Routledge
Taylor & Francis Group

NEW YORK AND LONDON

Designed cover image: © Matt Schoch

First published 2024
by Routledge
605 Third Avenue, New York, NY 10158

and by Routledge
4 Park Square, Milton Park, Abingdon, Oxon, OX14 4RN

Routledge is an imprint of the Taylor & Francis Group, an informa business

© 2024 Sheila P. Vakharia

The right of Sheila P. Vakharia to be identified as author of this work has been asserted in accordance with sections 77 and 78 of the Copyright, Designs and Patents Act 1988.

ISBN: 978-1-032-29474-2 (hbk)
ISBN: 978-1-032-29473-5 (pbk)
ISBN: 978-1-003-30174-5 (ebk)

DOI: 10.4324/9781003301745

Typeset in Galliard
by SPi Technologies India Pvt Ltd (Straive)

Contents

Acknowledgments

Writing this book was one the most challenging and rewarding experiences of my life. I could not have done it without the loving support and patience of my husband, family, and friends. I am still in awe of the extensive support system that wrapped me in love and care throughout this process. I could never express what you all meant to me.

A special thank you to my husband, Mike, whose unconditional love and support saw me through the ups and downs of the writing process every single day from the very beginning. We did it!

I am so fortunate to have parents who have always believed in me, even when I didn't believe in myself. For as long as I can remember, they told me I would write a book one day. I never thought it was possible. I never knew I wanted it. They did.

Thank you to Dimple, Rajesh, and Asha, for providing me with love, laughs, board games, and good food when I needed a weekend getaway from the city. And a special shout-out to my cat, Nova, who would snuggle into my lap on cold mornings as I grumpily typed away at my laptop and wished I was in my cozy bed.

Thank you to my friends, supporters, and co-conspirators at the Drug Policy Alliance, who inspire me daily. Kassandra Frederique, Dr. Jules Netherland, Stephanie Polito, Aliza Cohen, and Melissa Moore – you made me better, enriched my analysis, and were all integral to this. Thank you. And a very important thank you to Jeffrey Chen, who rescued my laptop from the brink of death on the night I submitted my manuscript!

Thank you to my friend Jeannie Little, whose loving guidance and helpful feedback on early versions of this book encouraged me to bring more of myself and my story into the book. You smartly urged me to "not just show but to tell" my audience what they needed to know. You helped me find my voice and use it. Thank you!

Dr. Lisa Munro and soon-to-be-Dr. Chris Vogel gave me the essential edits and feedback I needed over the 18 months I wrote this book. You made it better. You made ME better.

I am deeply grateful to Dr. Katy Peplin of ThrivePhD, whose writing coaching groups gave me the grounding and community I needed to feel less alone in this process.

Thank you to my talented friend Matt Schoch, who designed my beautiful book cover and figures. Although we said our monthly dinner dates were to "discuss the book cover," most of them gave us an excuse to gossip, chitchat, and bond. And I'm so grateful that we did!

This book would not exist without my Zoom writing buddies, who helped keep me accountable, disciplined, and productive. We wrote together on mornings before work, over the course of entire weekends, and even during the holidays. Seeing your faces on my screen made me feel less alone and inspired me to keep going, even when it was hard. This book could not have happened without you. Thank you to Dr. Heather Lee, Dr. Desirée de Jesus, Dr. Pooneh Sabouri, Dr. Helena Uhde, Dr. Amanda Latimore, soon-to-be Dr. Tracy Pugh, and Dr. Nadja Eisenburg-Gudot for joining me when you could. Most of us did not even know each other before this started. You are all my friends for life now.

A special thank you to Will Godfrey and Dr. Sean Allen for valuable content-specific edits during the drafting process.

Thank you to my friends who have been with me this whole time – Raquella, Becky, James, Sonia, Vidhya, and Tracye. Thanks for the dinners, drinks, texts, calls, laughs, and TikToks. You kept me grounded through the chaos and doubt.

This book would not have been possible without my harm reduction community. Thank you to my mentors, guides, teachers, friends, and peers in this space. You are saving lives every day and making the world a better place. My deepest wish is for this book to help others to see the value and essential value of the work you do every day.

A Note on Language

Welcome, and thank you so much for picking up this book. Before we get started, I would like to talk about some of the language and terminology I will be using in the book.

Words matter. How we use them can reveal our values, priorities, and perspectives. My use of certain language may differ from yours. I encourage you to reflect on how my choices align with yours and the reasons why we may use certain words differently from one another.

Language is so powerful that it can change how we view ourselves and others. It can shift our understanding of current circumstances and possible solutions. In this book, I want to offer an alternative way of looking at the issue of drug use in our communities that does not perpetuate stigma or judgment. My use of words and terms are designed to promote that conceptualization.

Words have weight and carry their own connotations, so they can also mean different things to different people. When reading this book, I encourage you to think about the words I use and what these words mean to you.

There is no clear consensus in the harm reduction movement on terminology, and many of us differ in our preferred use of language and terms. We often use different words to describe both our experiences and the experiences of those we serve, and our preferences can vary. There is also ongoing debate and discussion about language among drug policy reformers, drug researchers, treatment providers, and advocates about how we use terms. We do not all agree on the issue of terminology, and we have different frameworks for using that terminology. This is not unusual.

Language changes. Although I use current terms here in this book today, our language and conceptualizations will undoubtedly shift in the coming years. The terms used in this book are a snapshot of this current moment, but I hope that all of us can be open to removing certain words and terms from our lexicon and introducing new ones as our understandings change and evolve.

I use the word *drug* to mean a mood-altering substance. For the purposes of this book, it includes those that are currently legally regulated for adult use, such as alcohol, caffeine, nicotine, and, in a growing number of states, marijuana. It also includes drugs that many of us consider medications, such as Percocet, Adderall, Tramadol, Xanax, antidepressants, and others. I am also referring to the countless drugs that are highly controlled, banned, or illegal, such as heroin, cocaine, MDMA, psilocybin, and ketamine. There are also drugs that live in the gray area in between these categories, such as kratom, which is neither currently banned nor formally regulated.

There is ongoing debate across movements about the use of "person first" versus "identity first" language, including within the harm reduction movement. Recent shifts toward person-first language are intended to reduce stigma by putting the humanity of a person at the forefront rather than their disability or stigmatized identity. Aligned with this thinking, you will notice that I often will use *person or people who use drugs*, because many of us in harm reduction prefer person-first language. However, there is a solid contingent of harm reductionists who prefer identity-first language and proudly call themselves as *drug users* so as to resist stigma and reclaim their identities, much like people in the disability rights space who have reclaimed terms such as disabled, autistic, and neurodivergent. You will see both in this book.

People across the world and in all walks of life use drugs, yet we do not all face the same challenges, nor do we all have the same privileges afforded us to buffer us from drug-related harms. In this book, you may notice that I will sometimes use the phrase *marginalized person or people who use drugs*. In cases where I specify this specific subset of people who use drugs, I am specifically referring to people who use drugs who are also subjected to forms of societal, economic, legal, or cultural marginalization by dominant society. Marginalization is something that a group in power imposes onto another through policies, practices, and systematic exclusion. This group includes people who use drugs who are also unhoused or unstably housed, of low income, members of minority racial and ethnic groups, disabled, LGBTQIA+, currently or formerly involved with the criminal legal system, or sex workers, for instance. Notably, it includes people who use illegal or banned drugs. This is important because while all drug users share certain commonalities and experiences, some people who use drugs are privileged enough to be protected from certain drug-related harms and have access to resources that may allow them to stay safer than others.

People differ in their preferred terms when they talk about people who use drugs in ways that negatively impact various areas of their lives, including their physical and mental health, interpersonal relationships, employment, and education. Many of us colloquially use the term *addiction* in our day-to-day conversations. And at the time of this writing, the clinical or medical term for this diagnosis is *Substance Use Disorder (SUD)*. This diagnosis is made after the completion of a comprehensive assessment with a trained professional using established diagnostic criteria from the *Diagnostic and Statistical Manual of Mental Disorders*, 5th edition, known as the DSM-5. In the DSM-5, there are three levels of diagnosis: mild, moderate, and severe. These are based on the number of criteria that one meets, and I will break this down for you in the book. While some people prefer the precision of the medical term, I will interchangeably use both throughout this book.

I used to work at a *Syringe Service Program (SSP)*, and I will often use this term to mean a harm reduction–oriented program that distributes sterile syringes to people who use drugs. However, many of you may also know of these as *Syringe Exchange Programs* or *Harm Reduction Programs*. These are often brick-and-mortar sites where people may pick up sterile syringes and dispose of used syringes. These programs may provide a diverse range of other services in your community. However, they also often distribute other injection-related materials such as sterile cookers, cottons, antiseptic wipes, and Band-Aids. Depending on where you live and the funding source of the program, they may also provide free access to naloxone (the opioid overdose reversal medication), sterile smoking and snorting kits, referrals to treatment and other social services, case management, HIV and HCV testing, support groups, buprenorphine for opioid use disorder, meals, acupuncture, and much more. In many parts of the country, these programs are mobile and do outreach in communities directly providing services and picking up discarded syringes and other drug items. Because these programs do many of the same things, I will use these terms interchangeably.

I will be talking about *Overdose Prevention Centers*, which are places where people can bring pre-obtained drugs and use them on site under the observation of medical staff or peers. These sites are locations where people use and dispose of sterile drug-using equipment and where people can respond in case of a medical emergency, including an overdose. Many of these sites also employ social workers and case managers who can make referrals to social services and treatment, medical providers who can help with wound care and treatment, food, support groups, and other services. In many parts of the world, they are called *Supervised Injection Facilities, Drug Consumption Rooms*, or *Safe Consumption Sites*.

I may use the terms *clients, consumers, participants*, or *patients* at various points in the book to refer to the people who use harm reduction, treatment, and other medical services.

Introduction

This book is for you if you want to learn more about how to address the drug problems we face in this country. We are in an unprecedented overdose crisis that has claimed over a million lives. Tobacco and alcohol are leading drivers of early death and avoidable health harm. And we are all affected. We must do more if we want to keep our communities safe.

I believe there is a fundamental gap in our system – a harm reduction gap – into which millions of us fall every day. Those of us in the harm reduction gap have few tools and resources to navigate a world with drugs because our systems of care have focused on "Just Say No" drug prevention messages and abstinence-only treatment.

You may have heard of harm reduction before. Maybe you have not. You may have questions.

I hope you choose to read this book to learn more about this life-saving approach to care, and that it helps you to understand the fundamental role it can play in our communities.

If this book helps to change your mind, I hope you will join us in our fight to save lives. We need you.

DOI: 10.4324/9781003301745-1

1 "Just Say No" and the Harm Reduction Gap

My dad loves to tell the story about the day I stopped him from drinking and driving. Before I tell you this story, it may be helpful for you to know a little about me for some context. I was born in the 1980s and grew up in a small, predominantly white, rural town in upstate New York. I was a precocious, outspoken, and opinionated first daughter in one of the only Indian American families in the area. My teachers often commented on how much I loved learning, and my parents can attest that I would proudly share new facts and tidbits when I got home from school every day. So, of course, I was responsible for telling my father about the dangers of drunk driving soon after I learned about it myself.

Ronald Reagan was president during my early childhood. His two terms were characterized by numerous notable policy and cultural changes whose effects are still felt today, including his "trickle down" economic philosophy that led to dramatic tax cuts for the wealthy and his ramping up of the drug war through tougher enforcement and harsher penalties that disproportionately targeted low-income communities and communities of color. At the same time, First Lady Nancy Reagan launched her national "Just Say No" drug prevention campaign to warn kids and families of the ever-present threat of drugs. Magazine cover stories cautioned us about a new generation of so-called "crack babies" who would grow up to be a drain on public resources, and the term "crackhead" soon became a common insult hurled in schoolyards across the country, including my own. The nightly news cautioned suburban parents every Halloween about the dangers of unsupervised trick-or-treating. They urged parents to watch for used syringes and drugs hidden in their children's candy. It seemed like we were warned about drugs all the time and everywhere we turned. Drugs really did feel like "public enemy number one."

Like many kids of my generation, I spent thousands of hours each year in front of the television set. I was not only entertained during these hours, but I was also exposed to new ideas, new worlds, and new information. I would watch educational and enriching shows like Reading Rainbow, Sesame Street, and Mr. Rogers' Neighborhood on PBS, then click to

DOI: 10.4324/9781003301745-2

Nickelodeon for my favorite game shows and cartoons or sneak to MTV to watch music videos when my parents weren't in the room.

Looking back, I find it makes sense that some of the most epic drug prevention public service announcements (PSAs) were launched back then. Kids my age were a captive audience, and we were the first generation that probably got too much "screen time." My sister and I watched several of these different cautionary PSAs every night, tucked between cartoons and toy commercials, as we lay sprawled on our living room floor inches away from our family television after school.

I was five years old when the Partnership for a Drug-Free America launched its first PSA. In it, someone cracked an egg into a hot frying pan as the narrator explained, "This is your brain on drugs." I knew it was a serious message, but I had no idea what drugs were at the time other than an abstract, scary bogeyman that would damage my brain.

In contrast, the PSAs about the dangers of drinking and driving made more sense to me. "Don't drink and drive." *Got it.*

And so I thought I was doing the right thing when I chased my dad as he walked to the car one morning. I needed to stop him from drunk driving. I screamed, "Daddy, please don't drink and drive!" as I ran after him onto the driveway, barefoot in my pajamas, the screen door slamming shut behind me. At that point, I had been inundated with PSAs full of swerving cars and deadly crashes on a near-daily basis, and my 5-year-old self was in a panic.

But my father, in his suit and tie, was simply sipping a cup of hot black coffee as he unlocked the car door so he could go to work.

It would be years before I understood why he found it so funny.

***

Eventually, I was among the millions of kids who learned about drugs, what they looked like, and how they were used by a uniformed police officer who came into my middle school health classroom for my DARE (Drug Abuse Resistance Education) class. The officer was also the one who taught us about alcohol, so I did learn *which* drinks made driving more dangerous. I can still picture the drug identification display case he brought to class for his presentations, a portable drug cornucopia packed into some sort of briefcase. When opened, the clear plastic paneling displayed a rolled joint, various pills and powders, pipes, a tourniquet, a bent spoon, a syringe, and other drug-related items. The message was clear: *This is what drugs are. Just say no.*

Other trusted adults and authority figures added to this message and doubled down on it over the years. They told me I could get instantly addicted to a drug from the very first try and that only "bad" people and criminals do drugs. Drugs were the hot frying pan that would sizzle and fry my brain. Do. Not. Do. Drugs.

Of course, I am glad I eventually learned what "drugs" were and what drunk driving entailed. In that sense, my DARE classes were far more helpful than all the vague, scary, and developmentally inappropriate PSAs I watched on TV (although fear was a pervasive element of DARE class too). But was being lectured by a police officer the best and only way for me to learn about drugs? And did DARE prevent my generation from using drugs?

It turns out that the answer is no. And no.

According to national surveys at the time, rates of teen drug use (including alcohol) were high and on the rise in the 1990s.[1] Yet at the same time, hundreds of millions of federal, state, and local funds had been poured into DARE programs. Like my own, most schools across the nation were faithfully implementing the curriculum with local law enforcement in our classrooms. Little did I know that, as I was taking my own middle school DARE class, the National Institute of Justice (NIJ) was funding a major study to prove that the curriculum worked and that it was taxpayer money well spent (primarily because youth drug use remained so prevalent at the time). The research team was tasked to review all the published studies to date on the short-term outcomes of kids who completed the program.[2] Their results revealed an uncomfortable truth – while DARE did increase kids' drug-related knowledge, it had a minimal impact on their drug use. In fact, the researchers found that the lecture-based DARE curriculum was much *less* effective than other, more interactive and engaging drug prevention courses taught by trained teachers. Because the NIJ was so deeply invested in DARE, they were reluctant to publicize the mixed findings and instead chose to criticize the researchers' methods and try to bury the study's results. In fact, the study's methods were sound, and the results were ultimately published in a well-respected, peer-reviewed journal.[3] Yet, without the public backing of the study by the NIJ, the study got buried in the academic literature, and DARE continued to be taught in classrooms across the country. It was business as usual.

Fast forward to 2003, when I was a college junior. Youth drug use remained high nationally, and millions of federal taxpayer dollars were still bankrolling the DARE program. The US General Accounting Office (i.e., the "Congressional watchdog") was invited to review the latest research on DARE to see whether this was the best use of resources. They found that "DARE had no statistically significant long-term effect on preventing youth illicit drug use."[4] Instead, they recommended at least five other curricula with better outcomes and noted dozens of promising alternative curricula.

Despite the mounting studies challenging the effectiveness of the curriculum and a growing number of viable alternatives to it, DARE remained popular among law enforcement, policymakers, and the public because many believed that the tough message of the curriculum was what our young people needed to hear. They believed we just needed young people to listen to law enforcement and not do drugs. If anything, "these stakeholders viewed DARE as a way to promote personal responsibility, family values, a privatized solution to government responsibility, and respect for the police."[5] These other priorities were often highlighted as important achievements of the program beyond drug prevention alone.

Within a few years, however, federal funds for DARE shrank (although other public and private funds paid for these widely implemented programs), and the curriculum quietly underwent some changes to address these undeniable concerns about its effectiveness. In place of the old-school curriculum of my youth, DARE integrated an adaptation of an existing evidence-based curriculum called "keepin' it REAL" (KiR). Rather than being told to "just say no" to drugs, students in KiR received an alternative drug resistance approach: "Refuse, Explain, Avoid, and Leave." When DARE's leadership adapted and integrated KiR into their curriculum, they developed a new version for elementary school children. However, KiR was initially designed for and had been evaluated on middle schoolers only. DARE leadership also wanted to roll out the adapted curriculum in the nation's predominantly white classrooms even though KiR was initially designed for and had been studied on Latinx and multicultural students. And though KiR was designed for and studied with teacher-led instruction, DARE leadership kept their signature model that involved using police officers as instructors. While these may not seem like significant changes from the outside, when a curriculum is changed or used differently from its original design, it must be studied to show that it is still helpful in its new form and with different populations. And the research found that, in this case, these adjustments made the curriculum less effective than the original interactive, teacher-led version. A 2017 study determined: "We can conclude that the evidence basis for the DARE version of KiR is weak and that there is substantial reason to believe that KiR DARE may not be suited for nationwide implementation."[6]

Yet, despite this finding adding to over 20 years of data questioning its effectiveness, there remains an appetite for DARE nationally. At this point, DARE's popularity has more to do with our feelings than the facts.[7] I personally believe that many who promote these programs are well-intentioned, are concerned, and want to keep our young people safe. They think a severe message from a law enforcement officer will motivate young people to abstain and make different choices. However, the evidence is clear: fear-based messages eventually fall flat because young people benefit more from being engaged in open dialogue and discussion with trained teachers who know how to work with them.

* * *

Like many DARE graduates, I was not at all equipped to deal with the realities of drug use after my friends started experimenting. I was barely exposed to alcohol or cigarette use in my relatively conservative Indian immigrant household. All the bottles in my dad's liquor cabinet were gifts or souvenirs and either covered in dust or still in their boxes. Meanwhile, most kids in my classes were already living with drug use. Their parents drank beer or wine with dinner or at football games. Since it was the 1980s, it wasn't unusual for kids to come to school with the smell of their parents' cigarettes on their clothes and hair. With easy access to and little stigma about these drugs at home, some classmates snuck sips or stole cigarettes when no one was watching. Others had their first drink with their parents.

I remember being told to say no, but the people around me were already saying yes.

As I got older, I realized that specific claims from my DARE class were misleading or inaccurate. The sky did not fall when my friends and peers started using drugs. When I got to high school, I remember classmates would go out back behind our building to smoke cigarettes between classes. And I can still picture the guy in psychology class putting drops of Visine in his bloodshot eyes because he was often smoking – something else – before class.

I eventually learned that a few of my friends were also selling drugs. It forced me to rethink my assumptions about drugs and those who used and sold them. They were not the scary bad guys I was once warned about – they weren't even strangers. They were childhood friends, classmates, neighbors, and family members. They were not instantly addicted after simply experimenting, and their drug use alone did not somehow change their character or personality. And even though I had been warned about the dangers of peer pressure forcing me to use drugs, I don't remember ever feeling pressured into doing anything I didn't want to do.

When I headed off to college, cheap beer freely flowed every weekend at frat parties on the quad. Our campus had an annual spring tradition of celebrating Dandelion Day ("D Day"), a Saturday full of live music, games, activities, day drinking, and general debauchery on campus. But I barely remember my first D Day because I missed most of it. I had gotten up early with friends, and, thankfully, we ate the bagels that our Resident Advisors had provided us to ensure we did not start drinking on empty stomachs. Then the drinking (and drinking games) began. One of our friends got very sick before we made it to the quad because he drank too much, too quickly, and vomited everywhere. It was a mess, and I did my best to clean it up. After tending to him, I ran back to my room on the other side of campus to clean up and change into some fresh clothes. The shower made me feel drowsy since I was buzzed and had already been drinking for a few hours. A quick nap seemed like a good idea. I figured I would wake up in time to join my friends right before the concert started. Instead, I woke up hours later to a red flashing light on my telephone, alerting me to all the voicemails my friends had left me while I was asleep. I missed the concert.

When I went looking for my friends later, I had to step over vomit and garbage strewn in the hallways and on sidewalks as I made my way across campus. After drinking and partying all day, my friends had all passed out in their rooms. Looking around at the nearly abandoned campus as I walked back to my dorm room, I remember feeling disappointed and embarrassed that I missed the fun of my first D Day. It was as if I had missed out on a rite of passage.

In my teens and early 20s, people my age and in my social circles continued experimenting with different drugs, and a few went on to use them more socially or recreationally. Alcohol was, and remains, the most commonly used drug in all of my friend groups. I've noticed that the drugs we had positive experiences with were the ones we sought out and used again, whether on special occasions or on a regular basis. Meanwhile, drugs that came with negative experiences often taught us valuable lessons in what *not* to do (like my friend's D Day experience that, thankfully, never happened again). Sometimes we learned our limits and took steps to avoid experiencing the same problems the next time, or we decided that the main takeaway was not to use it again. For the most part, we walked away from our drug-related experiences relatively unscathed and more self-aware. We learned that there was a time and place to let loose and get high, but that there were other times when it would be best to avoid use. Most of us saw our drug use as a part of the bigger picture in our lives – sometimes, it was a small part, and sometimes it was a much larger one. This is because, as our life circumstances, social circles, and priorities changed, our relationships with drugs would often change too.

Within a few years of graduating from my DARE program, I learned that the directive to refuse and avoid drugs had an expiration date. But I also learned that so much of the content built around fear did not resonate with my experience and with what I saw in myself or my friends when we started using drugs. I saw firsthand that most people who used drugs could still pursue their goals. They didn't all get instantly addicted, and they didn't all fall into a life of violence and crime. We certainly didn't. But we had never been told this was the norm rather than the exception. I wish that instead of being instilled with fear in my DARE classes, we were armed with the knowledge and tools to keep ourselves and our friends safe so we weren't left to figure it out for ourselves.

***

Current surveys show that even though drug use among teens is significantly lower than when I was growing up, youth overdose death rates have skyrocketed since 2019.[8] This is because, even though drug use is comparatively rare among this generation of young people, they face an unpredictable and highly potent drug supply, unlike anything we've ever seen. So while generations before them outgrew the "Just Say No" advice of their youth and survived drug experimentation, this new generation faces potentially lethal consequences for doing the same thing.

How do they keep themselves, their friends, or loved ones who use drugs safe when they were never prepared for the reality of drug use in their abstinence-based drug prevention class? When they aren't taught that pills aren't necessarily safer than powder drugs since counterfeits look like the ones you get at the pharmacy? When they have not been taught how to recognize someone in crisis or to respond in case of an overdose? This tragic lack of information is the difference between life and death. It also exposes how our abstinence-based drug prevention classes are doing our young people a disservice by not teaching them the realities of how to stay safe if, at any point, they or their friends do go on to use drugs one day. A lack of information and preparation has put their lives at risk, and thousands of our young people have already died. Their deaths were preventable.

The Harm Reduction Gap

Hundreds of millions of people across the nation, teens and adults alike, eventually go on to use drugs. A 2021 survey (see Figure 1.1) indicated that 70% of the US population over the age of 12 had used alcohol, a tobacco or nicotine product, or an illegal drug in the past year. And nearly 60% of people in the nation, over 100 million people, had used one of these substances *in the past month*. The numbers speak for themselves – drugs are clearly a part of our culture. We use them to have fun, enhance our performance, take the edge off, numb pain, improve our mood, and fully experience ourselves and our lives. Drugs often play a role in how we socialize, worship, relax, and work. Sometimes people use drugs to get high or intoxicated. Sometimes they provide much-needed clarity and focus.

Our drug prevention programs focus primarily on teaching our teens enough about drugs so that they know how to refuse or "resist" them if offered. And we continue to do this with the full knowledge that many will eventually go on to experiment or potentially regularly use legal drugs like alcohol, and possibly illegal drugs, later in life. In our current approach, few to no resources are provided to help young people (or people of any age) learn how to stay safe today or in the future when they may use drugs. No one has explained the risks of mixing different types of drugs, how different drugs vary in the onset and duration of their effects, the strategies for moderating use, or how to administer naloxone if they witness an opioid overdose. For decades, people have had no other formal source of information about drugs after they completed their drug prevention courses in school.

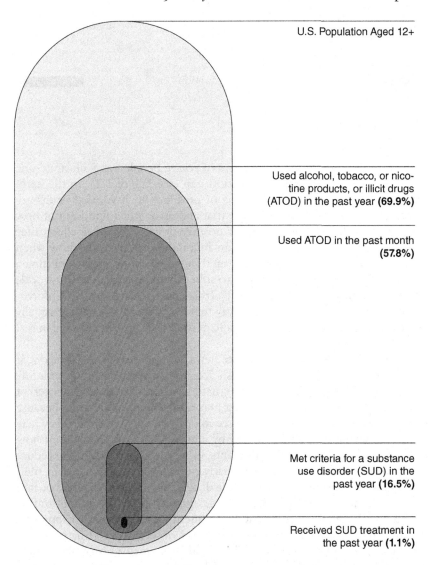

U.S. Population Aged 12+

Used alcohol, tobacco, or nicotine products, or illicit drugs (ATOD) in the past year **(69.9%)**

Used ATOD in the past month **(57.8%)**

Met criteria for a substance use disorder (SUD) in the past year **(16.5%)**

Received SUD treatment in the past year **(1.1%)**

Figure 1.1 Prevalence of substance use, 2021.

Source: Substance Abuse and Mental Health Services Administration. (2022). *Key Substance Use and Mental Health Indicators in the United States: Results from the 2021 National Survey on Drug Use and Health* (HHS Publication No. PEP22-07-01-005, NSDUH Series H-57). Center for Behavioral Health Statistics and Quality, Substance Abuse and Mental Health Services Administration. https://www.samhsa.gov/data/report/2021-nsduh-annual-national-report 2021 National Survey on Drug Use and Health (NSDUH).

Figure 1.2 The harm reduction gap.

My experiences and the experiences of young people today illustrate one side of what I call **the harm reduction gap** (see Figure 1.2). In the harm reduction gap, hundreds of millions of people who have used drugs are forced to rely on word of mouth or trial and error when figuring out how to stay safe as they also try to get the positive or enjoyable drug effects they seek. They may try a strategy they saw in a movie or television show when they don't know what to do when something goes wrong, such as putting a very drunk person in a cold shower to sober them up (this does not work!) or simply letting them "sleep it off" (this can be dangerous!). Unfortunately, many people learn the hard way that not all these sources are equally reliable, let alone helpful – in fact, some of what they see can be lethal in real life.

And in the era of the internet, fake news, and politicized social media, it can also be challenging to distinguish accurate, reputable sources of information from those which may perpetuate fear and confusion. An internet search about how to safely use a drug may result in mixed messages because so much drug-related content is censored or frequently removed. They may miss a life-saving post on Instagram by a group like DanceSafe about how to safely test one's drugs for adulterants, or a post from a local harm reduction group warning about a particularly potent batch of fentanyl in their community. Every day, many reputable drug-safety-related resources posted on the internet or social media are quickly taken down by administrators because of policies that censor and ban content that they deem "inappropriate" but that could save people's lives. I know of several expert harm reduction programs and advocates who have had social media posts taken down from platforms such as Facebook, TikTok, and Instagram because they provided essential harm reduction information flagged for supposedly promoting substance use. Many have had their social media accounts temporarily suspended or shadow-banned for posting essential information that could have reached countless people and helped keep people safe.

People who get to use with someone who is more experienced may be fortunate enough to pick up helpful tips and warnings: "Go slow," "Avoid taking an upper and a downer together," "This could make you feel nauseous, so don't use it right after eating," or "focus on your breathing because your heart is going to start beating really fast." Someone might be there to model safer strategies by using a sterile syringe or testing their drugs for adulterants first. Perhaps they recommend alternating a glass of water with every drink of alcohol. Some people are lucky enough to have someone willing to keep an eye on them because they know it's their first time. In fact, peer-to-peer support and education about safer use and risk reduction are how people have stayed safe while using drugs for millennia, and these are the very conditions in which harm reduction practices emerged, such as the distribution of naloxone and fentanyl test strips. People learned how to use drugs safely from others who used them, and they still do.

Unfortunately, well-intentioned and experienced users are themselves navigating the unpredictable and adulterated underground drug supply today. New and unexpected drugs continue to enter our underground drug supply, sometimes marketed as or mixed into known drugs, so users do not know what to expect. Experienced and novice users alike can get fentanyl when they think they bought heroin. Anyone could buy a counterfeit pill even if they thought they bought real oxycodone from a friend. And now, in some drug markets, fentanyl is being adulterated with novel sedative drugs and new opioids, such as etizolam, xylazine, and nitazene analogues, which can create stronger and more troubling effects.

Combine this with the fact that illegal use or underage use of substances can facilitate greater risk-taking than if the use was more socially sanctioned. For example, a person without stable housing may need to quickly inject heroin in a fast-food restaurant bathroom because they do not want to inject it in a public alley where a police officer may arrest them. But to avoid being harassed by staff or other customers for being in the bathroom too long, they may rush their shot and not have time to wash their hands and find the best vein to inject. This can result in vein damage or skin and soft tissue infections, and can also run the risk of overdose from injecting the whole thing all at once. Meanwhile, underage alcohol use can also be higher risk because high school and college students are often initiated into drinking practices like bingeing or playing drinking games by their fellow inexperienced peers because they are away from the watchful eyes of adults. However, they are also not necessarily equipped to know how to respond if someone experiences alcohol poisoning or if something goes awry.

Alcohol, tobacco, and other drugs have contributed to countless instances of preventable disease, harm, injury, and death worldwide. We are two decades into a drug overdose crisis that has claimed over a million lives in North America alone, including over 100,000 in 2021 and 2022.[9] But it doesn't have to be like this. Too many of our drug-related harms are driven by policies restricting education about staying safe in a world with drugs, criminalizing many harm reduction programs and tools, and keeping our underground drug supply unpredictable and unregulated. When we do not have open and frank discussions about drugs, safety, and health in our culture, people are left ill-equipped, ashamed, and unaware of what they can do to protect themselves and their loved ones.

These tragically common experiences should compel all of us to ask ourselves: why must we make it a gamble between life and death for an activity that millions of people engage in every year?

If we filled the gap left by traditional abstinence-only drug prevention messages with accessible harm reduction information, tools, supports, programs, and strategies, we could make it less of a gamble when it comes to drug use in the United States. People could learn about the real risks of the drugs they are taking, how to reduce them as much as possible, and how to ask for help without fear. Filling the harm reduction gap with more judgment-free resources and support is one critical step toward keeping people as safe as possible. But most of us live in parts of the country where this harm reduction support is inaccessible, nonexistent, or illegal.

Today, our formal addiction treatment system is the only recognized place where people can turn for any substance-related services or support in most of the country. However, our treatment system is built primarily to serve people with addictions or diagnosable substance use disorders (SUDs). Treatment services are specifically for those whose drug use has contributed to or exacerbated difficulties in their lives, whether it has affected their mental or physical health, or created problems in their relationships, at school, or work. And the majority of addiction treatment programs work with their clients toward a goal of abstinence from all drugs.

As a result of this focus on abstinence, our treatment system is not designed to teach young people (or people of any age) the basics of safer drinking, like the importance of counting the number of drinks they consume per hour or using the buddy system so you are not intoxicated and alone away from home. Our treatment system will not help someone who wants to learn which precautions to take before using MDMA at a music festival. Our treatment system is not equipped to help someone who doesn't like how much more frequently they are smoking marijuana and wants to cut down on their use to avoid future problems. Our treatment system will not help a pack-a-day cigarette smoker transition to vaping.

The harm reduction gap is the void in our current continuum of care between abstinence-based prevention programs and abstinence-only treatment programs, where people who currently use drugs are left without access to the knowledge, skills, and tools to stay safe. The problem is that our focus on preventing drug use and treating the addicted has overlooked the reality that these combined approaches neglect the needs of a critical population: people who use drugs. There is nothing for those of us who ultimately said yes to drugs and are most at risk for experiencing potentially devastating drug-related harms because we lack information or the tools to stay safe.

This large and diverse group includes the experimental user, the social user, and the binge user. But it also includes those with addictions who are not ready, willing, or able to stop, so they are not motivated for treatment. It also includes those who want treatment but cannot afford it, those who are currently on a waiting list for the next available treatment slot in their community, the hundreds of thousands who enroll in treatment in any given year but never complete it, and those who have completed a treatment program but return to drug use soon after.

Unfortunately, our current system gives this group of hundreds of millions of people few options for support or information if they want to stay safe and alive. This is a major reason why so many of our societal drug-related problems persist, and why some are getting worse. Our system has no contingency plan to help young people (and adults!) stay safe if they try or use drugs after completing their required school drug prevention curriculum. Our system offers nothing to social or recreational users who may be interested in simply cutting down or moderating their use so they can continue to enjoy the drug effects they seek. Our system has no holding space for people with addictions waiting for treatment or for whom treatment is inaccessible. And our system has no safety net for those that fall through the cracks of treatment because they dropped out, were discharged, could not continue to pay, or left for some other reason.

* * *

The aim of this book is to illustrate where harm reduction may be of use in our continuum of care and who may be best served when these resources and supports are available. The target audience for harm reduction is most people who use drugs: those who use them socially or recreationally, and those who experience drug-related problems, including people with diagnosable SUDs who are not in treatment.

Our system was not built to help people to stay safe while using drugs. Instead, our system was designed to prevent the initiation of drug use on one end, and to get those who use drugs problematically to stop using them altogether on the other. While we have had some degree of success at both ends, the current system will not eliminate all drug use in our society. More specifically, it will not improve the health and well-being of those who have started using or continue to use drugs. We could positively impact far more lives if we incorporated harm reduction into our continuum of care, but because many of these types of harm reduction services are illegal, stigmatized, or extremely rare, many people do not even have the option. By incorporating and investing in harm reduction, we can positively impact far more lives and save those who have fallen into the harm reduction gap.

I learned about the need for harm reduction firsthand. My first job was as a clinical social worker in a traditional abstinence-only addiction treatment setting, but I soon grew disenchanted with and demoralized by that approach. Few of my clients attended treatment voluntarily, most did not think they had a drug problem, and most never completed the program because they could not maintain abstinence and comply with our tight structure. I dreaded administering random urine drug screens to my clients even though I otherwise enjoyed other parts of my job, like conducting intake evaluations and running weekly group therapy sessions. I was required to report positive drug test results to case workers, parole officers, or the drug courts, and, as a result, many got sent back to jail or prison or lost custody of their kids. Hundreds churned through the revolving door of our program every year, often repeat clients, because our strict program rules made it easier to dismiss than to retain them in care. But instead of adapting our approach to meet our clients' needs, we doubled down on our strict policies and blamed our clients for lacking the motivation to change fast enough and on our terms. Like my clients, I did not last there for very long.

I left to work at a syringe service program and drop-in center at an organization that helped people living with HIV/AIDS get access to housing, healthcare, and other supports. I was hired to provide voluntary mental health counseling to our participants. It was a total 180-degree change from the dominant approach at my previous job. There were no mandates and no intrusive monitoring. Clients came to our site six days a week because they wanted to be there, not because they were forced to attend. They also wanted sterile injecting and smoking equipment to avoid infections, naloxone to reverse opioid overdoses, support groups and counseling to develop coping strategies, and referrals to treatment and other services to improve their circumstances. Most importantly, they wanted to be a part of a community where they were respected. I learned many valuable lessons there about the life-changing impacts that are possible only when people are welcomed, treated with dignity, and given honest, accurate information they can use to keep themselves safe. Over time, many of my clients cut down on their risky drug use practices, got housing, started attending medical appointments, and made numerous other positive changes due to their involvement in our program and other services. It was remarkable.

It may be uncomfortable or scary to think about anyone using drugs, especially illegal ones. You may believe that there is no safe way to use drugs and that abstinence should still be our ultimate goal since drugs carry too many risks. I understand. But allow me, in these following few chapters, to introduce you to a new way of thinking about the mood-altering substances that we commonly call "drugs" and their related risks and harms. I will also explain how much of what we think and know about drugs is because of our drug policies and history. Please stick with me. I plan to examine some common misconceptions and beliefs about drugs and offer you an opportunity to understand how harm reductionists think about drugs. Then I will introduce you to a conceptual model that offers us a helpful way to look at our relationships with drugs, including whether these relationships are helpful or harmful and what this model offers us in terms of keeping people safe. We will also talk about how and where treatment fits into our continuum of care.

Notes

1 Johnston, Lloyd D., Richard A. Miech, Megan E. Patrick, Patrick M. O'Malley, John E. Schulenberg, and Jerald G. Bachman. *Monitoring the Future National Survey Results on Drug Use 1975–2022: Overview, Key Findings on Adolescent Drug Use*. Ann Arbor: Institute for Social Research, University of Michigan, 2023.

2 Ennett, Susan T., Nancy S. Tobler, Christopher L. Ringwalt, and Robert L. Flewelling. "How Effective Is Drug Abuse Resistance Education? A Meta-Analysis of Project DARE Outcome Evaluations." *American Journal of Public Health* 84, no. 9 (1994): 1394–1401. https://doi.org/10.2105/AJPH.84.9.1394.

3 Marlow, Kristina, and Steve Rhodes. "Study: DARE Teaches Kids about Drugs but Doesn't Prevent Use." *Herald-Journal*, Chicago, IL, November 6, 1994.

4 US General Accounting Office. *Youth Illicit Drug Use Prevention: DARE Long-Term Evaluations and Federal Efforts to Identify Effective Programs*. Marjorie E. Kanof. GAO-03-172, Washington, DC, January 5, 2003.

5 Felker-Kantor, Max. "DARE to Say No: Police and the Cultural Politics of Prevention in the War on Drugs." *Modern American History* 5, no. 3 (2022): 313–37. https://doi.org/10.1017/mah.2022.19.

6 Caputi, Theodore L., and A. Thomas McLellan. "Truth and DARE: Is DARE's New Keepin' It REAL Curriculum Suitable for American Nationwide Implementation?" *Drugs: Education, Prevention and Policy* 24, no. 1 (2017): 49–57. https://doi.org/10.1080/09687637.2016.1208731.

7 Siegel, Zachary. "DARE 2.0 Is 'Keepin' It Real' in US Schools." *Substance Substack*, June 3, 2022. https://tanag.substack.com/p/dare-20-is-keepin-it-real-in-us-schools

8 Friedman, Joseph, Morgan Godvin, Chelsea L. Shover, Joseph P. Gone, Helena Hansen, and David L. Schriger. "Trends in Drug Overdose Deaths among US Adolescents, January 2010 to June 2021." *JAMA* 327, no. 14 (2022): 1398–1400. https://doi.org/10.1001/jama.2022.2847.

9 Hedegaard, Holly, Arialdi M. Minino, Merianne Rose Spencer, and Margaret Warner. *Drug Overdose Deaths in the United States, 1999–2020*. NCHS Data Brief, no. 428. Hyattsville, MD: National Center for Health Statistics, 2021. https://doi.org/10.15620/cdc:112340.

2 How the War on Drugs Created the Harm Reduction Gap

For millennia, civilizations across the globe have used plants with psychoactive or mood-altering effects for various purposes. Andean peoples found many uses for the coca plant growing on the mountainside, and even call it Mama Coca today because of its significance in the culture. Communities in Central Asia cultivated the cannabis plant and used it for several purposes, and tribes in the Americas continue to use tobacco to mark important occasions. Eventually, both plants spread worldwide across international trade routes, and demand for the plants grew. In many regions, grains and grapes were fermented into alcohol, and people learned that diverse plants and fungi had psychedelic effects. Opium was first cultivated in the Middle East, and its use spread to other regions due to its medical utility. While we can trace the roots of coffee to Ethiopia and tea to China, these substances are now widely consumed daily nearly everywhere. Our ancestors consumed these plants and substances for medicinal purposes, celebration, productivity, relaxation, enlightenment, and so much more. We continue to use many of these drugs today for similar reasons.

At the turn of the 20th century, advanced technology allowed us to extract and synthesize certain compounds from these plants, and we soon invented entirely new drugs made in both above-ground research laboratories and underground, clandestine labs. Semi-synthetic drugs like heroin and cocaine were invented by extracting and synthesizing plant compounds into more potent forms. Over the next several decades, new synthetic mood-altering drugs were made entirely from chemical precursors or building blocks. Well-known examples of synthetic drugs include methadone, PCP, ketamine, and MDMA. While some newer drugs share effects similar to those of well-established plant-derived drugs, many fully synthetic drugs have complex or multiple effects on the body that we are still trying to understand. Due to developments in chemistry, new drugs seem to be emerging in our underground markets every day. As a result, people today have access to a much wider array of legal and illegal drugs than were available to earlier generations.

DOI: 10.4324/9781003301745-3

While drug use is not new, how our society views and responds to various drugs has shifted dramatically. In fact, what we even classify as "drugs" has changed too. How and when did certain substances become "drugs"? Why do we trust medical professionals to dictate when and why we take certain mood-altering substances while there are others we can freely buy at the corner store? And why has law enforcement become the most trusted authority for all things related to illegal drugs?

I simply assumed that some drugs were legally available for recreational use because they were relatively safe, and others were illegal because they were dangerous. Some were medications because they could treat health issues but required medical supervision. And although I knew that legal drugs like alcohol and tobacco products carried health risks, I assumed that illegal drugs are banned because they are even more harmful. Perhaps you thought the same thing too. I thought these distinct categories must have been made based on a careful evaluation of different drug characteristics. I soon learned that the truth was more complicated.

During my doctoral program, I studied American drug policy history. I saw that the line between mood-altering medications and illegal drugs was always blurry and often nonexistent on a pharmacological level. I also learned that some of the most readily available legal drugs were, in fact, more harmful than many illegal ones. My research revealed that, for over a century, many policy decisions that drew legal distinctions between different drugs were guided not by in-depth research into drug effects and risks, but by xenophobia and racism. I was surprised to learn that, until the early 1900s, most Americans could legally buy tonics and tinctures containing cocaine, marijuana, and opium at local drug stores and through mail-order catalogs without prescriptions. They were often marketed as patent medicines to treat a wide range of ailments – from menstrual pain to sore throats – and were commonly used by Americans from all walks of life. It may be hard to imagine how drugs that are currently illegal were so normalized and readily available at any point in our nation's history – but they were.

In this chapter, I will provide an overview of the history of our drug policies and how these policies laid the foundation for our current harm reduction gap by banning some drugs and regulating others. Nearly a century after some of the earliest bans were implemented, our government has spent billions of dollars enforcing punitive policies to eliminate the underground market that emerged after these drugs were criminalized. Over the years, authorities doubled down on policies to eliminate the illegal drug supply by conducting frequent drug seizures or "busts," disrupting transnational drug networks, incarcerating drug sellers, and destroying drug crops domestically and abroad. At the same time, they funded various tactics they believed would eventually end American demand for these drugs. They made the personal possession of these drugs and the equipment to consume them a crime, developed programs to scare young people from ever using them, and funded abstinence-based addiction treatment services so that people with substance use disorders (SUDs) would stop using them altogether. Harm reduction programs that provided sterile drug equipment and safer use education to people who use drugs did not fit into this approach. In fact, these programs remained illegal for decades.

Let's talk about how we got here. It started with opium over a century ago.

Opium, Cocaine, and Our Two-Tiered Drug Policies

We can track some of the earliest drug laws by starting with opium. Opium was first imported into the United States in the 1700s. Doctors quickly found numerous applications for this multipurpose drug since it helped alleviate pain and had promising effects on cough and other symptoms. The import of crude opium reached its peak in 1896.[1] It was a common ingredient in many medications and was later processed into the more potent opium derivative morphine. Many do not know that "heroin" was the brand name of a potent opium-derived medication that Bayer Pharmaceuticals invented. People commonly consumed opium and opium-derived drugs in tonics, syrups, or lozenges to treat various health issues, including anxiety and nervous disorders, gastrointestinal problems, respiratory problems, menstrual cramps, and other ailments.

Population surveys in the 1800s showed that white Americans from all walks of life were using opiates – Civil War soldiers, housewives, working men, the educated, and the wealthy alike. During this time, middle-class white women emerged as the dominant consumers of opium products for both psychological and health issues. Though these drugs were legally available, production and sales were not regulated, so people often did not know how much they were consuming or whether the contents of these patent medications had been verified or tested. They also received no education or warnings about opiate-related risks. This meant that people could easily purchase opiates and use them as a cure-all but were unaware of potential harm. As opiate use became more prevalent, it soon came to be viewed as a social problem since growing segments of the population developed physiological dependence upon these drugs, needing larger and more frequent doses to get the same effects and experiencing uncomfortable withdrawal symptoms after the effects wore off. Combined, these symptoms drove people to use more opiates more frequently. Estimates suggested that roughly 250,000 Americans had become physically dependent upon these drugs by the turn of the century. Despite growing public concerns about opiates, no bans were proposed on widely used patent medications.

In fact, the only form of drug use that garnered significant scorn and stigma among the public was opium smoking. This was because smoking was associated with Chinese immigrants who came to the United States during the 1850s for the Gold Rush but also eventually worked on the railroads and in other industries in California and along the West Coast. Chinese people had a complicated place in American society at that point in history, since they were seen as competition for jobs during high domestic unemployment. Anti-Chinese sentiment was prevalent because their different culture and practices were perceived as threatening the American way of life. Chinese immigrants were frequently subjected to racial discrimination in their day-to-day lives, and waves of xenophobic laws were passed to target and exclude them from privileges afforded to white citizens.

At the time, it was common for Chinese immigrants to visit opium dens where they could recreationally use opium, as was practiced in China. While most of these dens predominantly served Chinese clientele, opium smoking had a growing appeal to white locals, rich and poor alike. But there were fears about the interracial socializing that could occur at these dens; some believed that Chinese opium dens would corrupt white women by getting them addicted to the drug so that Chinese men could sexually abuse them. Eventually, these fears motivated ordinances that banned white Americans from visiting opium dens altogether. San Francisco passed a general ban on opium smoking in 1875, the first anti-drug ordinance in the United States.[2]

Over the next several years, other jurisdictions nationwide passed similar laws targeting opium dens fueled by anti-Chinese motives. This marked the beginning of a two-tiered and racialized approach to drugs: the idea that drug use for health purposes should be accessible and available to predominantly white populations, but racialized others who sometimes used these same drugs recreationally could not be trusted and were, in fact, a threat to public safety.[3]

Cocaine was first extracted from coca leaves in the 1850s and was introduced to the United States soon after. Though the stimulating effects are relatively mild when coca leaves are consumed by chewing or brewing them into teas, cocaine is a far more potent stimulant. Cocaine quickly became popular, and cocaine imports peaked around the same time as opium imports. Cocaine was thought to increase worker productivity because of its stimulating effects. It was also seen as having great medical potential (Sigmund Freud loved it!). Like opium, cocaine was also added to beverages, patent medicines, and medicinal tonics. It was used as a temporary topical pain reliever and was even promoted as an effective treatment for morphine and alcohol addiction. And yes, the urban myth is true – the earliest Coca-Cola recipe contained coca derivatives and was marketed as a tonic until 1903, when they were removed, and Coca-Cola became what we now call a "soft drink."

While cocaine addiction was not unknown during this period, it was downplayed compared to opioids since there were no serious physiological withdrawal symptoms. However, much like opium smoking, cocaine quickly became associated with its own racialized fearmongering that motivated restrictive policy changes. Cocaine was cheap, and as its use spread into the South, white Americans became concerned about how cocaine would turn the freed Black community into a violent threat, even though white Americans were the dominant users of the drug at the time.

A clear example can be found in the 1914 *New York Times* cover story "Negro cocaine 'fiends' are a new Southern menace."[4] The article sensationalized anecdotes from sheriffs about supposedly dangerous Black men under the influence of cocaine who became better marksmen and were somehow impervious to traditional bullets. Because of this, law enforcement argued that they needed larger-gauge bullets to stop supposedly cocaine-fueled Black men from wreaking havoc. Using the racialized dimension of drug use to stoke fears was not an accident and was persuasive to the primarily white public. It did not matter that cocaine use among Black communities was rare or that there was no way to confirm that any men in the *New York Times* story were under its influence. Articles like this, along with films like *Birth of a Nation*, perpetuated the myth that Black men (both on cocaine and sober) were predators who, in the case of the film, would rape white women when given a chance. In one of the film's most memorable scenes, a Black man chases a white woman to the edge of a cliff, and she ultimately throws herself off to avoid being raped. "The fear of the cocainized black coincided with the peak of lynchings, legal segregation, and voting laws all designed to remove political and social power from him."[5] From the beginning, drug-related stigma was created and then weaponized to oppress Black communities further and to justify stripping them of legal rights, even as predominantly white populations of cocaine users maintained their legal access to the drug.

Early Federal Drug Laws Upheld and Restricted Medical Access

As I mentioned, one of the significant problems with patent medications and other related products was that, though they were legal, they were not regulated to ensure they contained the contents on the labels. As a result, consumers often used unknown quantities of various substances. So within a few decades, local and state laws were rightly passed to regulate these patent medications to protect consumers. Laws were also passed to tax certain drugs and allow only approved medical use, starting with cocaine and opium, and later marijuana, to control and limit who could use these drugs and under which conditions. Eventually, laws were passed to punish those who used or sold these drugs nonmedically.

An early and lasting tactic to gain mainstream support for these increasingly restrictive laws was associating the nonmedical use of certain drugs with intoxicated and dangerous racial and ethnic "others" who needed to be controlled for public safety. Restricting their access to these drugs was one way to do this.

By the last decade of the 19th century, most states had already begun to pass drug restrictions due to problems associated with the use of cocaine and morphine, including addiction. New state laws required prescriptions for the medical use of each substance. However, some over-the-counter patent medication manufacturers took advantage of loopholes and continued adding them to their products for some time. In 1906, the Pure Food and Drug Act was passed to ensure accurate product labeling so that patent medication manufacturers could be held accountable and be clear about which substances were in medications. The Food and Drug Administration (FDA) was formed to enforce the 1906 Act. Regulating acceptable medical use of these drugs was an early step toward restricting their use for social or recreational purposes. It also laid the foundation for our current harm reduction gap, because regulating the production and labeling of certain drugs let medical consumers know what they were consuming and how much, but unregulated versions of these drugs had no oversight. As a result, people who used these unregulated drugs were at risk for drug-related harm. There was no way for these consumers to stay safe as they navigated this unpredictable drug supply of unknown quality and potency.

In 1909, Congress passed its first real federal drug prohibition law, the Opium Exclusion Act, which banned imports of opium for nonmedical uses (i.e., for recreational smokers) but not the opium commonly consumed by white Americans for medical purposes.[6] In 1914, increased fears about the ongoing nonmedical use of opiates and cocaine led to the passage of the Harrison Narcotics Tax Act, the first federal law restricting the use of these drugs without a prescription. By allowing certain forms of consumption, the policy aimed to restrict opium smoking among Chinese immigrants and prevent imagined cocaine use in Black communities.

Eventually, even doctors' prescriptions came under scrutiny. A historic 1919 court case, *Webb v. United States*, and several subsequent cases narrowed the definition of acceptable medical treatment with opiates. Ultimately, the ruling deemed that doctors could not maintain patients on a steady supply of opiates to treat their withdrawal and manage symptoms of opioid use disorder (OUD).[7] Thousands of physicians were targeted after this ruling, and soon the last clinics where patients with OUD were treated with opiates closed. These patients were left to turn to the underground supply to manage their needs because they were pushed out of the medical system and denied access to regulated opiates – they were pushed into the harm reduction gap and forced to turn to the underground drug supply as well.

By this time, it was becoming clear that the nation was on a policy path to eventually restricting access to cocaine and opium altogether. Subsequent federal laws like the Jones-Miller Narcotic Drugs Import and Export Act of 1922 delineated fines and prison terms for violators of the Harrison Act and made possessing these drugs without a prescription a federal crime. Now, people who did not or could not access their drugs through the medical system faced the harms associated with using unregulated drugs that had potentially unpredictable effects and the prospect of another significant harm – incarceration – for simply using drugs that others could buy with a prescription. Eventually, the Heroin Act of 1924 made heroin manufacturing illegal while keeping access to similar opiates like morphine legal again, creating harm and risk for some opiate users while insulating others from these consequences. In 1934, the Uniform State Narcotic Drug Act was passed. It pressured all 50 states into codifying penalties for people who sold, manufactured, or used these drugs for any reason in their states, and the Act gave states the authority to enforce these laws within their borders. By officially pushing cocaine and heroin out of the medical system and into the underground market, our policies made it so that patients who used these drugs now joined the ranks of those excluded from medical access for decades. They were all in the harm reduction gap, with no alternative source of these drugs and nowhere to turn for help if needed.

The Alcohol Prohibition Experiment

Although some activists wanted to include alcohol in the 1914 Harrison Act, it remained widely available and exempt from prohibition for several decades. Alcohol had a unique association with social and recreational use in American society. However, growing numbers of states began to pass their restrictions in the early 1900s in response to alcohol-related problems and harm. Temperance advocates believed abstinence from alcohol was the most effective way to prevent alcoholism and that banning the substance would restrict its use. Some even believed that any drinker could potentially become addicted and were very concerned about alcohol's easy availability.[8,9] Yet it took them years to convince legislators, and the predominantly white, Anglo-Saxon, Protestant American public who generally accepted moderate beer, cider, and ale consumption. But things were changing. Around this time, these white Americans were concerned about growing numbers of new Jewish and Catholic immigrants along with those from Eastern and Southern Europe. This new wave of immigrants brought the nation different languages, cultures, and practices. Certain xenophobic temperance advocates viewed alcohol consumption by these new immigrants as a threat to American culture.

Though the 1914 Harrison Narcotics Act prohibiting nonmedical opiate and cocaine use was passed with relatively little dissent among legislators, recreational alcohol use was widespread. So its prohibition was highly contested by politicians and the public and reached several impasses. Ultimately, the Act passed in 1919, six years after its inception. It was first formalized in the 18th Amendment, and then an infrastructure for enforcement was created in the Volstead Act passed later that year. However, alcohol prohibition only lasted on the federal level from 1920 until 1933 and it soon lost public support since many Americans continued to drink alcohol from the underground market. These Americans fell into the harm reduction gap and, since they had no safer alternatives, experienced high rates of blindness, botulism, and other health issues from drinking potent and unpredictably sourced alcohol. The illegal status of alcohol also contributed to the proliferation of organized crime and bootlegging. Yet, unlike the cases of cocaine and heroin before, policymakers and the public were willing to do something to reduce the harms that resulted from making this drug illegal. They chose to close the harm reduction gap when the 21st Amendment repealed the 18th Amendment federally, allowing states to either develop their alcohol regulatory systems or continue prohibiting alcohol within their borders. Giving states a choice to legalize and regulate this drug once again was one way to reduce the most significant health and public safety harms associated with this drug. Re-legalization brought users out of the shadows and the alcohol industry, their products, and profits under regulatory control.

Marijuana, Following Cocaine and Opium's Example

Hemp was already a commonly grown crop among farmers used to make durable industrial fabrics and clothing, plasters, and rope long before opium or cocaine arrived in the United States. It is the same cannabis plant that we call marijuana, but it is bred and grown differently from marijuana, which has a higher THC content and psychoactive effects. It was not widely used or recognized as a mood-altering drug for a long time because the most prevalent forms were grown for industrial purposes. But by the turn of the 20th century, psychoactive cannabis was believed to have medicinal uses, and it was available in tonics and various other patent medications, sometimes even in combination with opiates or cocaine. As the backlash against opium and cocaine grew, some advocates attempted to include cannabis in early drafts of the Harrison Act. However, cannabis did not make it into the final legislation because there was no clear consensus about the harms of the drug on the federal level – yet. Recreational use did not become a concern to the general public until the 1900s, when some doctors and legislators in the South and Midwest warned about its habit-forming potential. But there was little political urgency for federal marijuana policy, since many policy-makers did not hear about problems in their communities.

Like government policy on opiates, cocaine, and alcohol before it, marijuana prohibition eventually gained more support due to xenophobia and fear. In the 1920s, concerns grew in the Southwest and along the southern border as Mexican immigrants entered the country due to the Mexican Revolution and in response to American demands for agricultural workers. Like the Chinese workers who arrived decades before, Mexicans were viewed as competition in the labor force and as foreigners who were culturally different. White Americans associated recreational marijuana use with Mexican immigrants, and the media led them to believe that marijuana made these outsiders prone to violence and criminality. This belief persisted even though marijuana use was not common among Mexican people. At the time, marijuana was also associated with other racial and ethnic minority groups and groups outside of the cultural mainstream, such as artists and entertainers. These groups, outside of respectable white society, were seen as threats to traditional American values and norms. And, again, these people ran the risk of corrupting white women.

States and jurisdictions began to pass laws to ban the recreational use of the drug in 1913, and they eventually pressured the federal government to pass the 1937 Marijuana Tax Act, which required marijuana sellers to pay taxes and for both users and sellers to be registered. The assumption was that medical providers and patients would willingly register themselves but that this system would restrict access for the groups who wanted to use the drug recreationally. The Act notably used the Spanish word "marijuana" instead of the more widely used word "cannabis" to exoticize it to the American public and instill fear that this seemingly foreign drug had infiltrated its borders (even though hemp had been grown domestically for decades). The first director of the Federal Bureau of Narcotics, Harry Anslinger, drafted the Marijuana Tax Act and played a significant role in its passage. He was one of the people credited for the language shift from cannabis to marijuana and helped to fan the flames of fear that led to this law. In fact, he said the following:

> There are 100,000 total marijuana smokers in the US, and most are Negroes, Hispanics, Filipinos, and entertainers. Their Satanic music, jazz, and swing result from marijuana use. This marijuana causes white women to seek sexual relations with Negroes, entertainers, and others.[10]

The Marijuana Tax Act was later ruled unconstitutional because it created a registry for sellers and users, violating their Fifth Amendment rights against self-incrimination. But marijuana was eventually made illegal on the federal level when the Boggs Act passed in 1951. The Boggs Act also created the nation's first mandatory sentences for people found guilty of violating any state or federal drug laws. In 1956, Congress passed the harshest federal drug legislation to date, the Narcotic Drug Control Act, which created minimum prison terms of up to several years and allowed for longer sentences in the case of multiple convictions for drug offenses. The drug war had already begun, and those that fell into the harm reduction gap were on their own to navigate the unpredictable drug supply and manage the threat of arrest and incarceration.

The "War on Drugs"

Fast forward to 1970. Most of us mark the "war on drugs" as starting when President Nixon signed the Comprehensive Drug Abuse Prevention and Control Act (CDAPCA) into law. The events of 1970 are noteworthy, but it is important to recognize that the nation had already been inching toward this level of enforcement for almost a century. What made the CDAPCA unique was that it was the most comprehensive and far-reaching federal policy to address the issue of drug use and it did several things that earlier laws did not. Notably, it focused on reducing the illegal drug supply by funding domestic law enforcement and international interdiction efforts to stop drugs from being brought into the country. Interestingly, it also rolled back some of the harsh mandatory minimums of the 1951 Boggs Act that had received backlash. Instead, it just formalized other punitive penalties.

The CDAPCA was also the first federal law that allocated federal funds toward drug prevention, research, and treatment efforts – components that were notably missing from all previous state and federal drug laws that solely aimed to punish people who used or sold certain drugs. The CDAPCA marked the first time the federal government invested in these critical efforts, and the US government continues to fund them to this day. The federally funded National Institute on Drug Abuse (NIDA) is now the world's largest funder of drug-related research. Federal funds for prevention were eventually used to expand access to abstinence-oriented DARE and other programming in schools and communities. Federal grants also helped increase treatment access and capacity in many states nationwide, which was a historic infusion toward building our treatment infrastructure. Although there were some clinics for alcohol use disorders, treatment for other drug addictions was not commonplace. Many Americans still saw addictions as a moral failing. Addiction was only starting to be viewed as a health issue, so these grants were a big step forward. Nixon also oversaw the first federal expansion of methadone as a treatment for opioid use disorder (OUD) because some Vietnam veterans returned home with heroin addictions and needed help. There was already a heroin addiction crisis in many of our cities at the time, and we had few effective treatments to offer. Allowing for methadone treatment was a historic accomplishment, given the legal precedents set a few decades earlier that criminalized many physicians for maintaining patients with OUD on opiates. These essential components of the CDAPCA are often overlooked but should be recognized for helping thousands of people with untreated SUDs get the help they wanted and needed. This investment narrowed the harm reduction gap by allowing those who wanted treatment to get it.

Notably, Title II of the CDAPCA, the Controlled Substances Act, instituted a five-level federal scheduling system to rank drugs by medical value, harmfulness, and potential for abuse and dependence and detailed the penalties for drug violations at each level. Federal scheduling was meant to standardize drug policy across the nation while still allowing healthcare providers to prescribe some of these drugs to patients during treatment or surgery. While it might have seemed like a sound system in theory, there was no significant body of research on all the drugs at the time, and no formal examination was conducted to accompany their categorization.

Schedule I drugs were deemed to have no medical utility and high abuse potential, so users or sellers who possessed these drugs were subject to some of the harshest penalties. Schedule I drugs included marijuana, LSD, psilocybin, and heroin. Drugs in Schedules II, III, IV, or V were deemed to have some accepted medical uses but were also thought to carry a degree of addiction potential. Penalties for violations involving these drugs were still harsh but not as severe as for Schedule I drugs. For example, Schedule II drugs included cocaine, methamphetamine, methadone, and stimulant medications commonly used for narcolepsy and ADHD, as well as opioid pain medications. Access to most of these scheduled drugs was highly controlled and allowable only within the medical system. This meant that social or recreational users and sellers in the underground market would be subject to penalties.

The drugs I listed in Schedule I may sound strange to some of us now, and the fact that they *remain* Schedule I at the federal level may also seem odd. Are they all highly addictive, and do they really have no medical uses? Today, medical marijuana is available to over 100 million Americans in over 75% of states nationwide. A growing research base suggests that drugs like LSD and psilocybin have therapeutic potential for psychiatric disorders such as PTSD, and there are parts of the world where heroin is still used medically. Claims that these drugs remain in the Schedule I categorization because they have no medical use are false. In addition, research suggests that marijuana and some of these psychedelics are associated with significantly lower rates of SUDs among users than a legal drug like alcohol, so claims about the high potential for addiction are overstated and incorrect.[11]

How did some of these specific drugs end up in Schedule I rather than at any other level? Nixon's Chief Domestic Advisor John Ehrlichman answered the questions decades later when he said the following in an interview in the 1990s:

> We knew we couldn't make it illegal to be either against the war or black but by getting the public to associate the hippies with marijuana and blacks with heroin and then criminalizing both heavily, we could disrupt those communities. We could arrest their leaders, raid their homes, break up their meetings, and vilify them night after night on the evening news. Did we know we were lying about the drugs? Of course we did.[12]

Like the other policies discussed in this chapter, the passage of the CDAPCA was not motivated solely by a desire to improve public health by reducing drug-related harms, even though it made a historical allocation of funds toward treatment, research, and prevention. Ehrlichman's statement reveals that racial and social control were critical drivers of selecting certain drugs for the most restrictive punitive level of federal scheduling. It also revealed that policymakers remained deeply invested in preserving medical access to certain mood-altering drugs for some, while leaving others to fend for themselves in the underground market and risk criminalization. The harms these drug users would face were deemed an acceptable consequence of these policy choices – and perhaps that was the whole point.

Within a few years, drug-related arrests increased as drugs became a domestic law-enforcement priority, and the promise of extra funds and military-grade equipment helped incentivize police to focus on drug crimes. Eventually, the Drug Enforcement Agency (DEA) was formed to oversee domestic and international drug control efforts to end the production, manufacture, and distribution of illegal scheduled drugs. Notably, the DEA was also charged with maintaining the list of federally scheduled and controlled substances and ensuring that the drugs allowed for medical use were properly produced, distributed, prescribed, and dispensed. Rather than giving that authority to a federal health entity such as the FDA or a federal research institute, the CDAPCA gave the DEA, a law enforcement entity, the authority to manage the system that determined which drugs were illegal and which could be medications. Overnight, law enforcement came to be viewed as drug experts. Drugs were now their domain.

Criminalizing Paraphernalia

States began passing statutes to criminalize drug tools and equipment in the early 1900s, starting with opium pipes and eventually including syringes and other heroin drug equipment. Many states also had syringe prescription laws, meaning they were legal to purchase only with a doctor's prescription for medical use. Yet "head shops," where people could buy pipes and bongs and other items to smoke drugs like marijuana, had increased in many parts of the country throughout the 1970s because they were in a legally unregulated policy "gray" area. Estimates suggest that it was a multimillion-dollar industry that operated through storefronts and via mail order across the country, since many of these products could arguably also be used to smoke tobacco, a legal substance.

Still, persistent and vocal community parent groups were concerned that easy access to these items would normalize drug use and encourage kids to use drugs. Although some state statutes were passed to criminalize "paraphernalia" sales, many of merchants successfully challenged these convictions because the language in many state statutes was vague, and they presumed that sellers could know whether customers intended to use these items to consume illegal drugs.[13] So in 1979, the DEA introduced the Model Drug Paraphernalia Act to offer standard language to states so they could criminalize various items deemed as drug paraphernalia within their borders. The Act was also written in a manner that protected the states from constitutional challenges that had been brought against earlier state statutes. Most states implemented the Model Act or similar anti-paraphernalia laws within several years. The Act defined "drug paraphernalia" as

> all equipment, products, and materials of any kind which are used, intended for use or designed for use in planting, propagating, cultivating, growing, harvesting, manufacturing, compounding, converting, producing, processing, preparing, testing, analyzing, packaging, repackaging, storing, containing, concealing, injecting, ingesting, inhaling, or otherwise introducing into the human body a controlled substance.[14]

Under the Model Act, targeting manufacturers and distributors of various drug equipment became easier. It also allowed police to arrest people who possessed these items for their personal drug use. Subsequent laws passed in the 1980s restricted access to drug equipment even more, making it a crime to bring supplies across state lines or send them in the mail.[15] This criminalization even further solidified the harm reduction gap for people who used illegal drugs: these people risked arrest for possessing the drugs; the drugs themselves were unpredictable, so they risked overdose and other potentially harmful effects for those using them; and the tools to use these drugs were now illegal too.

Adopting this Act in most states meant that, in the years leading up to the peak of the AIDS crisis, people who injected drugs were more likely to share used syringes since new sterile syringes for nonmedical use were increasingly difficult to acquire. The widespread sharing of syringes and other equipment quickly spread blood-borne viruses like HIV and hepatitis B (HBV) and C (HCV) among people who injected drugs and their sexual partners.

The dull tips of the reused needles damaged veins and led to skin and soft tissue infections. Other bacterial infections, such as endocarditis, became common because injecting with used equipment or in unsanitary conditions could introduce various bacteria into the bloodstream.

When advocates tried to narrow the harm reduction gap by trying to help people who injected drugs to stay safe, they put themselves at risk for arrest. Paraphernalia laws meant that the first underground syringe exchange programs (SEPs) in the late 1980s and 1990s were engaging in an illegal activity simply by acquiring syringes and supplies they knew would be used for drugs. It meant that freely distributing syringes, cottons, cookers, and other supplies for safer injection to reduce the spread of HIV were criminal activities because they facilitated illegal drug use. According to language in the Model Act that states adopted, SEP staff admitted they provided people with "paraphernalia" by giving participants educational materials to show them how to use these supplies safely. Dozens of program volunteers were charged across the country.

The Model Act and similar policies expanded the grounds that law enforcement could use to arrest people so that visibly homeless and marginalized people who were already disproportionately harassed by police were now deterred from acquiring too many new sterile syringes from underground SEPs. The fact that syringes and other drug equipment were deemed paraphernalia encouraged people to dispose of these items wherever they could as quickly as they could, whether in an open garbage can, a park, or on the sidewalk. These laws created a dangerous situation in which people were now afraid to do the right thing: hold on to their used supplies long enough to return them to the SEP. At the exchange, these supplies could be properly labeled as hazardous waste and disposed of appropriately, but many people could not wait until they made it there.

The adoption of the Model Act meant that, decades later, when fentanyl and other adulterants entered our underground opioid supply, the fentanyl testing strips and advanced drug-checking equipment used by harm reduction advocates and people who used drugs would be illegal. After all, the Act explicitly states that "testing equipment used, intended for use, or designed for use in identifying or in analyzing the strength, effectiveness or purity of controlled substances" would be criminalized as drug paraphernalia. Though some states did not copy all of the exact language from the Model Act, this equipment was criminalized in most states.[16]

Criminalization Created the Harm Reduction Gap

Since the War on Drugs began, many drug-related challenges that motivated prohibition have remained, while new challenges have emerged. Illegal drug use remains prevalent across the country, drug-related health harms (i.e., infectious and blood-borne diseases, drug overdose, etc.)

continue to take lives and reduce life expectancy for people who use drugs, the drug supply is as unpredictable as ever, drug-related arrests and criminalization disrupt lives, and people have few places to turn to for help. Prohibition has also created an entire underground and unregulated drug economy worth billions in revenue. This economy has been associated with violence, corruption, and destabilization of governments worldwide for over half a century. Meanwhile, the tools and equipment that could help one to use drugs safely became criminalized, so illness and other health harms became common among people who used illegal drugs.

Reagan-Era Policies and Crack Cocaine

In the 1980s, we also saw dramatic increases in drug-related arrests and a ramping up of punitive enforcement strategies in the name of the drug war. President Reagan signed the Anti-Drug Abuse Act of 1986, which solidified this approach. It was partially motivated by a highly publicized crack cocaine crisis in several major American cities that largely impacted communities of color and low-income communities. Interestingly, the public's fear of crack cocaine intensified even though powder cocaine remained a widely used party drug among the wealthy white elite in the same cities where crack cocaine was also used.

Crack cocaine was falsely portrayed as different from other drugs because it was depicted as uniquely harmful and addictive. Yet "crack was not a new drug; its active ingredient is entirely cocaine. Nor was it a 'new' way of using cocaine; smoking cocaine freebase had been practiced since the 1970s."[19] Through sensationalized coverage, the media depicted crack cocaine as a scourge ravaging predominantly Black communities and that it led to child maltreatment, violence, and crime. At the same time, movies showed powder cocaine used by wealthy white people with glamorous and lavish lifestyles. In the media, experts warned that crack could end up in seemingly safe American suburbs next.

This polarized perception eventually translated into public support for harsher penalties and greater policing of these communities rather than prioritizing funding for healthcare and treatment. Under Reagan, the penalty for possessing one gram of crack cocaine became just as harsh as 100 grams of powder cocaine. Policymakers provided five problematic reasons for the ratio: crack cocaine was more addictive than powder cocaine; crack cocaine use was related to violent crime; crack cocaine use by pregnant women impacted fetuses; crack cocaine use was growing among young people; and "the low cost of crack cocaine made it especially prevalent and more likely to be consumed in large quantities."[20]

These problems could have instead been solved with a public health approach to crack cocaine use and the recognition that many of the problems these communities faced had nothing to do with the drug. In reality, the notable differences in outcomes among users were because those who could afford powder cocaine had access to resources that buffered them from experiencing severe problems to begin with. Middle-class and high-income people who developed cocaine use disorders could afford to seek the help they needed. In contrast, many of the problems facing low-income inner-city communities of color attributed to crack were rooted in heightened surveillance, over-policing, systemic racism, food and housing instability, a lack of well-paying jobs, disinvestment, and years of Reagan's austerity policies that weakened the public welfare system. These were all structural problems that could be addressed only with more resources.

Within a few years of the new law's implementation, the number of Black people targeted and arrested for minor crack cocaine possession offenses dramatically increased, contributing to mass incarceration and the disruption of their families and communities. These policies created new harm.

Federal Funding Bans for Syringe Exchange

The drug war created the harm reduction gap that enabled this public health crisis to flourish; it placed thousands of people who injected drugs at risk of catching HIV – an infection that would turn into a terminal condition that, at the time, had no treatments.

In the late 1980s, the federal government was reluctant to acknowledge that SEPs were helping communities because of the stigma of injection drug use. Lawmakers believed it was immoral to provide people with illegal tools to stay safe while they engaged in the criminal act of illegal drug use.[18] Many did not see any reason for the federal government to fund such programs, and a federal funding ban was instituted until there was enough research to prove their efficacy. Yet at the same time, NIDA would not allow their federal research dollars to pay for the research to see whether these programs effectively reduced HIV transmission rates.

People who injected drugs and their allies continued this lifesaving work as a form of radical, loving, and defiant mutual aid, and they creatively found the funding to pay for it. At the same time, sympathetic researchers found alternative funding streams to study outcomes and build the American evidence base for these programs throughout the 1990s. By the time President Clinton was in office, the domestic and international evidence of the benefits of SEPs was undeniable. Yet politics (and a lack of courage) prevented the Clinton administration from using its power to lift the ban. So when Republicans pushed to make the ban permanent, Clinton (who personally supported needle exchange) signed off on it to maintain the peace. Over the years, although federal agencies took advantage of loopholes and used other strategies to support expanding syringe access, both directly and indirectly, the symbolic and actual impact of the federal funding ban revealed the deep stigma against these lifesaving programs.

The Obama Years

Obama and Democratic leadership in Congress temporarily lifted the federal funding ban for SEPs in 2009, before the Republican Party took control of Congress and reinstated it in 2011. But by 2015, red and blue states faced the overdose crisis and increased injection drug use. Several significant HIV outbreaks occurred in communities with no harm reduction infrastructure due to bans, which motivated bipartisan support to finally lift the ban so programs could receive funding for operations. But the money could not be used to purchase the syringes themselves.

Decades after Reagan instituted the harsh powder and crack cocaine sentencing disparity, Congress under the Obama administration moved to reduce the disparity to 18:1 in recognition of how differential sentencing for chemically similar drugs contributed to racial disparities in the criminal legal system. However, the fact that any disparity remains for this chemically analogous drug is due to social and cultural factors (namely, racism and classism) and not science.[17]

An Unpredictable Drug Supply for Some

In our quest to try to eliminate the nonmedical use of certain drugs, our policies created the conditions for an unpredictable, potent, and highly adulterated underground drug supply. Drug prohibition has driven illicit drug production and supply chains underground, creating an entire economy run by domestic and transnational drug distribution networks.[21] Although global estimates of illicit drug revenues are difficult to calculate, an analysis of drug consumption trends suggests that Americans spend an estimated $100 billion per year on the four most commonly used illicit drugs – cocaine, methamphetamine, heroin, and marijuana.[22] The global underground drug trade employs a workforce of tens of thousands of people, including those who grow drug crops, synthesize drugs in clandestine laboratories, transport drugs within and between countries, and sell drugs to consumers.[23] The drug economy may be the most lucrative option for those denied or excluded from work in the above-ground economy or who live in communities where existing options do not provide a living wage. For many people worldwide, the drug economy may be the best or only option for paid work because few other alternatives exist. However, this work places people under the constant threat of arrest and law enforcement contact, does not provide them with job stability and employee protections, and subjects them to stigmatization. In addition, some are involved in this economy under coercive or exploitative arrangements or through threats of violence or extortion from influential drug-involved actors.

Underground drug supply networks have no regulatory oversight, so people who use drugs purchase them at inflated street-level prices and with unknown purity and composition. Much of what determines drug price can be attributed to drug supplier monopolies, ongoing drug demand, and the scarcity of products. Law enforcement places drug suppliers at high risk of drug seizure, supply disruption, and arrest. These costs of doing business are reflected in prices.[24] Drug seizures or drug busts can also impact the quality and composition of the product because these disruptions reduce the amount of drugs that ultimately make it to the street-level drug seller, who may then be compelled to mix or add adulterants to compensate for lost products and maximize profits. As a result, people who purchase illicit drugs often spend more money on products of unknown quality, composition, and potency that can potentially harm them. Meanwhile, consumers of legal and regulated drugs (many of which are chemically similar to illegal drugs) always know what they are going to get and how much they will have to pay for them.

The Iron Law of Prohibition suggests that increasing police interdiction and drug busts incentivizes suppliers to produce and transport compact and more potent forms of drugs in order to avoid detection while still meeting demand. In the case of the North American overdose crisis, the growing number of heroin-involved overdose deaths in the early 2000s during the "second wave" of the crisis led to increased interdiction and seizure efforts by law enforcement to crack down on supplies of prescription opioids and heroin across the country and at legal points of entry.[25] The increasing demand for opioids and more frequent drug busts and seizures incentivized suppliers to shift to the cheaper, rapidly produced synthetic fentanyl, which didn't require suppliers to wait to harvest opium poppies. The smaller bricks of potent fentanyl were also far more discreet to transport into the country than larger quantities of heroin.

Fentanyl was first mixed into heroin in small amounts to stretch the supplies to meet increased demand, but also to account for the fact that much of the heroin entering the country was seized, resulting in less heroin reaching the consumer. By around 2013, people who used heroin in Northeast and mid-Atlantic states began to notice that their heroin was changing in color, and they also noticed that the effects were more potent and had a quicker onset and a shorter duration.[26] The potency and faster onset of effects contributed to more overdoses among otherwise seasoned users who knew their heroin tolerance. People were also beginning to report the earlier onset of withdrawal symptoms requiring more frequent use than heroin. By 2014, illicitly manufactured fentanyl and its chemically similar analogs were increasingly being seized in drug raids. They were identified in larger numbers of overdose deaths across major cities in the Northeast and mid-Atlantic, thus starting the "third wave" of the overdose crisis.[27] In the following years, fentanyl almost entirely replaced heroin in these regions while being found in higher quantities in heroin and counterfeit prescription pills sold in the South, the Midwest, and more Western states. Correspondingly, fentanyl-involved overdose deaths increased, and fentanyl became the drug involved in most overdoses nationally in mid-2017. In many parts of the country, fentanyl has now become an entrenched part of the drug supply and an indicator that the drug market is shifting toward more synthetic drugs and away from historically plant-derived drugs.[28]

The highly unpredictable supply has put people purchasing drugs on the underground market at risk for unintentional overdose and other adverse health effects. Unlike people who use legally regulated alcohol or medical-grade pharmaceuticals of known quality and potency, those who use drugs from the underground market need tools and strategies to mitigate the unpredictability of their drug supply and stay safe. It has created a need for harm reduction approaches to help people to test their drugs for their contents (a practice known as "drug checking"), as well as Overdose Prevention Centers (OPCs) where people can use their pre-obtained drugs on site at a facility staffed by people who can respond to an overdose or other adverse effects. It is also why many harm reduction advocates are calling for a safe supply – they argue that the only way to eliminate the harms of an adulterated underground drug supply is to provide people who use drugs with pharmaceutical-grade alternatives. The harm reduction needs of people who use drugs from the underground market are a direct result of drug criminalization.

Criminalizing Some People Who Use Drugs

Our attempts to deter certain drugs by criminalizing them have forced people who use those illegal drugs to the margins of our society or into the shadows to hide their use. They then became criminals for what they chose to put in their bodies, even as our systems allowed millions access to chemically similar, if not identical, drugs through our healthcare system. (And all this happened while other risky drugs like alcohol and tobacco products remained legal and readily available to the public.) We created a two-tier system of "criminals" and "patients," many of whom use chemically similar substances but experience very different consequences for their drug use. As soon as one group of drug users were deemed criminals, it became easy to justify targeted policing to enforce our drug laws. It is acceptable, even politically popular, to impose harsh penalties upon those arrested.

In 2020, drug-related offenses were the leading cause of arrest in the United States, with an estimated 1.1 million drug-related arrests that year.[29]

Of those arrests, over 85% were for possession of small amounts of drugs for the arrestee's personal use. That year, there were more arrests for possessing small amounts of drugs than murder, violent crime, rape, car theft, arson, and aggravated assault *combined*. It is not because any of those crimes are rare. This arrest disparity exists because minor drug possession charges are often prioritized over other offenses that significantly impact public health and safety because they are easy open-and-shut cases, since it is clear whether the person had the drugs on them. The other offenses I listed require police to do more investigative work to identify the perpetrator and gather the evidence to build a case against them. And it takes a lot more skill, time, and resources to build the case and convince a district attorney to press charges against someone for these types of crimes. (And, as I mentioned earlier, our drug laws have incentivized law enforcement to prioritize drug offenses because police are promised money, military-grade equipment, and other supplies to "fight" the drug war on our streets.)

Drug arrests are easy to make when police simply target low-income neighborhoods or homeless encampments where people are already outside and exposed. In addition, inflated drug arrest numbers can make a precinct's case clearance rates look high, so it seems as though they are doing "real police work." But law enforcement's prioritization of drug possession charges reveals a mismanagement of already expensive and limited resources at the local, state, and federal levels when police could be trying to solve the cases that matter most to victims.

The effects of drug policing are not equally felt by all communities across the nation, even though people of all races and ethnicities report similar rates of illicit drug use. Black, Indigenous, and Latinx communities are arrested disproportionately more than white communities. In addition, low-income people are more likely to be arrested on drug charges than high-income people. This is because police are more likely to be patrolling and targeting minority and low-income communities than higher-income communities where similar rates of drug use may be occurring. Even when higher-income people are arrested, they are better able to afford a robust legal defense to dispute the charges or negotiate some other type of arrangement with the court.

Due to significant reforms in the criminal legal systems in recent years, drug possession arrests alone do not result in the high rates of incarceration as they did in the 1980s and 1990s. However, a new drug conviction can lead to harsher, enhanced sentences and incarceration if a person is charged with drug possession and another offense like paraphernalia. Someone may also be penalized more if they have multiple past drug charges or a history of other charges. This is because of "three strikes" laws and other similar policies that justify stricter penalties for people seen as "repeat offenders" or mandatory minimum sentencing laws that require judges to impose imprisonment for certain crimes regardless of extenuating circumstances. Given that communities of color and low-income communities are disproportionately targeted by law enforcement for drug charges, these harsh penalties can compound the drug war's harms for some groups over others.

When people with SUDs are incarcerated, enrolled in a drug court as an alternative to incarceration, or placed on probation, research shows they are less likely to access evidence-based treatments like methadone and buprenorphine for OUD than the general population. These medications are still not readily accessible in prisons and jails across the nation, often due to stigma and a lack of policy, funding, infrastructure, and political will to allow the dispensing of these highly controlled medications to all who may need them. Many are lucky if they can even get on-site Alcoholics Anonymous or Narcotics Anonymous self-help meetings when incarcerated, because access to counseling or any other treatment is rare.[30] However, when people with OUD do not get access to these medications while inside jails or prisons, it dramatically increases their risk of a fatal opioid overdose soon after release. Studies have shown that those released from incarceration are 27 times more likely to overdose within the first two weeks of release than the general population.[31] In addition, local drug court and probation policies are no better – although many refer participants to treatment in the community, they may not allow participants to take these medications as part of treatment while they are under court supervision, often due to stigma rather than evidence.[32]

In addition, there are still myriad harmful collateral consequences associated with even a single drug possession arrest that can have lasting effects on someone's life even if they are never incarcerated.[33] Some people must pay costly tickets, fines, or fees, while others may be subject to community supervision programs such as probation. Once a drug possession charge ends up on a person's criminal record, it can also lead to challenges and discrimination for a lifetime. A drug conviction can result in a loss of child custody and voting rights and can lead to deportation for noncitizens, even if they have been in the United States since they were children and had no prior law enforcement contact. A drug conviction can make it hard to pass a background check for a job or a new apartment, even decades later. A drug conviction can mean you cannot pursue specific professional licenses or credentials, locking you out of a potentially higher-paying specialized field of work you are passionate about. A drug conviction can get you and your entire family evicted from public housing and make you ineligible for some social services. Essentially, the criminalization of drug use negatively impacts social determinants of health, the very things that most individuals and communities need to thrive, like housing, employment, social connection, community, and education.[34] And when specific communities, such as communities of color and low-income communities, are disproportionately impacted by these factors, criminalization of drugs can further disrupt their progress, suppress them from advancing economically, and entrench health disparities between them and more privileged groups.

The harms associated with drug criminalization are not experienced by people who use regulated and legal drugs or controlled medications. For people with SUDs who are arrested, then incarcerated, or involved with community alternatives to incarceration like drug courts or probation, this involvement with the criminal legal system can mean that people may not have access to any treatment, or they may not have access to the most effective treatments. Meanwhile, regardless of whether someone has an SUD, the collateral consequences of encounters with the criminal legal system can stay on one's record for a lifetime, long after release, or even if they never spend time behind bars. These harms could be reduced or eliminated if certain drugs were not criminalized, either through formal decriminalization of drug possession or through policy change that treats it as a civil offense like a traffic ticket.

Drug Equipment Deemed Paraphernalia

Our drug war policies also made the equipment used to consume illegal drugs illegal (i.e., syringes, pipes, cookers) so that people were forced to share or reuse them, which increased the risk of bacterial and viral infections. Together, these policies and practices laid the foundation for the conditions that contributed to the HIV crisis that wreaked havoc on people who injected drugs during the 1980s and 1990s (and contribute to outbreaks right now during the overdose crisis). Sadly, governmental apathy and inaction were an expected response after decades of demonizing and admonishing people who injected drugs as dangerous criminals on the nightly news. People who injected drugs were seen as disposable, since they shouldn't have been using drugs to begin with. Offering them assistance or sterile syringes was wrongly viewed as a waste of resources and encouraging illegal behavior rather than an investment in public health for a marginalized group. A growing body of research has found that the "criminalization of drug use has a negative effect on HIV prevention and treatment."[35] The major international journal *The Lancet* published an editorial in its HIV specialty issue with the provocative and succinct title "The War on Drugs is Incompatible with the Fight Against HIV."[36]

In response to their unmet needs, people who injected drugs and their allies started underground SEP networks to address this crisis in their communities. Many organized into advocacy coalitions, like ACT UP, to pressure public officials to face the crisis by legalizing and funding harm reduction solutions to save lives. After tireless efforts, some state laws were changed to allow SEPs to operate legally or, at least, caused states and local jurisdictions to deprioritize enforcing criminal penalties against them. Some states also protected participants from being arrested for syringe possession by decriminalizing needles or allowing legal exemptions for card-carrying SEP participants. These policy changes also allowed legally operating programs to seek local and state grants to sustain themselves. However, private foundations and donor funds were (and still are) needed to keep most programs afloat. Meanwhile, other states kept syringes illegal so that SEPs operated illegally and underground, if at all. To this day, many programs face challenges even in localities where they are legal because of restrictive local and state policies that can limit the types of services they offer and threaten them with shutdowns.

When the overdose crisis hit in the early 2000s, our existing harm reduction infrastructure from the HIV/AIDS crisis was all we had to support people injecting drugs and at risk of heroin- or fentanyl-involved overdoses. The provision of sterile injecting and smoking equipment was a way to help them reduce the risk of infections, but also a great recruitment tool to engage them in other services on site. During the overdose crisis, SEPs became known as Syringe Service Programs (SSPs) because they came to be seen as sites where people who use drugs could get a variety of other services on site too, including HIV/HCV testing, naloxone to reverse overdoses, fentanyl test strips and other drug-checking services, wound care and other medical treatment, referrals to treatment, and so much more. However, the ongoing drug war makes it difficult for these programs to survive and expand to reach the communities that need them the most.

Reflections on Our Drug Policy

Learning the history of drug enforcement complicated what I had assumed was a clear and long-standing line between illegal drugs, medicines, and legal drugs. But I learned that this line did not exist for most of the history of the United States and began to be drawn only in the 20th century. I also imagined that early American drug laws gained traction and were passed because of evidence that these substances were uniquely addictive or deadly compared to other readily available drugs. However, in actuality, the lines were first drawn due to fears that intoxicated users were a threat to public safety – more specifically, men of color posed a violent and dangerous threat to white women, children, and men while they used certain drugs. These fears contributed to increased support among the white population for restricting minority access to these drugs by banning products associated with these groups. It also linked these drugs to specific racial, ethnic, and social groups in the mainstream white American psyche, even if they were not using them at high rates (or at all). These groups became "faces" of various drugs. They also became associated with ideas of drug-related criminality and danger.

I have come to see that medicalizing certain drugs has always served a gatekeeping function. American drug policy always intended to maintain some people's seemingly legitimate access to specific versions of these drugs while limiting their widespread recreational use among the masses, especially among racial and ethnic minorities. Medicalization helped draw racialized lines between desirable and deserving patients versus everyone else. And although I started this chapter by describing an opiate crisis at the turn of the 20th century that involved Bayer-marketed heroin, it is hard to overlook the parallels between what happened at that time and what occurred during the turn of the 21st century with Purdue-marketed oxycodone.

What do we do now that we know that the lines between different drugs have always been subject to change? That the categories and labels that we have grown comfortable with – legal drugs, illegal drugs, and medications – were not initially made based on science or evidence? That emotions like fear led lawmakers and voters to support policies that drew new lines in the sand? That the concept of "good" drugs versus "bad" drugs and even "therapeutic" versus "dangerous" drugs were socially constructed and subject to change? That racial disparities in our criminal justice system, especially those fueled by the drug war, were made by design?[37] How do we reconcile that the disproportionate policing of communities of color in the name of the drug war was not simply a tragedy of misdirected enforcement priorities, but instead, because racism and xenophobia were baked into our US drug laws from the start? When do we acknowledge that the drug war has been working as designed?

The history shows us why we all may overestimate the harms of illegal drugs while underestimating the relative harms of legal or medical drugs. There are not, and never have been, fixed or permanent groupings of "good" versus "bad" drugs. And these "good" and "bad" drug categories are not universal. Drug perceptions, as well as policies, can and do change dramatically all the time.

Within the context of ever-changing public views and policies, harm reductionists consistently understand that all drugs serve unique functions for users and potential risks and harms. They recognize that many people may choose to avoid or abstain from certain drugs to avoid the actual or perceived health risks, to avoid the stigma associated with using them, because of their illegality, or for other reasons. But, most importantly, harm reductionists also acknowledge that *there will always be a subset of people in our population who will choose to use drugs anyway*. These people are entitled to tools to stay safe.

Harm reductionists resist the false dichotomy of the drug war, which tells us that there are good drugs whose use should be exempt from punishment and bad drugs that should be banned. Since all drugs fall along a continuum of potential harm, creating a line between so-called good drugs and bad drugs is arbitrary and unhelpful. Research shows that all drugs, regardless of their legal or social status, come with risks of harm. In the next chapter, I will describe how harm reductionists propose that we reduce drug-related harm in our communities.

Notes

1 Musto, David F. *The American Disease*. New Haven, CT: Yale University Press, 1973.
2 Davenport-Hines, Richard. *The Pursuit of Oblivion: A Global History of Narcotics 1500–2000*. London: Weidenfeld & Nicolson, 2001.
3 Herzberg, David. *White Market Drugs: Big Pharma and the Hidden History of Addiction in America*. Chicago: University of Chicago Press, 2020.
4 Williams, Edward Huntington. "Negro Cocaine 'Fiends' Are a New Southern Menace." *New York Times*, 12, February 8, 1914.
5 Musto, David F. The *American Disease*. New Haven, CT: Yale University Press, 1973.
6 Ibid.
7 Fiscella, Kevin, E. Sarah, and Leo L. Beletsky. "Buprenorphine Deregulation and Mainstreaming Treatment for Opioid Use Disorder: X the X Waiver." *JAMA Psychiatry* 76, no. 3 (2019): 229–30.
8 Jellinek, E. Morton. *The Disease Concept of Alcoholism*. New Haven, CT: Hillhouse Press, 1960.
9 Schneider, Joseph W. "Deviant Drinking as a Disease: Alcoholism as a Social Accomplishment." *Social Problems* 25, no. 4 (1978), 361–71.
10 Solomon, Robert. "Racism and Its Effect on Cannabis Research." *Cannabis and Cannabinoid Research* 5, no. 1 (2020): 2–5. https://doi.org/10.1089/can.2019.0063.
11 Nutt, David, Leslie A. King, William Saulsbury, and Colin Blakemore. "Development of a Rational Scale to Assess the Harm of Drugs of Potential Misuse." *The Lancet* 369, no. 9566 (2007): 1047–53. https://doi.org/10.1016/S0140-6736(07)60464-4.
12 Baum, Dan. "Legalize It All: How to Win the War on Drugs." *Harper's magazine*, April 2016. https://harpers.org/archive/2016/04/legalize-it-all/.
13 Johnson, Kenneth E. "The Constitutionality of Drug Paraphernalia Laws." *Columbia Law Review* 81, no. 3 (1981): 581–611. https://doi.org/10.2307/1122259.
14 Model Drug Paraphernalia Act (United States Drug Enforcement Administration 1979), reprinted in Drug Paraphernalia: Hearing Before the Select Committee on Narcotics Abuse and Control of the House of Representative, 96th Congress, 1st session, 88–95, 1979.
15 National Research Council (US) and Institute of Medicine (US). *Panel on Needle Exchange and Bleach Distribution Programs. Proceedings Workshop on Needle Exchange and Bleach Distribution Programs*. Washington (DC): National Academies Press (US), 1994.
16 Ibid.
17 At the time of this writing, Attorney General Merrick Garland released a memo that instructed federal prosecutors nationwide to sentence people for possession of crack cocaine using the same thresholds as cocaine and reserving mandatory minimum sentences only for cases with certain aggravating factors. Legislative efforts are underway to reduce these sentencing disparities as well.

18 Showalter, David. "Federal Funding for Syringe Exchange in the US: Explaining a Long-Term Policy Failure." *International Journal of Drug Policy* 55 (May 2018): 95–104. https://doi.org/10.1016/j.drugpo.2018.02.006.

19 Reinarman, Craig, and Harry G. Levine. *Crack in America: Demon Drugs and Social Justice.* Los Angeles: University of California, 1997.

20 Beaver, Alyssa L. "Getting a Fix on Cocaine Sentencing Policy: Reforming the Sentencing Scheme of the Anti-Drug Abuse Act of 1986." *Fordham Law Review* 78 (2010): 2531–75.

21 Vakharia, Sheila P. *Drug Policy Reform. Encyclopedia of Social Work.* London: University of Oxford, 2021. https://doi.org/10.1093/acrefore/9780199 975839.013.1426.

22 Midgette, Gregory, Steven Davenport, Jonathan P. Caulkins, and Beau Kilmer. *What America's Users Spend on Illegal Drugs, 2006–2016.* Santa Monica, CA: RAND Corporation, 2019. https://doi.org/10.7249/RR3140.

23 This material was originally published in *The Encyclopedia of Social Work* by Sheila P. Vakharia and has been reproduced by permission of Oxford University Press: http://global.oup.com/academic. For permission to reuse this material, please visit http://global.oup.com/academic/rights.

24 Wilson, Laura, and Alex Stevens. Understanding Drug Markets and How to Influence Them. *Beckley Foundation Drug Program.* Beckley Foundation, 2016. https://www.beckleyfoundation.org/resource/understanding-drug-markets-and-how-to-influence-them/

25 Beletsky, Leo, and Corey S. Davis. "Today's Fentanyl Crisis: Prohibition's Iron Law, Revisited." *International Journal of Drug Policy* 46 (2017): 156–59. https://doi.org/10.1016/j.drugpo.2017.05.050.

26 Ciccarone, Daniel. "Fentanyl in the US Heroin Supply: A Rapidly Changing Risk Environment." *International Journal of Drug Policy* 46 (2017). https://doi.org/10.1016/j.drugpo.2017.06.010.

27 Voelker, Rebecca. "As Heroin Death Rates Rose, So Did Illicit Drug Seizures." *JAMA* 318, no. 14 (2017): 1315. https://doi.org/10.1001/jama.2017.14433.

28 Pardo, Bryce, Jirka Taylor, Jonathan P. Caulkins, Beau Kilmer, Peter Reuter, and Bradley D. Stein. *The Future of Fentanyl and Other Synthetic Opioids.* Santa Monica, CA: RAND Corporation, 2019. https://doi.org/10.7249/RR3117.

29 Federal Bureau of Investigation. "Crime Data Explorer 2020 National Incident-Based Reporting Systems Tables." https://crime-data-explorer.app.cloud.gov/pages/downloads (accessed December 27, 2022).

30 Weizman, Shelly, Joanna Perez, Isaac Manoff, Melissa Baney, and Taleed El-Sabawi. *National Snapshot: Access to Medications for Opioid Use Disorder in US Jails and Prisons.* Washington, DC: O'Neill Institute for National and Global Health Law at Georgetown Law Center, July 2021.

31 Cooper, Janine A., Ifeoma Onyeka, Christopher Cardwell, Euan Paterson, Richard Kirk, Dermot O'Reilly, and Michael Donnelly. "Record Linkage Studies of Drug-Related Deaths among Adults Who Were Released from Prison to the Community: A Scoping Review." *BMC Public Health* 23, no. 1 (2023): 826. https://doi.org/10.1186/s12889-023-15673-0.

32 Khatri, Utsha G., Benjamin A. Howell, and Tyler N. A. Winkelman. "Medicaid Expansion Increased Medications for Opioid Use Disorder among Adults Referred By Criminal Justice Agencies." *Health Affairs* 40, no. 4 (2021): 562–70. https://doi.org/10.1377/hlthaff.2020.01251.

33 To learn more about the harms associated with a criminal record in general, I encourage you to visit the National Inventory of Collateral Consequences of

Conviction website at https://niccc.nationalreentryresourcecenter.org/. To learn more about the harms of drug-related convictions and drug enforcement outside the criminal legal system, I recommend you check out the Drug Policy Alliance's six-part video and report series, *Uprooting the Drug War*, at https://uprootingthedrugwar.org/.

34   Cohen, Aliza, Sheila P. Vakharia, Julie Netherland, and Kassandra Frederique. "How the War on Drugs Impacts Social Determinants of Health beyond the Criminal Legal System." *Annals of Medicine* 54, no. 1 (2022): 2024–38. https://doi.org/10.1080/07853890.2022.2100926.

35   DeBeck, Kora, Tessa Cheng, Julio S. Montaner, Chris Beyrer, Richard Elliott, Susan Sherman, Evan Wood, and Stefan Baral. "HIV and the Criminalisation of Drug Use among People Who Inject Drugs: A Systematic Review." *The Lancet HIV* 4, no. 8 (2017): e357–74. https://doi.org/10.1016/S2352-3018(17)30073-5.

36   Editorial Board. "The War on Drugs Is Incompatible with the Fight against HIV." *The Lancet HIV* 6, no.5 (2019): e269. https://doi.org/10.1016/S2352-3018(19)30112-2.

37   Alexander, Michelle. *The New Jim Crow: Mass Incarceration in the Age of Colorblindness.* New York: New Press, 2010.

3   What Is Harm Reduction?

Harm reduction is a reality-based approach that recognizes that drug use and other risky behaviors are a part of our everyday lives. Harm reductionists recognize that although abstinence may be a safe strategy, it is not feasible, appealing, or practical for all people in all situations. Despite our efforts to ban certain drugs or restrict certain behaviors, harm reductionists acknowledge that people will continue to use drugs and engage in high-risk practices. Harm reductionists believe we must do what we can to ensure that anyone using drugs has the tools to stay as safe as possible. People who practice harm reduction acknowledge that drug use carries a degree of risk for users, their loved ones, and their communities. Some of these harms are inherent to drugs – alcohol is a known neurotoxin – while others are policy-driven. For example, we can reduce legal drug-related harms if people are taught strategies for lower-risk use, including moderation, or can access lower-risk alternatives. Meanwhile, the illegal and unregulated status of other drugs creates and compounds drug-related risks, since such a status makes it extremely difficult to practice safer use strategies, and the threat of arrest and incarceration can drive people into the shadows to avoid punishment.

Even if you've never heard of the term "harm reduction" before, you have probably benefited from some harm reduction tools and practices in your day-to-day life. For instance, social distancing, wearing a mask, and vaccination are harm reduction strategies many of us have used to stay safe during the COVID-19 pandemic. Since we cannot eliminate the risk of catching the coronavirus, we learned which steps to reduce that risk as much as possible. Some familiar drug-related harm reduction examples include having a designated driver when drinking alcohol, and switching to nicotine gum instead of smoking cigarettes. There are hundreds of different, lesser-known harm reduction strategies for these and other substances that could be useful to many of us, and I will be discussing some of them in this book.

Harm reductionists know it is possible to arm those who use drugs with the tools and skills to stay as safe as possible *right now*. And they believe that this is far more practical and realistic than simply hoping people who use

DOI: 10.4324/9781003301745-4

drugs can figure out how to keep safe on their own after they outgrow the "Just Say No" and abstinence-only messages they've been inundated with since they were kids. Harm reductionists believe that anyone can be supported in being safer, including people who do not meet the criteria for a substance use disorder (SUD) diagnosis and those who may not need formal treatment. It also means that harm reductionists are willing to help people without fixating on the unrealistic and overly idealistic belief that people with SUDs can be helped only if they agree to stop all drug use.

According to the National Harm Reduction Coalition, harm reduction is "a set of practical strategies and ideas aimed at reducing negative consequences associated with drug use."[1] It is grounded in the understanding that people can and will make informed choices to keep themselves and their loved ones safe when empowered to do so. While harm reduction options are readily available and widely supported in many parts of the world, they are underfunded, inaccessible, highly stigmatized, and illegal in much of the United States.

Yet, harm reduction is not only the sum of its tools and strategies. Harm reductionists advocate for dozens of broader policies at the local, state, and federal levels to promote community health and safety, such as those that provide supportive and affordable housing, guarantee a living wage, reform our criminal legal system, fund the social safety net, and expand access to healthcare and other lifesaving services. In addition, harm reductionists support drug policy changes that would end the criminalization of people who use illegal drugs. They also want policies to allow for a safer supply of drugs, be it through a legally regulated model and/or by having access to tools to test and check what is in the drugs they may choose to use. Harm reductionists want access to various non-stigmatizing, trauma-informed, evidence-based treatment options if they seek formal assistance for medical or mental health needs. Harm reductionists are critical of the widespread use of the criminal legal system to punish people through incarceration, surveillance, and lifelong criminal records when those resources could be more wisely spent on community enrichment for greater public safety and well-being. Together, these policies can help save lives by addressing our current health and social issues, improving the material conditions of our communities, and ensuring people feel safe when they seek help.

Harm reduction is grounded in a compassionate stance that all people deserve help and support. At its core, it is a philosophy that affirms that every human life has value and that all people deserve unconditional support as they navigate challenges. And harm reductionists believe that this is true regardless of which psychoactive substances a person may choose to put in their body. It also respects the autonomy and self-determination of people by helping them on their own terms and timelines in realistic and manageable ways. Most importantly, harm reduction challenges our cultural norms about who is entitled to a dignified life. Unfortunately, our policies and systems often distinguish between those who are "deserving" or "undeserving" of help to meet their basic needs, but harm reductionists fundamentally believe that no one is disposable.

There are many incredible leaders, both past and present, who have made an impact on the movement.[2,3] Someone might reference the Young Lords and Black Panthers, who fought for community-driven care and shared resources in the 1960s and 1970s when government institutions failed to address poverty, food insecurity, and lack of healthcare in their communities. Others may look to the drug user union *Junkiebond* in the Netherlands that started the first needle exchange for injection drug users in the 1980s during hepatitis B and HIV outbreaks. Many of us were introduced to harm reduction by the LGBTQIA+ and sex worker mutual aid groups who passed along the first "bad date" lists and helped one another stay safe on the streets, or we may draw inspiration from the ACT UP activists who fought for access to HIV/AIDS treatments and funding in the 1980s and 1990s. Others were moved to do this work by great individuals like Edith Springer, Imani Woods, Joyce Rivera, Alan Marlatt, Keith Cylar, Dan Bigg, and Dave Purchase. Others followed the lead of the Vancouver activists who opened the first Overdose Prevention Centers (OPCs) in North America, or the harm reductionists who started underground naloxone distribution among people who use drugs. Meanwhile, some of us joined the movement because it saved our lives; perhaps the local harm reduction program supported us when we needed it the most. Regardless of the individuals or groups one credits as their inspiration or entry point into harm reduction, many core values and principles guiding early harm reduction practice and advocacy still inform the work today.

Harm reduction is an ethos of unconditional care with deep roots in mutual aid and a commitment to building power within communities through shared knowledge and resources. It was born from low-income communities that were criminalized, marginalized, and subjected to structural violence due to their drug use, as well as from their racialized identities, being LGBTQIA+, engaging in sex work, working in other underground economies, and/or being unhoused.[4] In the face of criminalization and oppression, these communities developed strategies to navigate myriad risks and dangers, such as:

- The unpredictability of the illicit drug supply
- A lack of sterile syringes and other drug-using equipment
- Interpersonal and state violence
- The constant threat of police contact and criminalization
- Poverty and financial instability
- A lack of safe and stable housing

- The risk of HIV and other blood-borne or sexually transmitted infections
- A lack of access to health and mental healthcare
- And much more

It should also be noted that thousands were doing this work and helping one another to stay safe long before the term "harm reduction" was coined in 1987, and countless people are doing this work around the world every day without using the term or label. The "harm reduction movement," as we know it, is simply an extension and a recent iteration of generations of resistance, advocacy, and mutual aid movements among marginalized communities who could not rely upon formal institutionalized structures and systems to meet their needs. For decades, harm reductionists have taken matters into their own hands while navigating systems that did not acknowledge their humanity and actively threatened their fundamental rights to health and safety. Harm reductionists have always understood that we are all safer when we find solutions together and resist the forces that oppress us, marginalize us, and neglect our needs.

Harm Reduction in the United States and Abroad

What examples of harm reduction programs and approaches have emerged over the past several decades? What are the characteristics of each, and who is best served by them? What gap do they attempt to fill in our current continuum of care? Is there research or evidence to support their efficacy? In this chapter, I will describe six main types of drug- and alcohol-related harm reduction programs and approaches currently available in the United States and abroad so that we are all on the same page about the types of programs and approaches discussed in this book. Some may sound familiar, but others may be new to you.

Syringe Service Programs

The most common and well-known harm reduction programs in the United States and globally are Syringe Service Programs (SSPs), sometimes called syringe or needle exchange programs. Some SSPs are in brick-and-mortar locations, while others are mobile or online. Nonprofit groups run most SSPs, and many receive support from city or state public health departments. SSPs distribute sterile syringes and injecting equipment to people who inject drugs, including sterile cookers, cotton, Band-Aids, alcohol wipes, and tourniquets.[5] In some states, SSPs can legally distribute safer smoking kits, including new glass pipes for smoking drugs like crack cocaine, methamphetamine, heroin, and fentanyl. They may also distribute various other items for safer smoking.[6] In addition, SSPs distribute condoms and lubricant to promote safer sex practices, because sex and drug use often go together; reducing risks associated with both behaviors can help keep people safe all around. Many SSPs also provide rapid HIV testing and hepatitis C testing, since people who inject drugs are a high-risk population for these infections. Some SSPs also distribute other items and provide other services, such as snacks, bottled water, clothing, showers, acupuncture, case management, and on-site counseling.

SSPs are a significant distribution source of the opioid overdose reversal medication naloxone[7] that revives people after an overdose involving a drug like fentanyl, heroin, or opioid pain medications. SSPs often conduct overdose response training and distribute naloxone to SSP participants, their loved ones, and community members.

Depending on state policies, SSPs also provide participants access to tools or machines to check their drugs to see what substances they may contain, since the drug supply is unpredictable.[8] As I mentioned in the last chapter, many state laws deem these tools "drug paraphernalia." In states where this practice is decriminalized or legal, SSPs can distribute fentanyl test strips, small strips of paper to dip into a diluted drug solution and indicate whether fentanyl is present. And since xylazine has entered the drug supply in recent years, programs are also beginning to distribute xylazine test strips. Providing these services is essential and lifesaving because the average person buying drugs in the underground market cannot know whether the drug they purchased is what they think it is. Armed with information about what one's drugs actually contain can help inform drug-related decision-making. With this knowledge, the person may choose to use less than usual, they may not mix it or take it along with other drugs, they may choose not to use it alone, and they could ensure that they are using it with someone who has naloxone on hand in case they overdose.

There are approximately 450 legally operating SSPs across the nation.[9] Though 450 SSPs may sound like a lot, it is not nearly enough. For reference, the United States has approximately 16,000 publicly funded addiction treatment programs. We have one legally operating SSP for every 35 treatment facilities, a ratio that, for several reasons, is even more skewed in many states. The few SSPs nationally are disproportionately concentrated in major cities and coastal blue states. Relatively few operate in predominantly rural, midwestern, or southern states, and many of these states do not even have a single legal above-ground SSP in operation.[10] While SSPs can operate legally and above ground in some parts of the country, are illegal and try to stay under the radar in their communities to avoid arrest. Unfortunately, this means that people in most communities nationwide do not have a safe source of sterile equipment. And this disparity contributes to our nation's harm reduction gap.

We have relatively few SSPs because of restrictive local and state policies that make it difficult or illegal for them to do their lifesaving work. Since possessing syringes or glass pipes to smoke drugs is a drug paraphernalia offense in many states, many harm reductionists have not opened SSPs for fear that staff and participants could be targeted by law enforcement. As of this writing, *SSPs still cannot legally operate in 20% of US states*, and many states with legal SSPs still do not provide complete legal protection to clients who use these services.[11] In addition, vocal "Not in My Backyard" (NIMBY) community members and politicians have forced some legally operating SSPs to shut down or suspend services, and many SSPs remain under attack because of community hostility and stigma against people who use drugs. Lastly, funding disparities and differential funding streams also explain why there are significantly more operating treatment and prevention programs than harm reduction programs across the nation. Until recently, SSPs could not receive federal funding to do their work. Since SSPs are largely mutual aid efforts led by impacted communities rather than by formalized medical centers, they cannot bill insurance plans and rely on grants and donations to operate.

However, there has been some progress in advancing policies to support SSPs in recent years, and there were more operating SSPs in 2023 than there were in 2013. Decades of advocacy and increased injection drug use caused by the current overdose crisis have contributed to this enormous step forward. And more must still be done to expand access to these vital supports and services. Also, just because a state allows for the operation of SSPs does not mean there are enough operating programs to meet community needs across the state. Unfortunately, few SSPs in the nation can afford to be open for as many hours per day or days per week as they need, and tight budgets and policy restrictions may mean they cannot provide as many supplies or services as possible. It also often means that people who work for SSPs are not well-compensated for their work, and unpaid volunteers primarily staff many programs.

Why SSPs Are Essential in Our Continuum of Care

In much of the United States, it is challenging to acquire new sterile syringes unless you go to a pharmacy with a prescription for an injectable medication. While more states allow pharmacies to sell syringes without prescriptions, there are barriers to access. Cost and transportation are common obstacles, in addition to the stress of having to navigate stigmatizing attitudes among pharmacy staff. Sometimes your dealer may sell syringes, or you can borrow/share a syringe from a friend who injects drugs.[12] In any case, there is no guarantee that you will have a sterile new syringe, which may place you at risk for harm every time you inject yourself. Infectious diseases like HIV and hepatitis C spread very quickly among people who share syringes, since one's bloodstream has direct contact with the needle, and small amounts of blood in the needle or barrel can then be unintentionally injected into the next person who uses the syringe.

You can also get sick or injured by reusing your own syringes, even if you never share a syringe with anyone else. It is difficult to keep them clean, and they gradually become damaged from repeated use. Without an SSP, you might not have access to alcohol wipes, Band-Aids, and tourniquets. These are supplies that can make each injection safer, much like any injection you would receive in a medical setting. This is why programs work so hard to ensure that people have their own supplies, do not share them, and use a new sterile syringe and equipment *every single time*. Depending on one's drug use patterns and which drugs they use, some people can need sterile equipment for up to 6–10 injections per day, because every single injection poses a potential risk for infection and other health risks.

Most SSPs teach participants about these risks and help them learn about the precautions they can take to stay safe. SSP participants learn the importance of rotating injection sites on the body so they do not cause further damage by repeatedly injecting in the same place, especially if they already have a wound or injury. They also learn about the lowest-risk and highest-risk veins for injecting and are taught vein care strategies to avoid collapsed veins or incurring new damage.

Sometimes SSPs can also give people the tools to switch from injecting to a lower-risk route of consumption. A recent study found that an SSP helped people who primarily injected heroin transition to smoking heroin by providing them with sterile pipes.[13] Though smoking drugs is not entirely 100% safe, it is a lower-risk route of administration than injecting because it reduces the risk of certain blood-borne infectious diseases and injection-related harms such as skin and soft tissue infections. Switching away from injecting can also reduce the risk of overdose because it is easy for some people to inject too much. For them, smoking drugs may help them pace themselves.

SSPs also encourage participants to dispose of used syringes and equipment on site, and research shows that communities have fewer publicly discarded syringes after opening SSPs.[14] SSPs hand out medical sharps disposal containers so participants can collect and safely store their used syringes until they dispose of them at the program. Participants are also taught how to safely dispose of syringes if they cannot wait to return to the SSP, for instance at pharmacies or at public kiosks.[15] Community syringe cleanup is also a common practice for most SSPs, and outreach teams go into alleys and nearby neighborhoods to pick up and dispose of publicly discarded syringes. Many SSPs have become valued members of their communities for providing this service regularly or when requested.

During the early months of the COVID-19 pandemic, some states classi-fied SSPs as essential healthcare programs, allowing them to operate and keep participants engaged in health-promoting behavior during lockdowns. And given the widespread misinformation and confusing guidelines for CO-VID-19 prevention, SSPs used their established trust and credibility with their participants to be a reliable source of accurate health information. They developed accessible and easy-to-understand materials to teach par-ticipants about the virus, how it could be spread, and how to stay safe. They even taught participants COVID precautions for when they respond to an overdose. Many provided participants with personal protective equipment (PPE), masks, and hand sanitizer and even conducted rapid COVID tests. When the vaccines were made more accessible, some SSPs vaccinated their participants on site. When COVID-related telehealth provisions were passed, many SSPs could also provide more mental health and primary care services.[16] Given that a significant number of marginalized people who in-ject drugs have multiple comorbidities and COVID-19 risk factors, it is likely that thousands of members of this high-risk population avoided infec-tion because they received information and support to stay safe from their SSPs.

Lastly, SSPs are an unparalleled lifeline in our communities for people us-ing illegal and highly stigmatized drugs like heroin, fentanyl, crack cocaine, and methamphetamine. People who actively use these drugs are often shunned, shamed, and disqualified from most types of programs and ser-vices in our communities. SSP staff, peers, and volunteers can engage them in a community of care and support by creating a welcoming environment. They are not pressured to comply with strict enrollment or attendance re-quirements, so they can utilize these services as needed on their terms. And whenever they show up, they can get the supplies they need, check in with people who are happy to see them, share their day-to-day struggles, and work toward their goals. Given the success of SSPs in engaging an otherwise hard-to-reach population, some have built linkages with broader healthcare systems to provide more services on site. A growing number of SSPs have contracted with providers to provide medical treatments such as hepatitis C treatment and low-threshold buprenorphine, a medication used to treat opioid use disorder (MOUD).[17]

Over 30 years of domestic and international research shows that access to SSPs and sterile drug-using equipment can dramatically improve the health of people who inject drugs. SSPs are a referral source for other services, in-cluding healthcare and treatment.[18] [19] SSPs reduce the incidence of HIV, hepatitis C, and other injection-related harms among people who inject drugs in communities.[20] In fact, several of the most notable HIV outbreaks among people who inject drugs in the United States were in communities without SSPs or those that restricted or recently shut down their SSPs. The success of SSPs shows that it is possible for people who inject drugs to stay safe; they simply must have the resources and support to do so without the threat of arrest.

Overdose Prevention Centers

The first OPC was opened in Switzerland in 1986, and over 100 OPCs operate worldwide in more than a dozen countries. These are also known as Supervised Injection Facilities, Drug Consumption Rooms, and Supervised Consumption Sites. OPCs are legally sanctioned sites where people can bring pre-obtained drugs and use them on site with new sterile equipment under medical supervision, so that any drug-related adverse events can be addressed and opioid overdoses can be reversed immediately. People predominantly inject drugs at these sites, but there are sites where smoking is also permitted. OPCs are often staffed by various medical professionals who can respond to medical needs and treat injuries or wounds. However, they also employ peers and other staff who can respond to emergencies and make referrals for treatment and provide support and resources on site. Many sites also provide participants with showers, laundry facilities, bathrooms, snacks, drinks, and support groups.

At the time of this writing, there are only two sanctioned OPCs in the United States. Both opened in December 2021 in New York City with the support of local policymakers and neighbors and an agreement with the police department to not intervene in operations. In their first year of service, hundreds of guests *per day* used the facilities. While over 700 overdoses occurred on site, not a single guest died, because the staff could reverse these overdoses on site with naloxone or oxygen. There was one outdoor, legally sanctioned OPC in San Francisco for much of 2022 that was permitted to operate by local policymakers and law enforcement. No one died of an overdose at the site, and the staff reversed over 300 overdoses while serving thousands of participants. In 2021, the governor of Rhode Island signed a bill into law to allow OPCs to open in the state, yet no sites have opened there as of this writing in 2023. There are no other legally operating OPCs in the United States, although advocates in over a dozen cities across the country have expressed interest in opening these sites in their communities. One of the barriers to opening these sites is that many advocates fear federal interference since OPCs technically violate federal law.

In 2019, community members in Philadelphia came together to explore plans to open an OPC called Safehouse. The Trump administration argued that the proposed OPC would violate the federal 35-year-old so-called "crackhouse statute" and filed a civil lawsuit. Written in the 1980s, when racialized fears of crack cocaine use and crime in major cities fueled harsh federal and state laws and penalties, the crackhouse statute made it illegal for landlords and property managers to knowingly operate a site where people manufactured, distributed, or used illegal drugs. However, Safehouse advocates successfully made the case in court that OPCs were medical sites that provided healthcare and other support to participants. The judge ultimately ruled in their favor. But soon after, federal officials filed an appeal and won, overturning the initial ruling and deeming these sites federally illegal. Despite this, federal law enforcement entities under the Biden administration never intervened at New York City or San Francisco's sites, both of which opened during the early months of his presidency. Other jurisdictions may open their sites soon if they get enough local support and buy-in – and as long as the federal government does not go after them.

Why Do We Need OPCs?

One of the key populations that OPCs serve is people who are homeless, unstably housed, or live in unsafe environments. Most shelters and structured housing programs prohibit drug use on site and will kick people out if they are found using drugs on the premises. This can mean that they may end up using drugs in alleys, abandoned buildings, restaurant bathrooms, libraries, or other public places. When using drugs in these scenarios, fear of getting caught or arrested may lead someone to quickly inject and not take precautions to reduce the risk of an infection or an overdose. And if they do overdose, a bystander or passerby may not immediately notice or be equipped to respond effectively. Using drugs in these situations also increases the likelihood that someone will end up using nonsterile equipment, missing their vein, or injecting too much too quickly because they were rushed. An OPC can provide a clean environment with sterile equipment and good lighting. There is no rush, and people can take their time to do it right. Trained staff are available to respond if anything happens. Research shows that injecting drugs in these conditions reduces the risk of bacterial or viral infections, fatal overdose, and skin and soft tissue damage from improper injecting practices in unsafe environments.[21]

OPCs also serve an essential function for communities because they bring drug use inside. These sites afford people who use drugs the dignity to safely and comfortably use in a setting where they are supported and cared for rather than a sidewalk, where they may receive stares and unwanted attention.[22] When OPCs operate in easily accessible neighborhoods and are operational for as many days and hours as possible, people are more likely to use drugs on site rather than in public places.[23] In addition to reducing public drug use, OPCs can help reduce drug-related litter in neighborhoods, since many people who use drugs outdoors may be unable to safely dispose of their drug equipment quickly or may not be able to hold onto syringes, pipes, and other items long enough to return them to an SSP.

When people can use on site and safely dispose of drug equipment at the OPC, it reduces public drug use and drug litter in communities.[24] These beneficial outcomes help garner greater community support for OPCs because people can see the immediate benefits in their neighborhoods.

OPCs also appeal to people who have safe housing. Many people choose to use drugs alone, whether due to personal preference, to hide their use from others, or for some other reason. But when someone ends up unintentionally using highly potent or adulterated drugs alone, there is no one there to respond if they need help. People who otherwise use drugs alone can benefit significantly from access to OPCs since they provide a safe and nonjudgmental space.

In addition, OPCs appeal to people who use drugs in groups or with others because people who use drugs together may worry about calling 911 during an overdose or medical emergency. Since the police are often the first responders at the scene and there may be illegal drugs and drug-using equipment lying around, many worry that calling 911 could mean being arrested for drug or paraphernalia possession, violating their probation or parole, being deported, or even being charged with a drug-induced homicide if the overdose victim cannot be revived. Sadly, the fear of punishment can deter people from doing the right thing.[25] That is why even people who use drugs with others may decide to visit an OPC – they can get the help they need, and no one will get arrested.

OPCs also provide people with a safe space beyond infection or overdose prevention. Women, LGBTQIA+ people, people with disabilities, and others often are targets for violence, exploitation, theft, and sexual assault when they are impaired on the street or in the community. At an OPC, participants can feel safe to remain on site until they feel ready to leave, whereas in other settings, their impairment could have made them vulnerable to other harm. In Canada, Spain, Germany, and other countries, specialized OPCs predominantly serve women, for example, to prevent these very situations. These specialized OPCs can also offer other services and programming tailored to their clientele and needs.

OPCs are also an essential touchpoint for people who may be exposed to new drugs or adulterants that have entered the underground drug supply. Novel opioids, benzodiazepines, and tranquilizers such as nitazene analogs, etizolam, xylazine, and other drugs have now been added to heroin and fentanyl in some parts of the United States. These new drugs can cause many unknown and unpredictable drug effects. Many OPCs offer drug-checking tools and technologies to inform people about "bad batches" or help them learn what to anticipate if they decide to use a given drug. It is essential that people are in a safe space when using these drugs so they can be monitored for adverse effects and offered help if they need it. With the increasing number of novel benzodiazepines and tranquilizers being added to the opioid supply more recently, OPCs are essential for people who may become highly sedated or incapacitated for hours and so would be vulnerable on the street or alone.

Lastly, OPCs also present a cost-effective and humane alternative to calling 911 and utilizing emergency medical services (EMS) in cases of overdose. Opioid overdoses can be lethal because the brain stops signaling the lungs to breathe. Naloxone is the best tool to reverse an opioid overdose, because a person will start breathing as soon as an effective dose is administered. However, naloxone can induce opioid withdrawal in people physiologically dependent on opioids, meaning they will wake up feeling extreme discomfort for hours until they use an opioid again. OPCs often keep oxygen tanks on hand to keep the overdose victim breathing until they regain consciousness. Sometimes oxygen is provided along with low doses of naloxone, or sometimes without needing to administer any naloxone at all.[26] Remarkably, using oxygen can end up being a highly effective strategy that does not induce withdrawal and helps keep the overdose victim breathing until they wake up.

In addition, the care the OPC staff provides after an overdose differs dramatically from what they may experience when revived by an EMT or a police officer. Overdose victims in an OPC wake up to see the familiar and loving faces of their relieved OPC staff rather than the face of a stranger or a cop. Unless they have additional medical complications, the overdose victim may simply remain on site at the OPC until they feel better. When this happens, taxpayers save thousands of dollars per overdose because the person does not need to utilize costly EMS services from a 911 call, and they do not need to go to the emergency room for monitoring.[27]

Decades of global research show that OPCs are essential for saving lives, engaging marginalized people who use drugs, and providing a linkage to care for people who may otherwise be disengaged from healthcare and supportive services.[28] As more OPCs open in Canada and other parts of the world, we must think about how the United States can expand the availability of this lifesaving intervention. The first step is to ensure they can legally operate without fear of government or law enforcement interference.

Harm Reduction Approaches for Treatment and Mutual Aid

In 2007, I was hired as the sole mental health provider at an SSP and drop-in center in New York City. It was part of a large HIV and homelessness advocacy organization providing case management, housing assistance, and medical services. When I started there, I was like a fish out of water because I was in a new environment, and the SSP operated very differently from what I was accustomed to. I was coming off a couple of years working at a traditional abstinence-only outpatient substance use treatment program in my hometown in rural upstate New York. In our individual and group therapy sessions with clients, we predominantly used a counseling approach known as Twelve-Step Facilitation (TSF). The TSF approach integrated the key tenets and values of Alcoholics Anonymous (AA) and Narcotics Anonymous (NA), the well-known free community-based mutual aid groups for people with substance-related problems, into paid treatment for clients seeking professional treatment services. The TSF approach included working with clients toward accepting that they were "addicts" and that they had become powerless over their substance use and addiction. Addiction was framed as a lifelong spiritual disease that could not be "cured." Still, clients were told that recovery was possible if they worked the 12 steps of AA/NA with a sponsor and regularly attended AA/NA meetings in the community while remaining abstinent from alcohol and illegal drugs for the rest of their lives.

Clients were required to maintain abstinence from alcohol and illegal drugs while in treatment, which was monitored through routine observed urine drug testing done by the same counselors who conducted the therapy sessions. (I hated handling my clients' urine!) Even if clients were seeking treatment for a drug like cocaine, they were instructed not to use alcohol or any other illegal drugs for the duration of treatment.

I knew I had a lot of unlearning and deprogramming to do if I wanted to engage with the clients at the SSP successfully. TSF would have been ineffective, tone-deaf, and unhelpful with my clients at the SSP. My clients often picked up syringes in the room attached to my office just minutes before they met with me, so clearly, they were still using drugs, and the message of lifelong abstinence was not helpful for them in their current circumstances. Most of my SSP clients were very familiar with TSF and AA/NA (even more than me!), since almost all had been in and out of substance use treatment programs for years if not decades. Because the approach only promoted abstinence as a solution, it offered little to them to stay safe outside of following the one-size-fits-all approach.

And the rigid expectations of a TSF approach and the requirement to attend multiple AA/NA meetings a week were unrealistic. Most of my clients at the SSP temporarily lived in shelters or single resident occupancy (SRO) hotels while waiting for housing vouchers to get their apartments. Some were still on the streets. They lived with HIV, hepatitis C, and other chronic health and mental health issues. They didn't always have a safe place to sleep, access to healthy and nutritious food, or strong family or friendship networks for emotional support. They often did their best to manage their complex health issues and housing instability. Coming to the SSP was the one consistent commitment that they could manage on a regular basis, which provided them with support, community, and health-promoting resources. They did not always have the stability to be able to keep their medical appointments, and it was difficult for them to always take their medications as prescribed. Not only would their medications often get stolen or lost on the street, but the side effects of heavy-duty HIV and psychiatric medications were not conducive to life on the streets – many medications could be taken only with food, and all of them came with uncomfortable side effects including drowsiness, diarrhea, nausea, and vomiting. The shelters also kicked them out every morning and expected them to line up to reserve a bed for the night in the afternoon, leaving them to wander the streets for six hours a day without access to a bathroom, meals, a place to sit or relax, and with limited job prospects for that narrow window of time every day. And if they missed the opportunity to line up or no open beds were available that night, they were left to endure the streets overnight until they could line up again the next day.

My clients were navigating challenging and, at times, impossible circumstances. Sometimes their drug use was the least of their problems – or it was often their survival strategy for coping with it all. So what can therapy look like when clients' lives are unstable and sometimes chaotic, and they may still be using drugs?

It can look like Harm Reduction Psychotherapy (HRP).

HRP is "an approach to psychotherapy for people who use substances in which abstinence is considered neither a prerequisite to treatment nor its predominant mark of success."[29] Using HRP with my clients at the SSP was freeing for all of us because it meant we could talk about what was most important and pressing to my clients first.[30] We could discuss how they slept the night before, or whether they were able to sleep at all. And I would get updates about their housing and health. I felt privileged to bear witness to their lives and experiences. For many of my clients, the SSP was a lifeline and a community where they were treated as valuable members. It was also the only place where they could be open about their circumstances and treated with dignity and respect. Clients often dealt with dehumanizing situations on the streets and with service providers. We talked about how they coped with shame and stigma, in addition to threats to their safety on the street. We talked about their mental health and psychiatric symptoms. We discussed how their substance use fit into the broader context of their lives and how they might take steps toward being safer.

HRP emerged during the 1990s in response to a growing demand for alternatives to traditional abstinence-based treatment for people who use substances, including those who experience substance-related problems.[31,32] HRP invites incoming clients who are still unsure about their substance-related goals but want to engage in therapy for other reasons. In most traditional treatment settings where people with SUDs seek care, abstinence is the goal, and one must commit to it on day one to receive any help. This upfront expectation can deter some people from seeking services because they know they will be expected to work toward a goal that may not be appealing or feasible at that moment.

Clients with SUDs may seek therapy to manage their mental health symptoms, learn how to cope with stress, and address problems in their relationships because those concerns are most pressing to them. However, many settings refuse to treat mental health or other problems because they believe the person's SUD should be addressed as the primary issue before anything else. In addition, many people who seek counseling primarily for anxiety, depression, and other life stressors often come to see that their substance use patterns may be linked to their mental health symptoms. Some may want integrative treatment to address their issues together rather than separately by going to a traditional addiction treatment center and a different mental health provider. Yet, in traditional treatment settings, even if clients are making progress in other domains of their lives, they run the risk of being terminated or discharged for not achieving or maintaining abstinence first.

Due to these and many other factors, increasing numbers of psychologists, therapists, and social workers began to take an alternative approach to work with clients who used substances and had non-abstinence goals. While HRP practitioners are a small minority in the field, there is an increased interest domestically and internationally among therapists willing to work with clients on treatment goals that include reduced use, moderation, or safer use practices. Within a few months of starting at the SSP, I attended the Harm Reduction Psychotherapy conference in Philadelphia, where I met many of the founding members of this movement, including Alan Marlatt, Jeannie Little, Patt Denning, Andrew Tatarsky, and others. I bought all their books and couldn't wait to read them. And when I got home, Alan Marlatt agreed to be my clinical supervisor to help me integrate HRP into my work.

HRP therapists often work in existing SSPs or OPCs, drop-in centers, and other grant-funded programs. However, they can also work in private or clinical settings. They vary in orientations and approaches, so some practitioners have integrated a harm reduction orientation into psychoanalysis or Cognitive Behavioral Therapy. Others have integrated it into their trauma-informed approach. Some harm reduction therapists provide individual therapy, while others use the approach with couples, families, or groups. In most states, practitioners cannot bill insurance for HRP services per se. Instead, they can bill to treat a primary mental health diagnosis or substance use disorder diagnosis if they are licensed and in network. Depending on the state and the insurance provider, there may be a requirement to submit a treatment plan and progress notes, which may be a barrier for some HRP practitioners who worry that a non-abstinence orientation could be a concern for insurers. As a result of these issues, some HRP practitioners do not accept insurance at all and accept only self-pay clients. Unfortunately, this limits access to this helpful treatment approach.

Why We Need HRP in Our Continuum of Care

In HRP, a client's substance use is one of the many potential topics to discuss during therapy, but it is not the only topic. And when clients do talk
about their substance use, it is often so that both the client and their therapist can better understand their substance-related decisions and behaviors
within the context of their lives. How often did they use since the last session, and which drug(s) did they use? Who were they with, what was their
mood, and what were the circumstances? Were they able to take adequate
precautions for safety? Did they use more or less than they anticipated? Did
they have positive experiences or encounter any adverse effects or
consequences?

The ongoing task for the HRP practitioner is to understand this client's
unique relationship with the drug(s) in their life – is it a coping strategy, a
social lubricant, a numbing and dissociative tool, or a way to alleviate bore-
dom and loneliness? Maybe it is all of the above and more. This rich and
deep understanding can help the client and practitioner consider substance
use without scorn or judgment, but with curiosity that can guide future
decision-making and goals.

HRP respects that someone's use of mood-altering substances is their
proactive attempt to manage their emotions and circumstances. Practitioners know that understanding these motivations can facilitate productive
conversations about safety and goal-setting. My clients often talked about
how getting high was a cost-effective and practical decision – sometimes,
they only had a few dollars in their pockets, and it made more sense to get
high than to buy a hot meal. While a meal would feel good at the moment,
it would mean hours later, they would be desperately seeking a nonexistent
public bathroom or waiting in a long line to use the shared shelter or SRO
bathrooms. And they would get hungry again sooner. But getting high
could suppress their appetite and keep them going for a few more hours.
Understanding a person's motivation for use can encourage more productive discussions about better meeting their needs within their circumstances
or, at least, staying as safe as possible when using drugs. It would have been
unhelpful to the client to tell them not to do drugs without understanding
their motivations for use.

I had a long-time client at the SSP, a Vietnam veteran who acquired HIV
in the 1990s due to injection drug use. He attended the local methadone
clinic and did not inject heroin anymore. He did, however, binge drink and
use crack cocaine occasionally. He told me that vodka was his "anti-freeze"
on cold nights in the streets; the false flush and warmth helped him tolerate
sleeping on the sidewalk or alley when he couldn't secure a shelter bed. He
explained how blacking out would numb him enough so he did not feel the
bugs or hear the cruel remarks of passersby. In this situation, was it really my

place to tell him that alcohol was the wrong way to cope with life on the streets? He could hardly ever scrape more than a few dollars together at a time because he was often robbed when he spent the night at the shelter and on the street because he could not defend himself. Was it my place to tell him that he shouldn't have spent the few dollars he had on a drink that provided him with some comfort for the night? Should I have scolded him for not trying to save it for a security deposit? Instead, it was much more helpful to him to hear my compassion and to be invited into a conversation about how he coped with these devastating circumstances. We could then also talk about whether he could take other strategies or steps to be safe while on the streets. And in our sessions, I could gently remind him when it was time to call his case manager to check the status of his housing application or suggest that he pop into our clinic to get someone to look at the new injury he got after a fight the night before.

Unlike traditional substance use treatment, practitioners and clients develop mutually agreed-upon goals for substance use, including reduced use, safer use, moderation, or abstinence. There is an understanding that goals may vary from drug to drug, so a client receiving HRP in a private practice setting may want to moderate their alcohol use and engage in harm reduction strategies when they occasionally use cocaine and MDMA. Meanwhile, a homeless client who uses fentanyl several times a day might receive HRP at the SSP whenever she picks up sterile injecting equipment. She may start talking about how she could start engaging in safer use practices with her therapist. And, for the first time in years, she might eventually feel ready to meet with a caseworker to fill out an application for one of the housing assistance programs she qualifies for. An HRP practitioner may help the client to see that these steps are positive since she had a long history of depression and hopelessness, which had made it difficult for her to see herself as worthy of safety, support, and a place to call her own. After all, it can take years to change how you view yourself – it does not happen overnight and cannot be forced. But the safety of the therapeutic relationship can help bring the process along in a way that does not shame or blame clients for not changing fast enough.

Harm Reduction Mutual Aid Groups

It is well known that mutual aid groups (also known as self-help or support groups) can play an essential role in people's journeys as they take steps to improve their health and well-being. It can be helpful to join others with shared experiences who can offer guidance and support beyond a formal treatment setting and outside one's immediate family and social network. These types of groups are particularly appealing because they are free and available in the community outside of business hours. There are also more virtual and internet-based options today, since the COVID-19 pandemic forced many groups to innovate to meet the needs of the community. These groups can offer an alternative to treatment for some who may never seek formal help due to cost, stigma, scheduling, or other reasons. And they can be a valuable point of contact for people currently in treatment but who have free time or want support outside of the facility. These groups are also very helpful for those who have completed treatment but want to maintain their gains.

Mutual aid is well-known in the field of drugs. AA, NA, and their spinoffs such as Gamblers Anonymous and Al-Anon, are some of the most popular support groups in the world. However, the expectation of abstinence from all drugs, the promotion of the disease concept of addiction, and some of their other practices may not appeal to all. Several promising alternatives have emerged in recent decades, including SMART Recovery, LifeRing, Secular Organizations for Sobriety, and Women for Sobriety, which provide support but without the spiritual underpinning and other elements of AA and NA.[33] In addition, a growing number of explicitly harm reduction-oriented mutual aid groups welcome people with abstinence goals as well. Some more commonly known options include Moderation Management for alcohol,[34] HAMS Harm Reduction for Alcohol,[35] and Harm Reduction Works,[36] which is a newer harm reduction support group that gained wider engagement via Facebook and Zoom during the COVID-19 pandemic because it is virtual.

Mutual aid can provide support to keep people alive and safe if they choose to continue to use drugs. In these groups, members are taught the risks and hazards of drug use while also acknowledging the role of drugs in how some people live, survive, thrive, and cope with their circumstances. People who use drugs and who practice harm reduction know how hard it can be to change harmful ingrained habits to safer ones, and they also know how important support and belonging can be when trying to make a change. For many, these groups can offer a safe space to express their concerns and explore harm reduction goals with support. While these treatment and support group alternatives are growing in popularity, they are still not readily available or accessible everywhere, and many people still do not know they exist.

Accurate General Drug Education

Accurate and developmentally appropriate drug education for older teens and the general public is another essential part of a harm reduction approach to drugs. Youth drug education should acknowledge that abstinence-only education has an expiration date and that older teens and young adults need tailored information on how to stay safe if they or their peers go on to use drugs. Safety First, a drug prevention curriculum rooted in harm reduction and youth educational empowerment, is an excellent example. It was developed by the Drug Policy Alliance and is now housed at Stanford University's Halpern-Felsher REACH lab (Research and Education to Empower Adolescents and Young Adults to Choose Health). Young people are taught coping strategies to address depression, anxiety, and other factors that often drive substance experimentation and are associated with escalating substance use into SUDs. They are also given the tools for improved online health literacy so they can identify and discern accurate drug information from misinformation. Teens also learn how to identify and respond to overdose and other drug-related harms.

Given how widespread alcohol consumption is in American culture, accessible programs and materials should be made more available to help young people and adults alike navigate the realities of alcohol use. We need to provide our communities with tools and strategies for safer alcohol use, help them to recognize alcohol-related risks and make appropriate responses, identify the signs when drinking may become a problem, and practice strategies to reduce harms. For the general public, this can look like "Rethinking Drinking" from the National Institute on Alcohol Abuse and Alcoholism, where people can learn about standard drink sizes and download tools and worksheets to reevaluate their drinking and goals.[37]

Billboards, public service advertisements (PSAs), and tailored messaging on social media can help to spread information and resources for a broader impact. Rather than the fear-based drunk driving PSAs of my youth, they can focus on sharing information about noticing one's drinking patterns, strategies for safer or reduced use, and more. Dry January (or Dryuary) is an increasingly popular initiative where adults are encouraged to take a monthlong break from alcohol to reset from the end of the boozy holiday season and get a fresh start to the new year. The popularity of Dry January shows us that there is an increasing interest in our culture to reevaluate our collective relationship with alcohol. We can build on this motivation to share more strategies and tools to help support safer use throughout the year. Given the numerous preventable health harms associated with alcohol consumption, we can narrow the harm reduction gap for drinkers with these types of resources for our communities.

Adults over the age of 26 have increasing rates of marijuana use after medical and adult use legalization in states, and few have received adequate education about the various products that are available, potency considerations, and how to stay safe. After legalizing the adult use of marijuana, the state of Colorado launched a great public health campaign called "Responsibility Grows Here," including a website full of harm reduction resources for adults, including strategies on how to store marijuana and edibles away from children and pets as well as tips for parents to talk to their kids about marijuana.[38] As more states legalize, PSAs and web-based public health education initiatives like this should be more accessible to ensure that communities are educated on how to stay safe with marijuana. Since marijuana is the most commonly used drug after alcohol and tobacco products, it is important for people with both legal and underground access to the drug to know how to take adequate precautions and protect their health.

Safe Supply

As I've mentioned throughout this book, an incredibly unpredictable and potent underground drug supply is driving overdose deaths. Experienced users, social/recreational users, and experimental users are all equally at risk for overdose and other adverse effects when they use drugs from the underground drug market. Though harm reduction strategies like making sure someone has naloxone on hand, using drugs at an OPC, and moderating one's use of drugs can help people stay safe, these are all strategies to mitigate the unpredictability of the drug supply. They do not reduce the risk altogether. If the drug supply is adulterated and potentially harmful, harm reduction programs can only do so much to save lives. The problem is the quality of the drugs themselves, and this was a decision policymakers made when they decided to criminalize some drugs and not others. An unpredictable drug supply is the natural result of a nonregulated market.

As discussed in Chapter 2, the quality and potency of the illegal drug supply are dictated by loose networks of thousands of underground drug manufacturers, suppliers, and sellers, and there are no checks and balances for quality control. A lot can go wrong when things aren't being monitored or regulated, and even well-intentioned sellers and members of the supply chain cannot account for what might have happened to a drug before they acquired it. By the time a drug is sold to the consumer, it has already passed through the hands of dozens of people in the drug supply chain who may have diluted it, added fillers to it, or cut it with other adulterants. In addition, the drug may have been accidentally cross-contaminated with other substances while being measured and packaged on shared surfaces or using the same equipment. And unfortunately, similar-looking powders or pills can be easily confused with one another if sellers or users are not paying attention or are inexperienced. Counterfeit pressed pills can easily be mistaken for legitimate pharmaceuticals because the colors and branding may look legitimate.

Most people do not realize how seemingly small decisions anywhere along the supply chain can dramatically change the quality of the drugs available to consumers. Imagine that you sell drugs on the side to supplement your minimum-wage job at a fast-food restaurant. Since you buy in bulk when you can, you can usually split up five grams of cocaine and sell it as five one-gram bags for a nice profit. You also pride yourself on selling good-quality products. But your rent is due soon, and you had to replace a flat tire last week. You need to make ends meet, and extra shifts at the restaurant will not be enough to cover this unanticipated expense. You may decide to increase profits by splitting up your cocaine more than usual so that you pack ten one-gram bags with only half a gram of cocaine combined with half a gram of cheap inert fillers and powders. But the following month, you feel bad that you shortchanged your customers, many of whom are your friends and acquaintances. So you don't cut your cocaine with filler this time because you want to make up for the low-quality product you sold them last month. But now, this batch of cocaine is twice as strong as the last one. As a result, one of your friends accidentally uses too much of this latest batch too fast, because they expected it to be as mild as the cocaine they purchased from you last month. This is how overdoses and other harmful effects happen every day.

Sometimes broader supply chain disruptions, like drug seizures or bans on precursor chemicals, can lead sellers to offset these losses by cutting their drugs with other substances to meet drug demand. This is how illicitly manufactured fentanyl entered our drug supply in the 2010s and started the "third wave" of the overdose crisis, as I explained in Chapter 2.[39] And a 2023 study using data from the state of Indiana found that local drug busts by law enforcement were associated with an increase in the number of opioid overdoses within a few hundred meters of the bust and within several days of the bust.[40] The researchers hypothesized that this was likely because the sellers' customers lived in the surrounding community and experienced immediate withdrawal and/or losses in tolerance after their sellers were arrested. It is possible that losing their trusted sellers led them to seek out new or alternative drug sellers whose drug supplies may have been more potent or different from what they were otherwise accustomed to.

A recent example of supply chain disruptions on a global scale was what occurred to the drug supply during the early COVID-19 lockdowns and travel restrictions in 2020. These disruptions played a role in the dramatic increase in overdose deaths in North America during 2019 and 2020 when over 90,000 deaths occurred in the United States alone. The underground drug supply became even more unpredictable and expensive as drug distributors attempted to travel over borders and state lines undetected. This pandemic-induced instability was why many Canadian advocates renewed calls for a safe supply of illicit drugs like heroin, fentanyl, methamphetamine, and cocaine to prevent overdose and other harmful effects. In this context, safe supply means "providing people who use drugs with pharmaceutical-grade alternatives to illicit drugs."[41] Though many had been sounding the alarm on the need for a safe supply for decades, the pandemic brought with it an urgency to respond.

The efforts of Canadian drug user advocates, researchers, and healthcare providers during the early months of the COVID-19 pandemic eventually resulted in key changes to clinical guidelines and exemptions to Canadian law. These changes allowed healthcare providers to legally prescribe pharmaceutical alternatives to street drugs to ensure that people with SUDs who used illegal street drugs could switch to using drugs of known quality and potency. Several opioids, benzodiazepine, and stimulant options were allowed to be prescribed as a safe supply for patients, including oral hydromorphone, oral morphine, and dextroamphetamine. The drugs were prescribed in pill form only and not intended for injection.

Safe Supply was intended to help people to avoid the unstable underground drug supply and reduce overdose risk during lockdowns when emergency staff and healthcare facilities were overburdened treating other patients. But safe supply was also meant to help keep people who used drugs safe and socially distanced at home to avoid COVID-19 exposure from going out and buying drugs several times a day every day.

Safe Supply became accessible in some of the major cities and in programs that already predominantly served marginalized people who use drugs. However, uptake has varied across the country and remained relatively low due to stigma among providers and logistical barriers for people in rural communities. To date, safe supply remains legal in Canada, and several thousand people who use drugs across the nation are receiving pharmaceutical-grade drugs to avoid the underground drug supply. Models vary, so there are some clinic-based programs, but there are also innovative programs, including vending machines that dispense medications to registered patients through identifying them by scanning the palms of their hands.

This medicalized model of Safe Supply is innovative at the current moment, but it is not the first time prescribers have offered pharmaceutical-grade drugs as an alternative to street drugs in Canada or in the world. (And, as I mentioned in Chapter 2, this occurred here briefly in the early 1900s until it was criminalized.) The "British system" allowed for injectable diamorphine (the chemical name for heroin) to be prescribed to people with heroin addiction as early as the 1920s, though the approach became less popular and unsustainable after key policy changes in the 1960s so that few patients have access today.[42] Heroin Assisted Treatment (HAT), also known as a form of Opioid Agonist Treatment (OAT), has been available in some parts of Europe since the 1990s and via clinical trials in Canada in the early 2000s. It is intended to be a humane alternative for qualifying patients with OUDs who do not respond well to methadone or other treatment options but who are at risk for overdose and harm. In these programs and trials, patients come to the clinic to inject heroin on site several times a day. Decades of research on international HAT programs have shown that patients experience lower rates of overdose, improved health, reduced use of street drugs, and other benefits.[43]

It is noteworthy that the current safe supply model and the HAT model are both highly medicalized. This still means that one must be consistently connected with a healthcare provider or HAT program to receive a safe supply, and depending on the provider or program policies, the prescribed dosage and take-home quantities can vary. Between these factors and the limited number of safe supply prescribers and HAT programs in the world, only a small portion of people who could benefit from safe supply or HAT can access it at any given time.

During the COVID-19 pandemic, drug user advocates called the Drug User Liberation Front (DULF) in the Canadian province of British Columbia launched over a dozen public actions, during which they distributed heroin, cocaine, and methamphetamine that was purchased on the underground market but that had undergone advanced drug checking to ensure they had no adulterants or contaminants in them.[44] These actions were conducted in part to show that it is possible to provide people with access to these drugs outside of a tightly structured medical model. The approach also embodies the harm reduction tenet that people who use drugs should be at the center of any efforts to meet their needs – they know what they need and what would work best for them.

Safe Supply Can Narrow the Harm Reduction Gap

Safe supply is a necessary next step if we want to fill the harm reduction gap and save lives during this overdose crisis. It can be offered in a variety of ways, whether through medical models, through a peer-driven model, or with some other combination of approaches. This is because safe supply addresses the unpredictability of the underground drug supply that contributes to unintentional overdose risk and other adverse drug-related effects for anyone who uses drugs. More widespread access to drugs of known potency and purity can allow for clearer harm reduction guidelines for safer use, since people can better titrate their drug use and plan to anticipate the effects. Safe supply would remove the current divide between those who are given access to legally regulated substances and those who must fend for themselves while managing a criminalized, unpredictable supply and avoiding contact with law enforcement.

Expanded access to safe supply or HAT would reduce community reliance upon naloxone, the opioid overdose reversal drug. Naloxone was always meant to be a drug of last resort – something to be used to bring someone back from the brink of death. Unfortunately, hundreds of people across the United States and Canada are brought to the brink of death every day because they only have access to a highly potent, unpredictable drug supply. Even those who do their best to go slowly and use a small amount may find that the pace and quantity that worked one day may not protect them on the next day, week, or month. Every time someone experiences an opioid overdose, they stop breathing. A few minutes without oxygen can lead to long-lasting and damaging effects on the brain and body, so even if the overdose is reversed, it still puts an extreme strain on the system that could have been avoided. Safe supply could help to create the conditions where opioid overdoses become less common, thereby putting fewer people in the position of accidentally overdosing and requiring naloxone.

A safe supply would also augment the benefits of SSPs to the community, because while SSPs help reduce the risk of HIV, HCV, and other infections due to sharing or reusing drug equipment, access to safe supply would reduce the risk of overdose. Combined, these two harm reduction approaches could help ensure that people who use drugs do not have to risk catching a harmful (potentially lifelong) infection *and* dying of a preventable overdose. Similarly, safe supply augments the benefits of OPCs as well. This is particularly for those marginalized people who are homeless or unstably housed, but also those who are hiding their use or who do not want to use drugs alone. OPCs are essential for anyone who does not have a safe, clean environment to use drugs and who want to reduce the risk of infectious diseases and overdose at the same time. When OPCs and a safe supply are available, it means even fewer people will overdose or have any associated health effects.

Safe supply would also make it easier to have conversations about harm reduction and safer drug use during HRP or in other preventative or educational settings. When practitioners and clients are both able to talk about the known potency of a drug, they can better discuss strategies to stay safe or how to taper one's use to reduce or moderate their use. The unpredictability of the underground drug supply is often the sole variable that no one can control or anticipate, which can make these conversations particularly challenging. HRP conversations can look very different for regulated drugs like alcohol, nicotine, pharmaceuticals, and, increasingly, marijuana. This is because these products are labeled for potency, so consumers know what they are going to get.

It's far easier to talk about harm reduction with someone who recently blacked out while drinking because an HRP therapist can begin by asking about the client's pattern of use and consumption of "hard" high-potency liquors. Due to alcohol's legal status and established research base, there is much we understand about alcohol metabolism and blood alcohol content. This means that the HRP therapist can initiate open conversations about the pros and cons of switching to lower-potency alcohol and other strategies like alternating alcohol with water, eating meals before drinking, avoiding alcohol with their psychiatric or sleep medications, and diluting high-potency alcohol to bring down alcohol content. Or, if someone is trying to give up cigarettes, they can choose to buy e-cigarettes with a higher nicotine content to help transition away from combustible tobacco use. And eventually, they may decide to purchase cartridges with increasingly lower nicotine concentrations as they phase down and transition away from regular use.

Given the unpredictability of the underground drug supply, these types of conversations are much more difficult to have for people who use criminalized drugs. And after discussing our drug policy history that created this dangerous divide between groups of drug users, there is no reason that some people should be allowed a regulated drug supply while others face criminalization and avoidable drug-related harms.

Safe Supply is the last essential piece of the puzzle when it comes to truly reducing drug-related harms and overdose risks for people who use drugs. This is because it complements and builds upon the other available harm reduction tools and strategies we have for disease and overdose prevention. It also removes the fear of arrest and criminalization, which can help people to get access to the tools and support they need in the community rather than being arrested and potentially incarcerated. It is one of the much-needed final steps toward truly treating drug use as a health issue rather than a criminal issue because it brings the drug supply chain above ground into the legally regulated market.

Conclusion

When combined and adequately scaled up to meet community needs, these key harm reduction interventions and programs could help us to make drug use safer for the millions of us who use any mood-altering substances. More widespread availability could help keep all users safe – including those who use drugs occasionally, recreationally, or daily. As I mentioned earlier in the book, the combination of these programs and interventions could take the gamble out of drug use and ensure that people can be adequately prepared and supported to stay safe from the beginning.

Though not detailed in this chapter, quite a few other programs and policies promote a harm reduction philosophy to keep people safe. This includes policy changes such as drug possession decriminalization, which was first instituted on a nationwide level at the turn of the 21st century in Portugal but was also passed in Oregon in late 2020. By decriminalizing the possession of drugs for personal use, we can reduce the contact between people who use drugs and law enforcement and keep people in their communities where they can get access to the support they may need. It also helps them to avoid the trauma of contact with police, such as potential incarceration or the lifelong impacts of a criminal record.

In addition, Housing First programs are those that are designed for homeless or unstable people who use drugs (including alcohol) and who often have other co-occurring mental health and physical health needs. Many traditional housing programs exclude or evict residents who actively use drugs due to strict policies, but this often leaves this group of marginalized people with nowhere to live and few options to stay safe. Housing First programs have been shown to help provide residents with stability and access to help, whereas those same residents may continue to deteriorate and face other life-threatening harms while staying on the street. While they do not exist everywhere, they should be viewed as an essential component of any community's approach to addressing homelessness.

This chapter provided an overview of several key harm reduction interventions and programs. They are not equally available or accessible across the United States, and their legal status varies from state to state. Although some of them are more accepted than others, none of them are fully mainstream or legal in the United States or in much of the rest of the world. Several types of harm reduction programs are still federally illegal at the time of this writing, notably safe supply and OPCs. SSPs are still illegal in many states. Unfortunately, because harm reduction programs have faced backlash, skepticism, and hostility, they are not scaled up to adequately meet community needs in most parts of the country. Some of these barriers to harm reduction implementation and expansion are unique to the US context and our drug war, but some barriers are more global. Regardless, there is much we can do to create the conditions where these types of harm reduction programs are legal, well-funded, and easily accessible to all.

Notes

1 National Harm Reduction Coalition. "Principles of Harm Reduction." https:// harmreduction.org/about-us/principles-of-harm-reduction/ (accessed June 29, 2023).
2 Szalavitz, Maia. *Undoing Drugs: How Harm Reduction Is Changing the Future of Drugs and Addiction.* New York: Hachette Go, 2021.
3 Hassan, Shira. *Saving OUR OWN LIVES: A Liberatory Practice of Harm Reduction.* Chicago: Haymarket Books, 2022.
4 Shira, Hassan. "Harm Reduction, Abolition, and Social Work: Reflections on 25 Years of Resistance and Cooptation." March 31, 2021. Network to Advance Abolitionist Social Work and Haymarket Books "Abolitionist Social Work" series webinar, 1:30:16. https://www.youtube.com/watch?v=_iFwX_Jzunk&t=101s.
5 Injecting equipment includes more than syringes alone, because bacteria and viruses can be spread by touching and sharing equipment or using nonsterile items. Reusing these items poses risks too. A cooker is a small container where a solution of a drug is mixed with water before drawing it up into a syringe. Depending on the drug, the cooker can be heated to prepare the drug solution. Sharing a cooker with others who are reusing syringes can mean that the tips of their syringes could deposit bacteria or viruses into the solution and then be drawn up and injected by others. SSPs try to ensure that people have their own cookers and discourage them from sharing when possible. Tiny cotton pellets are dropped

into the drug solution in the cooker, and people typically place the tip of the syringe into the cotton to draw the solution through it – it functions as a filter to avoid drawing up large particles into the syringe. SSPs provide participants with ample cotton so they do not have to share with others or reuse old cotton because it can harbor bacteria and cause something known as "cotton fever."

6 Smoking kits often include lip balm, alcohol wipes, and a rubber mouthpiece to attach to the pipe to prevent skin burns and reduce the risk of HIV/HCV transmission from sharing pipes with someone with bleeding, cracked, or dry lips. A screen or filter is also provided so drugs like crack or meth are not pulled into the mouth or throat when smoked. (A commonly distributed filter is referred to by its brand name Chore Boy because the copper scrubber can block pieces from being inhaled into the throat or lungs.) Screens and filters prevent painful throat or lung injuries. Meanwhile, new pipes prevent injuries from using makeshift crack or meth pipes made from household items that could break in the mouth or hands.

7 Many people are familiar with the brand name Narcan, a nasal spray formulation of naloxone recently approved for over-the-counter access. Some people use "Narcan" interchangeably with "naloxone," but that is incorrect. Some people have also incorrectly turned Narcan into a verb – "The EMT Narcaned the overdose victim." Narcan is just one brand and product type, but other companies also make naloxone, including formulations that can be injected intramuscularly and in higher dose formulations. Avoid using the brand name unless you specifically refer to the branded product. Also, try to avoid turning the brand name into a verb, and instead state, "We gave the overdose victim naloxone."

8 Depending on state laws, some SSPs can provide participants with access to information based on advanced drug-checking technology, including machines that use Fournier Transform Infrared Spectroscopy (FTIR) or Gas Chromatography Mass Spectrometry (GC-MS) to detect multiple substances, fillers, and adulterants that may be present in a drug someone purchased in the underground market. This type of advanced drug checking can inform participants whether the bag of heroin they purchased contains heroin. Certain types of analyses can also tell how much of the sample is heroin, how much is fentanyl, and any other adulterants.

9 North American Syringe Exchange Network. Harm Reduction Locations (2023). https://www.nasen.org/map/.

10 Dozens of underground and unsanctioned programs operate across the country in states where it may not be legal. These underground programs are run by courageous harm reduction activists committed to this lifesaving work.

11 Fernández-Viña, Marcelo, H. Nadya, E. Prood, Adam Herpolsheimer, Joshua Waimberg, and Scott Burris. "State Laws Governing Syringe Services Programs and Participant Syringe Possession, 2014–2019." *Public Health Reports* 135, no. 1_suppl (2020): 128S–37S. https://doi.org/10.1177/0033354920921817.

12 Pollini, Robin A., Catherine E. Paquette, Susannah Slocum, and Dean LeMire. "'It's Just Basically a Box Full of Disease'—Navigating Sterile Syringe Scarcity in a Rural New England State." *Addiction* 116, no. 1 (2021): 107–15. https://doi.org/10.1111/add.15113.

13 Fitzpatrick, Thomas, Vanessa M. McMahan, Noah D. Frank, Sara N. Glick, Lauren R. Violette, Shantel Davis, and Shilo Jama. "Heroin Pipe Distribution to Reduce High-Risk Drug Consumption Behaviors among People Who Use Heroin: A Pilot Quasi-Experimental Study." *Harm Reduction Journal* 19, no. 1 (2022): 103. https://doi.org/10.1186/s12954-022-00685-7.

14 Levine, Harry, Tyler S. Bartholomew, Victoria Rea-Wilson, Jason Onugha, David Jonathon Arriola, Gabriel Cardenas, David W. Forrest, Alex H. Kral, Lisa R. Metsch, Emma Spencer, and Hansel Tookes. "Syringe Disposal among People Who Inject Drugs before and after the Implementation of a Syringe Services Program." *Drug and Alcohol Dependence* 202 (September 2019): 13–17. https://doi.org/10.1016/j.drugalcdep.2019.04.025.

15 In addition, they learn that laundry detergent bottles are safe for disposal as long as they tape the bottles shut and mark them as "medical waste" before disposing them in the garbage.

16 Behrends, Czarina N., Xinlin Lu, Grace J. Corry, Paul LaKosky, Stephanie M. Prohaska, Sara N Glick, Shashi N. Kapadia, David C. Perlman, Bruce R. Schackman, and Don C. Des Jarlais. "Harm Reduction and Health Services Provided by Syringe Services Programs in 2019 and Subsequent Impact of COVID-19 on Services in 2020." *Drug and Alcohol Dependence* 232 (March 2022): 109323. https://doi.org/10.1016/j.drugalcdep.2022.109323.

17 Lambdin, Barrot H., Ricky N. Bluthenthal, Hansel E. Tookes, Lynn Wenger, Terry Morris, Paul LaKosky, and Alex H. Kral. "Buprenorphine Implementation at Syringe Service Programs Following Waiver of the Ryan Haight Act in the United States." *Drug and Alcohol Dependence* (May 2022): 109504. https://doi.org/10.1016/j.drugalcdep.2022.109504.

18 Gibson, David R., Neil M. Flynn, and Daniel Perales. "Effectiveness of Syringe Exchange Programs in Reducing HIV Risk Behavior and HIV Seroconversion among Injecting Drug Users." *AIDS* 15, no. 11(2001): 1329–41. https://doi.org/10.1097/00002030-200107270-00002.

19 Fernandes, Ricardo M., Maria Cary, Goncalo Duarte, Goncalo Jesus, Joana Alarcao, Carla Torre, Suzeta Costa, Joao Costa, and Antonio Vaz Carneiro. "Effectiveness of Needle and Syringe Programmes in People Who Inject Drugs – An Overview of Systematic Reviews." *BMC Public Health* 17 (2017): 309. https://doi.org/10.1186/s12889-017-4210-2.

20 Ruiz, Monica S., Allison O'Rourke, Sean T. Allen, David R. Holtgrave, David Metzger, Jose Benitez, Kathleen A. Brady, C. Patrick Chaulk, and Leana S. Wen. "Using Interrupted Time Series Analysis to Measure the Impact of Legalized Syringe Exchange on HIV Diagnoses in Baltimore and Philadelphia." *Journal of Acquired Immune Deficiency Syndromes* 82 (December 2019): S148–54. https://doi.org/10.1097/QAI.0000000000002176.

21 Roux, Perrine, Marie Jauffret-Roustide, C. Donadille, L. Briand Madrid, C. Denis, I. Célérier, C. Chauvin, et al. "Impact of Drug Consumption Rooms on Non-Fatal Overdoses, Abscesses and Emergency Department Visits in People Who Inject Drugs in France: Results from the COSINUS Cohort." *International Journal of Epidemiology* 52, no. 2 (2023): 562–76. https://doi.org/10.1093/ije/dyac120.

22 Kosteniuk, Brynn, Ginetta Salvalaggio, Ryan McNeil, Hannah L. Brooks, Kathryn Dong, Shanell Twan, Jennifer Brouwer, and Elaine Hyshka. "'You Don't Have to Squirrel Away in a Staircase': Patient Motivations for Attending a Novel Supervised Drug Consumption Service in Acute Care." *International Journal of Drug Policy* 96 (October 2021): 103275. https://doi.org/10.1016/j.drugpo.2021.103275.

23 Kennedy, Mary Clare, Kanna Hayashi, M.-J. Milloy, Miranda Compton, and Thomas Kerr. "Health Impacts of a Scale-Up of Supervised Injection Services in a Canadian Setting: An Interrupted Time Series Analysis." *Addiction* 117, no. 4 (2022): 986–97. https://doi.org/10.1111/add.15717.

24 Tran, Vincent, Sharon E. Reid, Amanda Roxburgh, and Carolyn A. Day. "Assessing Drug Consumption Rooms and Longer Term (5 Year) Impacts on Community and Clients." *Risk Management and Healthcare Policy* 14 (November 2021): 4639–47. https://doi.org/10.2147/RMHP.S244720.

25 Almost every state nationwide has passed a Good Samaritan Law (GSL) – intended to encourage bystanders to call 911 when they witness an overdose by providing them with some degree of legal immunity for a drug and/or drug paraphernalia charge. However, GSLs are not created equal, and many GSLs have limits to the immunity they offer and to whom. In some states, the GSLs protect the caller and the overdose victim from arrest. But in other states, one or both may be arrested but not prosecuted for drug or paraphernalia charges. Some states limit the number of times a person may receive immunity from calling 911, so somebody could be arrested after their second overdose call. Also, states vary in whether they provide immunity to noncitizens or people on parole or probation. There is still much confusion among law enforcement and the public, so GSL protection is not guaranteed. In addition, mistrust of law enforcement and fear can still deter people from calling 911, even if they may receive protection.

26 Rowe, Adrianna, Andrew Chang, Emily Lostchuck, Kathleen Lin, Frank Scheuermeyer, Victoria McCann, Jane Buxton, et al. "Out-of-Hospital Management of Unresponsive, Apneic, Witnessed Opioid Overdoses: A Case Series from a Supervised Consumption Site." *CJEM*, 24, no. 6 (2022): 650–58. https://doi.org/10.1007/s43678-022-00326-9.

27 Khair, Shahreen, Cathy A. Eastwood, Mingshan Lu, and Jennifer Jackson. "Supervised Consumption Site Enables Cost Savings by Avoiding Emergency Services: A Cost Analysis Study." *Harm Reduction Journal* 19, no. 1 (2022): 32. https://doi.org/10.1186/s12954-022-00609-5.

28 Levengood, Timothy W., Grace H. Yoon, Melissa J. Davoust, Shannon N. Ogden, Brandon D. L. Marshall, Sean R. Cahill, and Angela R. Bazzi. "Supervised Injection Facilities as Harm Reduction: A Systematic Review." *American Journal of Preventive Medicine* 61, no. 5 (2021): 738–49.

29 Milet, René C., Teresa López-Castro, Amy Leibowitz, Kevin McGirr, and Sheila P. Vakharia. "Defiant Hospitality: A Grounded Theory Study of Harm Reduction Psychotherapy." *Addiction Research & Theory* (March, 2021): 1–9. https://doi.org/10.1080/16066359.2021.1900129.

30 Vakharia, Sheila P., and Jeannie Little. "Starting Where the Client Is: Harm Reduction Guidelines for Clinical Social Work Practice." *Clinical Social Work Journal* 45, no. 1 (2017): 65–76. https://doi.org/10.1007/s10615-016-0584-3.

31 Denning, Patt. *Practicing Harm Reduction Psychotherapy: An Alternative Approach to Addictions.* New York: Guilford Press. 2000.

32 Tatarsky, Andrew. *Harm Reduction Psychotherapy: A New Treatment for Drug and Alcohol Problems.* Lanham, MD: Jason Aronson, Inc., 2007.

33 Zemore, Sarah E., Camillia Lui, Amy Mericle, Jordana Hemberg, and Lee Ann Kaskutas. "A Longitudinal Study of the Comparative Efficacy of Women for Sobriety, LifeRing, SMART Recovery, and 12-Step Groups for Those with AUD." *Journal of Substance Abuse Treatment* 88 (May 2018): 18–26. https://doi.org/10.1016/j.jsat.2018.02.004.

34 Moderation Management Webpage. https://moderation.org/.

35 HAMS: Harm Reduction for Alcohol. https://hams.cc/.

36 Lupick, Travis. "Harm Reduction Works: An Exciting New Alternative to Narcotics Anonymous." *Filter.* May 19, 2020. https://filtermag.org/harm-reduction-works-narcotics-anonymous/.

37 You can learn more by checking out all the resources at https://www. rethinkingdrinking.niaaa.nih.gov/ or by searching "Rethinking Drinking" in your preferred search engine.

38 You can learn more by checking out all the resources at https://responsibility growshere.com/.

39 Beletsky, Leo, and Corey S. Davis. "Today's Fentanyl Crisis: Prohibition's Iron Law, Revisited." *International Journal of Drug Policy* 46 (August 2017): 156–59. https://doi.org/10.1016/j.drugpo.2017.05.050.

40 Ray, Bradley, Steven J. Korzeniewski, George Mohler, Jennifer J. Carroll, Brandon del Pozo, Grant Victor, Philip Huynh, and Bethany J. Hedden. "Spatiotemporal Analysis Exploring the Effect of Law Enforcement Drug Market Disruptions on Overdose, Indianapolis, Indiana, 2020–2021." *American Journal of Public Health* 113, no. 7 (2023): 750–58. https://doi.org/10.2105/AJPH.2023.307291.

41 McNeil, Ryan, Taylor Fleming, Samara Mayer, Allison Barker, Manal Mansoor, Alex Betsos, Tamar Austin, Sylvia Parusel, Andrew Ivsins, and Jade Boyd. "Implementation of Safe Supply Alternatives during Intersecting COVID-19 and Overdose Health Emergencies in British Columbia, Canada, 2021." *American Journal of Public Health* 112, no. S2 (2022): S151–58. https://doi.org/10.2105/AJPH.2021.306692.

42 Dennis, Fay. "Advocating for Diamorphine: Cosmopolitical Care and Collective Action in the Ruins of the 'Old British System.'" *Critical Public Health* 31, no. 2 (2021): 144–55. https://doi.org/10.1080/09581596.2020.1772463.

43 McNair, Riley, Mark Monaghan, and Paul Montgomery. "Heroin Assisted Treatment for Key Health Outcomes in People with Chronic Heroin Addictions: A Context-Focused Systematic Review." *Drug and Alcohol Dependence* (April 2023): 109869. https://doi.org/10.1016/j.drugalcdep.2023.109869.

44 Drug User Liberation Front website. https://www.dulf.ca/.

4   What Are Harm Reduction Tenets and Beliefs?

I did not know what to expect when I showed up for my job interview at the Syringe Service Program (SSP) in 2007. It was my first time at an SSP, and I had only a vague idea of what they did on a day-to-day basis other than to give out needles. The only thing I knew for sure was that I was in desperate need of a change, and this job could be my way out.

I had just spent the past few years working at an outpatient substance use treatment program in my hometown, and I could not do it for a moment longer. Even though I adored my clients, I had started to feel like I wasn't really helping any of them. The program was grounded in an abstinence-only approach, and although some of our therapists used evidence-based treatments like Cognitive Behavioral Therapy, we predominantly used Twelve-Step Facilitation, as I described earlier. I always struggled to accept that addiction was a spiritual disease and that people had to follow specific steps to overcome their problems rather than have an individualized approach tailored to their needs. I did not always find this approach helpful, and I came to resent the lack of flexibility.

Although I did not entirely understand what a harm reduction approach truly entailed, there was one thing I knew about working at an SSP – that clients were there voluntarily because they wanted help and services. There was no threat or punishment hanging over their heads to coerce them into complying, like there were for the many mandated and coerced clients who received services at the treatment facility. No one would be calling me to check up on whether my clients were compliant or progressing fast enough. And since abstinence was not a prerequisite for my counseling services at the SSP, I knew that my clients would talk about their drug use more openly and we would work on mutually agreed-upon goals together. That was enough for me.

Little did I know that spending the next few years of my life at this SSP would turn me into a passionate and committed harm reductionist for life.

In this chapter, I will detail what I have learned about harm reduction since I started working at the SSP. I will clarify what I believe are the

DOI: 10.4324/9781003301745-5

distinguishing beliefs and foundational tenets of harm reduction that make it stand apart from other approaches towards drug use and high-risk behavior. You will also see that these also explain why harm reductionists support certain types of policies over others, and how this perspective informs how many of us view the world. It shows why so many harm reductionists promote approaches that affirm the dignity and worth of people who use drugs, and why we support the self-determination of people to make their own choices.

Managing Drug-Related Risks Is Similar to Managing Any Risk

We all navigate various risks and threats in our everyday lives, because a risk-free life does not exist in this world. But our exposure to risk and our ability to manage it can vary greatly from person-to-person. There are millions of people across the world who will engage in high-risk activities, while many will choose to engage in relatively lower-risk behaviors, hobbies, or income-generating activities. Due to the diverse risks that we all face and the different resources we may have to manage them, we need to consider a multipronged approach of harm reduction in our policies, structures, and individual-level behaviors to ensure people are able to stay as safe as possible in the world we live in.

Some of the risks we face are widespread and inevitably affect all of humanity. For instance, we all live on a planet that is actively undergoing climate change, and at the time of this writing, we are still living through a global pandemic. Neither climate change nor COVID-19 can be entirely avoided by any person on earth. Anyone alive right now as well as future generations will live in a world where the lasting effects of these crises will continue to be felt, and potentially intensified. Yet despite these shared risks of instability and illness, we vary in the intensity of our exposure to the harms of each and the tools we can use to mitigate them to keep ourselves safe. We also differ in how policies, systems, and structures can protect us from these harms, prevent the exacerbation of these harms, and help us plan for a safer future. In the meantime, many of us take steps at the individual level to reduce harm, whether it is through changing our consumption or travel habits to reduce our carbon footprints or through masking and vaccination to reduce our COVID risk.

In addition, there are those in our communities who must manage harms and risks that others simply do not experience in their day-to-day lives. Far too many, through no fault their own, are forced to navigate interpersonal and state violence, exploitation, homelessness, hunger, illness and disability, discrimination, oppression, isolation, alienation, poverty, and so much more. And people facing these risks do not often have the power and privilege to undo the entrenched systems and structures that have created these risks, so harm reduction is often the most feasible strategy to survive on a day-to-day basis, through shared resources, working off the books and in underground economies, and developing community networks of care outside of formal structures.[1]

There are also those who voluntarily choose to engage in risky behaviors because they find them fun, exhilarating, or otherwise worthwhile. Some people enjoy bungee jumping and skydiving, others like the rush of day-trading stocks and cryptocurrencies, and many people drive cars, motorcycles, and ATVs. People often risk personal bodily injury and harm to others, including financial instability, when choosing to engage in these behaviors. Yet most of these behaviors are legal for adults to engage in. Due to the relatively high risks associated with these behaviors, most who engage in them practice forms of harm reduction, whether through ensuring that they are using legally regulated equipment and products with trained professionals, by wearing helmets and other protective gear, and, in the case of financial risk-taking, by building emergency savings and other diversified investments to mitigate risks.

The choice to use drugs of any kind, either legal or illegal, should be viewed within the context of the myriad risks that we are navigating every day. Much as we differ in our risk tolerance in other parts of our lives, we differ in our degrees of risk tolerance when it comes to drugs. There will always be people who choose to abstain, and others may use only the drugs they are prescribed. Some may experiment with drugs that are stigmatized or illegal, while many will stick to those that are legal and socially acceptable. We all know many prescription drugs carry potential side effects, and that alcohol can impair our response time and decision making; yet we consume them anyway, because we already practice harm reduction when we consume these drugs. For instance, we may take certain medications only as prescribed, and we may reduce the risk of alcohol-related harms by avoiding alcohol before driving a car.

There are countless ways we can help to reduce the harms of both legal and illegal drug use while acknowledging that there will always be people who use drugs. For example, we can help people to shift their use patterns, reduce the frequency of use, adjust the social or situational risk factors that could be increasing harm, try out safer use methods, or set personal limits on use. Some may ultimately decide that they can no longer use certain drugs at all or will lose interest in some drugs as their circumstances change. Harm reductionists are open to exploring these and other options, helping people to decide what works best for them, and sticking with them as they figure out how to maximize the benefits they seek while staying safe.

A harm reduction approach is essential to managing all risk in our lives, and it should not be viewed as unique to drug-related risks. And, in the case of most of the risks we face, we need harm reduction policies at the international, federal, state, and local levels to facilitate conditions that help keep people as safe as possible and promote health on a broad scale. But beyond this, we also need programs and structures in place to implement these policies and directly provide support to individuals as they practice harm reduction strategies as well.

Harm reduction shows that there are a multiplicity of options and strategies to help people beyond the narrow and restrictive idea that abstinence is the only way to keep our communities safe from drug-related harms. And this reality applies to the social or recreational user as much as it does the person living with an addiction. Harm reductionists are willing to grapple with questions of how to best address drug-related harms, and they do so while being guided by a consistent set of values that prioritize compassion and autonomy. One of the strengths of a harm reduction approach is that it is nimble. After classifying the varying levels of harm, we can see how targeted interventions and strategies at the individual level, programs at the family and community levels, and/or broader policy solutions can lead to immediate changes that improve safety and reduce risk.

Harm reductionists also highlight that we could be prioritizing investments in social support structures such as affordable housing, job training and support, higher education, quality healthcare, childcare and family supports, steady access to nutritious food, and harm reduction and treatment services available on demand. Such investments would be far more effective at improving our collective physical and mental health than the disproportionate funds funneled into our criminal legal system and policing, which prioritize punishment and control over all else.

Harm reduction is an approach to helping individuals and communities stay safe by providing them with the support, tools, resources, and education to reduce risky practices, improve health, and enhance well-being. The most well-known applications of harm reduction are within the context of injection drug use and sexual behavior; however, harm reduction can be applied to other drug-related behaviors and practices, and so much more.

Harm reduction recognizes that the safest way to reduce risks associated with certain behaviors or practices is complete abstinence. However, abstinence is not desirable, feasible, or realistic for everyone. In cases where abstinence is not possible, harm reductionists can help people explore ways to reduce risks and harms while staying as safe as they can. Harm reduction approaches can be helpful to people who use alcohol, by helping them to develop strategies to pace themselves, alternate water, and plan for a designated driver. But harm reduction can also be helpful to reduce risks associated with other drugs, such as by ensuring people use sterile new glass pipes for smoking drugs. For instance, it is well known that condoms can prevent STIs and pregnancy for those who decide to engage in sexual activity. A harm reduction approach can even be useful for diabetes and high blood pressure management, since most of us cannot cut out sugar or salt out of our diets entirely, but we can develop strategies for moderation or reducing daily intake. Ultimately, harm reduction acknowledges that there are many ways to help people reduce the risks so they can live healthier lives.

Low Thresholds and Open Doors

Harm reduction programs are typically referred to as "low threshold," meaning that they have few requirements for entry. Unlike traditional addiction treatment or healthcare services, there are few hoops to jump through to get help and few prerequisites. Since these services are provided freely in the community, one does not need to pay to get help or provide an insurance card for services. Grassroots harm reduction programs operate on a walk-in model, so that anyone who shows up to a brick-and-mortar SSP looking for a sterile syringe or naloxone during operating hours can often get what they want that day. Or, if someone walks into an OPC, they can come in and use their drugs on site with no appointment. Depending on the program, some also provide other services such as drop-in support groups, snacks and water, case management and referrals, space for socialization and recreation, showers, toilets, and much more for anyone looking for help.

Harm reduction works because programs aim to make it as easy as possible for people to get the support they need at the moment they need it, without undue delays, bureaucratic barriers, and logistical challenges that otherwise characterize our current systems of care. Far too often, our current systems of care have rigid structures that are more convenient for providers rather than patients. Low-threshold assistance is essential because people should not have to jump through hoops to get help, and they should get what they need when they are most motivated. Harm reduction programs are unique because they give participants what they want with no strings attached and encourage them to keep coming back. This initial approach can help to build the foundation to a trusting, helping relationship. By proving themselves as reliable and helpful, harm reductionists can then offer additional services and referrals as needed.

Meet People Where They Are

Harm reduction works by first engaging with people on their own terms. It's an approach where the focus is on first identifying what the individual wants and then figuring out how to be of assistance. By meeting people where they are mentally and emotionally, harm reductionists are not trying to put the cart in front of the horse. That is, they figure out where each person wants to start and what they need in the moment. What concerns them? What motivates them? What is their top priority? Are they hungry or thirsty?

Would they want a granola bar and a bottle of water? Are they worried about fentanyl in their heroin? Would they like to get some fentanyl test strips and naloxone? Are they ready for new sterile syringes, and do they have old ones to dispose of? Do they need someone to help treat an abscess? Would they like to talk to someone about their recent eviction? Meeting people where they are means adjusting one's approach based on what the person is most motivated and interested in addressing first. It also means not setting unrealistic goals or expectations based on what the harm reductionist may think they need but seeing how and where to engage with the person right now. It can also open the door to future conversations down the road about long-term goals, like treatment, college, or family reunification.

Harm reductionists also go to meet people where they are physically. Mobile outreach services are increasingly common in both rural and urban settings because they are both more affordable to operate and can be more accessible to people without steady access to transportation. In these types of programs, outreach workers can distribute harm reduction supplies, socks, and water bottles directly to people "where they're at" in the community. Workers often hand out various items from their backpacks, trunks, or vans in areas where folks may congregate or live. Harm reduction workers may also provide wound care, conduct rapid HIV tests, or even engage in "sidewalk psychotherapy," as harm reduction psychotherapy pioneers Patt Denning and Jeannie Little call it. Mail-order harm reduction services are also growing, allowing people in an increasing number of jurisdictions to directly order syringes, naloxone, and other drug-checking tools online to be delivered to their home.[2]

This is a radical departure from how most systems of care work in the United States and many parts of the world. Most service providers, whether they are addiction treatment providers, mental health providers, social services, housing programs, or others, require the client to "start where the system is." This means that these programs often have clear requirements for enrollment, eligibility, and rules for compliance and adherence, and that people are expected to meet staff and program expectations to continue to receive help. That clients must be ready, willing, and able to change immediately in order to stay connected to services from the moment they walk through the door. It also means that the treatment plan or pathway to services is typically structured and predetermined, and there is little flexibility to account for individual circumstances or goals. Treatment goals are often built around pursuing and maintaining abstinence, complying with attendance requirements, and other rules. Programs can determine that the client is not changing fast enough or is noncompliant with the treatment plan so that clients can be deemed unmotivated or resistant to change and can lose access to services altogether, be referred to an even more intensive level of care, or be discharged. As I've said before, people in these settings are often told to "come back when they're ready."

"Any Positive Change"

Harm reductionists often talk about the importance of recognizing and celebrating "any positive change," coined by John Szyler, co-founder of the Chicago Recovery Alliance, but often credited to Dan Bigg.[3] This phrase was offered as a simple way to define recovery and progress. It is about celebrating the small wins on someone's journey to be safer and take care of themselves.

Most treatment settings and other systems of healthcare and services view abstinence as the only acceptable goal and outcome for people with substance use disorders (SUDs) or addictions. This reflects a broader challenge in the dominant addiction discourse that forces binary either/or thinking.[4] Either you are "clean" or you are "dirty"; either you are in recovery or you are in active chaotic use and addiction.[5] There is no middle ground.

There is a common assumption is that people who are actively using drugs are incapable of taking steps to care for themselves until they stop using drugs. Far too many wrongly believe that drug use itself is the main problem, so that promoting safety precautions is a distraction. Others incorrectly think that embracing any positive change is lowering one's expectations for behavior change when people should really aspire and devote their energy toward abstinence. However, abstinence-only thinking makes it easy to overlook or dismiss the seemingly small steps that people take to care for themselves and for others. And it overlooks how small changes can lay the foundation for larger changes in the future. Far too often, our systems view abstinence as the only way and the only marker of success, and this can mean that people stop seeing their own progress.

As a result, many people show up to the SSP for the first time with a lot of the same thoughts in the back of their minds. They believe that their ongoing drug use is a failing, so they may not see the harm reduction steps they take as an accomplishment or an achievement worth celebrating. Clients may minimize the fact that they showed up to the SSP a few days in the past month to pick up needles and participate in a few drop-in groups, even though it has been years since they participated in any type of service program. They may not see what an accomplishment it is that they didn't share syringes this week, or that they used new syringes every time they injected since their last visit to the SSP. But it is quite an achievement since their risky injecting gave them a staph infection six months ago, and it is how they caught hepatitis C eight years ago. Never underestimate the impact one can have by helping people to see that they're changing and doing better.

This is where harm reduction's focus on "any positive change" is a much-needed counterpoint to the status quo. Sadly, most people have not been taught to see harm reduction outcomes as progress or as viable goals. Because of this, it is important for harm reductionists to be clear with participants that using sterile syringes, not sharing used equipment, transitioning from injecting to smoking their drug, or using drugs at an OPC are all significant steps to reduce risky practices and take responsibility for one's and one's community's health. When people engage in these harm reduction practices, they are celebrated and praised for the important steps they took to care for themselves. It is important for everyone to receive reinforcement that they have made responsible choices for themselves and that they can make even more in the future. All of this feedback is combined with the invitation for clients to come back to the program whenever they would like, as often as they would like, because showing up also counts.

Redefining Relapse and Recovery

In dominant models, the key characteristic of recovery is abstinence, and a single return to use can be viewed as a "relapse." In fact, most AA/NA meetings and treatment settings count one's recovery time in terms of "days abstinent" so that your check-in or introduction at the beginning of every meeting includes stating your name, stating aloud you're an "addict" or "alcoholic," and then reporting the number of days, weeks, months, or years you have remained abstinent. If you use again, even once, it can mean that your metaphorical recovery tracker is set back to zero. You must report this use at your next AA/NA meeting or group session, and you have to start counting your recovery days all over again from scratch.

This is the exact opposite of "any positive change" – it is "any use is a failure."

This narrow view of recovery breeds an environment of secrecy because it becomes a survival strategy in a world that looks at drug use in such a narrow way. Why risk being honest when there are such serious negative consequences for telling the truth about one's ongoing drug use or one's return to use after a period of abstinence? Sadly, this secrecy can be lethal. Countless people have died of overdose because of hidden use after periods of abstinence because they returned to use, but their tolerance was so low and/or they used a highly potent fentanyl-adulterated bag. In many of these cases, loved ones look back and wish they could have helped, but abstinence-only expectations create an environment where people cannot be honest when they struggle or return to use. Relatedly, these strict definitions of relapse and recovery make some feel like failures. Many people who use drugs have low feelings of confidence when it comes to behavior change or are reluctant to pursue treatment again after past attempts. We must wonder whether some reluctance for people to attend treatment is because they have been given strict rigid definitions about what health and wellness mean, and they are unsure they can muster the courage to try again.

A harm reduction perspective acknowledges that any behavior change is difficult, and that many factors should be considered when looking at someone's return to use. A single occasion of use may be called a "slip," to soften the language and introduce less judgment into the process. It helps us to acknowledge someone's efforts to change deeply ingrained drug-related patterns, and it recognizes that they had an occasion when they slipped into old habits. After all, what do we all do after we slip and fall? Most of us get up again. Early days of recovery are like walking on black ice, we should anticipate and prepare everyone to slip even if the person is doing everything to avoid falling. So many providers in abstinence-only settings focus on relapse prevention alone without also discussing the importance of safety if one were ever to return to use again. Some of this is because of fear that they may "plant the seed" for relapse or tempt someone to use again, but this silence can be deadly and contribute to harmful or lethal slips or binges if someone returns to use.

One of the greatest strengths of harm reduction is that these conversations about slips or relapses are at the forefront of the work even when abstinence is the primary goal, and everyone is provided with preparation. This means that everyone is taught about overdose risk and the importance of keeping naloxone on hand and never using alone. Clients are always encouraged to keep sterile and new equipment on hand and are invited to come back no matter what. By staying as safe as possible during this slip, one can see that they can care for themselves even during difficult situations. And later, they can explore which feelings or situations triggered them to use that day so they may cope with those moments differently in the future.

Beyond Disease Models of Addiction

The need for lifelong abstinence to preserve recovery is also deeply tied to disease models of addiction. The dominant thinking in addiction research and treatment is that addiction is a chronic relapsing brain disease, while AA/NA characterizes addiction as a spiritual disease. Both disease models presume the lifelong course of addiction and that it is best addressed by maintaining an abstinence-based recovery. Among those who ascribe to either disease model, there is often also a belief that individuals are incapable of ever returning managed or moderate substance use, even after years of abstinence.

Harm reductionists are open to the fact that some definitions people may find these disease models helpful, but the prescriptive definition may not be helpful for others. Instead, they allow for greater flexibility in how someone may define both their problems and their path to recovery. Harm reductionists recognize a client may not find that an occasional drink is a violation of their recovery, since they have successfully abstained from cocaine, the drug associated with the most negative consequences in their life. Harm reductionists can understand how some might view marijuana as their "exit drug"[6] that helped them stop using other drugs problematically. They can see how the use of psychedelic drugs can help some people to cut down on their drinking.

In addition, harm reductionists encourage people to decide whether or not they are in recovery at all. For some, it can be helpful to think of their addiction in the past tense so that they may see themselves as "recovered" rather than "in recovery." Others may reject the concept of recovery entirely and simply say they stopped their unhealthy or risky drug habits. After all, if you have not used heroin in 15 years, you may find "recovery" to be an unhelpful lens to look at your current lifestyle and circumstances since the past is long gone. And harm reductionists could see how someone in their 40s can now appreciate a nice bottle of wine even though their drinking was incredibly self-destructive in their teens and early 20s.

Everyone Deserves Help, and No One Is Disposable

Harm reduction is more than its interventions or policies; it's about the spirit that drives the work and how people treat one another. Harm reductionists believe at their core that people who continue to use drugs matter, because many of them used the same drugs themselves (or still do!). Drug use is relatively prevalent in our society, but some users have the safety of a regulated supply of known quality and composition, while many do not. Some have the privilege of legally sanctioned use without fear of arrest or punishment. Some people who use drugs can do so openly, while others are forced into the shadows. Harm reductionists believe that all people who use drugs, especially the most marginalized (i.e., those who inject drugs, who use illegal drugs, who are unhoused, who live in poverty, etc.), deserve to be treated with dignity and respect because their lives have worth and meaning. Every single participant who attends an SSP or OPC is a valued member of the community who has much to gain and much to contribute.

Unlike traditional abstinence-based treatment providers, harm reductionists actively pursue and maintain ongoing relationships with people who continue to engage in a broad range of drug-related risk behaviors. They aim to keep communication open and build rapport, rather than expecting participants to immediately change in order to qualify to get help or services. Because of this, harm reduction programs can be a valuable point of contact for people who are otherwise disconnected from other services and supports. Harm reductionists fill an important gap in the continuum of care by targeting those who need to help to reduce risky drug use practices or do not have access to the tools to stay safe.

The most marginalized people who use drugs are often disparaged for continuing to use drugs. Many people look at them and justify their own hard-heartedness by saying that if these people choose to use drugs, why should the public fund services to help them? Others wrongly ask why we should keep them safe when so many other groups need help too? Since I began my work for the SSP, people have expressed these very sentiments when they find out about what I do for a living. I am reminded every day that we live in an era where many people do not have a lot of compassion to spare – there are so many others struggling that are deemed more "worthy" of our time, energy, and resources that people who use drugs are often viewed as the least deserving of them all. But pitting different marginalized groups against one another based on their so-called worthiness of our help only hurts us all.

This is exactly why harm reduction is so essential in the world today. Harm reduction programs are a vital touchpoint for people who may not have anywhere else to turn. Sadly, the near-universal stigma against people who use illegal drugs often locks many people into self-destructive cycles because they stop seeing themselves as being worthy of caring and compassion. A quote by Pastor Rayford Johnson, a prominent faith leader from a small town in Tennessee, will forever stick with me: "In the society in which we live and in the culture in which we live, I think 100%, most definitely, Jesus would have been carrying Narcan with him."[7][8] This simple statement shows how harm reduction, at its core, is about saving lives and helping those who are overlooked. In fact, harm reduction has always had an interfaith coalition of members, including clergy, people of faith, and spiritual leaders.[9] As a practicing Hindu myself, I do this work because I want to help reduce suffering in the world.

Harm reductionists are most helpful because they are willing to be there for others and, often, it is because they have had similar experiences themselves. They don't give up on people, and they keep inviting them back because someone did this for them – or because they wish someone had been there. They understand that change is hard, especially for people who have high-risk practices and patterns of use. They also recognize that not everyone will change enough for some people's standards or change at all, but everyone deserves a community of support.

Harm Reduction Is for Anyone Who Uses Drugs

Harm reduction is not just for those who are addicted to drugs. The vast majority of people who used drugs in the past month did not have diagnosable SUDs or addictions. However, one can still be at risk for drug-related harms if not prepared with the tools and information to stay safe. The clearest example for most people comes from college. Many college freshmen spend their first semester away from home experimenting with alcohol. These experiments can involve risky behaviors that can cause harm. I know this well because I was once a college freshman myself and, later in my junior and senior years, a Resident Advisor to incoming freshman in the dorms. Naivete and lack of alcohol tolerance, combined with peer pressure and high-risk practices, often led many young people to drink beyond their limits, black out, get sick, and, at least once a month, resulted in a campus-wide notification that someone was transported to the hospital for alcohol poisoning. These novice drinkers may not have met criteria for an alcohol use disorder, but their drinking sometimes caused harm.

The more we are armed with tools and strategies *before* using drugs, the more likely we will know what to do to avoid or mitigate certain risks from the beginning. And there is no reason to believe that this type of education will encourage drug use among people who would not otherwise use these drugs. In fact, it can teach people to ensure their peers are safe so they can respond effectively, or it can prepare them if they decide to use these drugs later in life. If experimentation and early use experiences can be safer and less harmful, it may prevent future problems down the line because people develop safer or more responsible habits. Beyond this, harm reduction is also helpful for the social, occasional, or infrequent user who may not use regularly but who wants to ensure those few times are enjoyable and as safe as possible.

"Nothing About Us Without Us"

A disability rights slogan also embraced by harm reduction advocates, "nothing about us without us" expresses the foundational conviction that people with lived experience should be at the table in policy discussions and when decisions are being made that will affect their lives. It is a radical stance because, in reality, so many life-altering decisions at the policy and programmatic levels are often made by a select few and behind closed doors. This can include elected officials and special interest groups, sometimes with the input of professionals, experts, or researchers. Unfortunately, the impacted populations themselves rarely have a seat at the table to talk about their needs and concerns. For instance, when a new treatment center is proposed in a community, neighbors and local business interests can play an outsized role in determining where it is located due to the potential impact on property values and fears about public safety, rather than the convenience of its location for clients who may rely upon public transportation to get there. Impacted communities are simply expected to comply when treatment and social service programs are open only during traditional working hours and have set protocols for intake and enrollment, even though they may be challenging for clientele with nontraditional schedules or who have instability in their lives (i.e., the people for whom these services could be most helpful!).

Harm reduction was started by current and former drug users who helped one another to stay safe when public institutions failed to meet their needs or outright denied them assistance. It took years of advocacy and tens of thousands of deaths to convince the government to pass policies and expand funding to address the HIV/AIDS crisis. When Reagan ramped up Nixon's drug war in the 1980s, the proposed solutions were based on politics rather than what communities actually wanted to address drug use in their communities. People who use drugs and communities of color have long understood that top-down solutions led by people without personal stakes in the issue often are imperfect and can increase harms.

To this day, most grassroots harm reduction programs are founded by current or former drug users who first decided to start handing out supplies from their backpack, their garage, or their car trunk. The harm reduction strategies and wisdom they often share with one another are also the result of their own experimentation and ingenuity. Many harm reductionists taught themselves how to write grant applications for funding, did their own outreach, designed 'zines and pamphlets to raise awareness and teach each other how to stay safe, and built relationships in the community to do the work. And for many, doing harm reduction work cannot be separated from activism to change the conditions around them.

Though the field of substance use treatment and recovery do have a significant representation of people with a history of addiction, most medicalized treatment settings do not always have people with direct experience of the issue at hand.

In contrast, in harm reduction programs across the world, people who use drugs are involved in the operations and/or leadership. This is because they intimately understand the needs of the community and want to give back. The usual categories of professionalized staff and client may not exist as they do in other types of settings, like treatment. People who use services are often hired as peers or volunteer their time to help with outreach activities, doing neighborhood syringe pickup and cleanup, or assembling harm reduction kits. There is a communal aspect to harm reduction work that distinguishes it from many other services in the community.

An Anti-Racist and Social Justice Orientation

Harm reduction's roots in mutual aid by communities facing oppression cannot be overlooked. This has also been an intersectional movement for racial and social justice by people forced onto the margins of society due to their drug use and who did not receive the help that they needed. Major pushes for health equity have often been driven by marginalized people who have never had their needs met adequately by systems that were never designed to meet their needs to begin with. Reducing harms associated with drugs cannot be disentangled from the way systems harm. This can include the criminal legal system, the healthcare and treatment system, the public welfare and social services system, the educational system, the family regulation system (i.e., the so-called child welfare system), and other systems. While these institutions proclaim to improve public health and safety, their benefits or positive effects are often felt more among certain segments of society than others. Often these systems are not exempt from racism, sexism, heterosexism, transphobia, xenophobia, and classism, so that they often end up disproportionately surveilling and punishing some people more than others.

For instance, harm reductionists understand that although drug use occurs among people from all walks of life, certain drug-related risks are not necessarily equally distributed across society. Higher-income people who use drugs are not necessarily subjected to routine policing and surveillance as people who live in low-income or predominantly minority communities are. And even when higher-income people experience drug-related policing and criminalization, they are most likely to be able to afford a strong defense, negotiate fewer penalties, and get a less punitive response than lower-income people. Similarly, middle-class and higher-income people are more likely to have the social and financial resources to access quality treatment, get paid time off and medical leave to address their health issues, and have family resources they can depend on in case of emergencies.

This is why harm reduction service delivery cannot be seen apart from political advocacy and activism. Harm reductionists support drug policy changes that would allow for the decriminalization of the possession of syringes, pipes, fentanyl test strips, and other drug-related equipment. They also support the decriminalization of drug possession, sex work, and other low-level crimes of survival, since police often use these charges to disproportionately target low-income communities of color. If anything, the criminalization of these activities puts people at greater risk of harm and exploitation, while driving people underground and in the shadows. Harm reductionists also support policies that would allow for a safer supply of currently illegal drugs, be it through some sort of regulatory model and/or through drug decriminalization and easier access to drug-checking tools to detect adulterants and contaminants in the underground drug supply. They also want access to non-stigmatizing, trauma-informed, evidence-based treatment options for those who may seek formal assistance for substance use, mental health concerns, or other health issues. Together, these kinds of policies can help to save lives by reducing the negative consequences of drug criminalization, improving the material conditions of people's lives, and helping people to feel safe coming out of the shadows to seek help.

Harm reductionists advocate for dozens of broader policies at the local, state, and federal levels to promote community health and safety. This is because many harm reductionists understand that a number of the challenges facing our communities have only intensified, and new threats have emerged, such as income inequality, housing inaccessibility, gentrification, climate change, racial and ethnic inequities, an increasingly toxic and unpredictable drug supply, mass surveillance, militarized policing, a rollback of reproductive rights, a global pandemic, and so much more.

The harm reduction movement has evolved over decades as younger generations have taken the reins and built upon the lessons of the elders who came before. And in light of the current challenges facing our communities today, new generations of harm reductionists continue to develop innovative tools and strategies to reduce harm and increase safety while also building intersectional power and cross-coalition alliances to affect social and policy change. They are fighting for policies that allow greater access to supportive and affordable housing, guarantee a living wage, reform our criminal legal system, fund the social safety net, and expand access to healthcare and other life-saving services.

Conclusion

Harm reduction is not only about the tools to help people safe, but about the underlying values and principles that guide a diverse movement of people to serve one another and help keep our communities safe. As highlighted in this chapter, harm reduction offers a humane, kind, and compassionate view of people who use drugs and does not affirm binaries of who is and is not "worthy" of help and support. Harm reductionists aim to meet people where they are, both physically and mentally, so that they can be most effective and helpful to the communities they serve. Although there is so much that can be said about the foundational tenets to this approach, I hope this chapter helped to provide even greater context and understanding for why harm reductionists do what they do. I also hope readers can reflect upon how they can apply harm reduction into how they approach the people in their families and communities who engage in high-risk practices.

Notes

1 Boucher, Lisa M., Zoë Dodd, Samantha Young, Abeera Shahid, Ahmed Bayoumi, Michelle Firestone, and Claire E. Kendall. "'They Have Their Security, We Have Our Community': Mutual Support among People Experiencing Homelessness in Encampments in Toronto during the COVID-19 Pandemic." *SSM – Qualitative Research in Health* 2 (December 2022): 100163. https://doi.org/10.1016/j.ssmqr.2022.100163.

2 You may have an SSP near you that offers pickup or mail-order supplies, so I first recommend you check the NASEN directory at https://nasen.org/ and contact your nearest program so you can find out if this option is available to you.

Beyond this option, Next Distro is a mail-order harm reduction program that delivers supplies to residents of certain states, and you can learn more by visiting their website: https://nextdistro.org. Remedy Alliance mails low-cost naloxone to harm reduction programs in many parts of the United States, and you can learn more by visiting their website: https://remedyallianceftp. You can order drug-checking tools such as fentanyl test strips and chemical reagent tests from DanceSafe, and you can learn more by visiting https://dancesafe.org.

3 Szalavitz, Maia. *Undoing Drugs.* New York: Hachette Go, 2021.

4 Miller, William R. "What Is a Relapse? Fifty Ways to Leave the Wagon." *Addiction* 91 (1996): S15–27. https://doi.org/10.1046/j.1360-0443.91.12s1.6.x.

5 Harm reductionists avoid using terms like "clean" and "dirty," and I use them here to illustrate the dichotomous but also value-laden way that our systems use such terms. Harm reductionists resist this language because we do not believe that the presence of a chemical in one's body makes them "dirty" or "contaminated." As mentioned earlier, drug use is a morally neutral act, and it does not dictate someone's worthiness of help.

6 Lucas, Philippe, Amanda Reiman, Mitch Earleywine, Stephanie K. McGowan, Megan Oleson, Michael P. Coward, and Brian Thomas. "Cannabis as an Adjunct to or Substitute for Opiates in the Treatment of Chronic Pain." *Journal of Psychoactive Drugs* 44, no. 2 (2012): 125–33. https://doi.org/10.1080/027910 72.2012.684624.

7 Keeling, Jeff. "Pastor, City Leader Call for Narcan Vending Machine in Johnson City." *WJHL News*, 15 December 2022. https://www.wjhl.com/news/local/pastor-city-leader-call-for-narcan-vending-machine-in-johnson-city/amp/.

8 Narcan is the brand name of a form of naloxone, the opioid overdose reversal medication, that is available as a nasal spray.

9 To learn more about the interfaith movement of harm reduction leaders and get involved, you can look up Faith in Harm Reduction: https://faithinharmreduction.org/.

5 Why Harm Reductionists Embrace the Drug, Set, and Setting Model

Why do some people develop drug problems while others do not?
Why are some people able to stop using while others cannot?

I am often asked questions like these when I tell people I am a former addiction counselor and currently work in drug policy. Perhaps you have wondered the same thing too. Why do people have such distinct experiences with the same substances?

Scholars have devoted their entire careers to uncovering the answers to these questions. While we know a lot about how drugs work in the body, we still have many unanswered questions about why some people struggle with drug use, and others develop addictions. There is also more we can learn about why some achieve recovery while others do not. Experts from a diverse range of fields – from sociologists to psychiatrists, from anthropologists to criminologists, and from psychologists to neurobiologists – have offered a variety of theories to try to explain why different people can have such different relationships with drugs. There is still no clear consensus, but quite a few theories have persisted because they have some evidence to support their utility. Meanwhile, others continue because influential actors in treatment, research, and recovery promote them. Although each theory provides a piece of the puzzle, finding a single explanation for so many unique experiences can be challenging.

You may be familiar with several common theories of addiction. The well-known self-medication theory posits that some people develop substance use disorders (SUDs) after regularly using drugs to cope with trauma, adverse childhood experiences, or untreated mental health or medical issues. Self-medicating can create drug-related problems if the underlying conditions do not improve or worsen due to ongoing use. There is some evidence to support this theory. Research suggests that people with SUDs have higher mental health diagnoses and health issues rates than the general population.[1] And many people with SUDs say that using drugs helped them

DOI: 10.4324/9781003301745-6

cope with depression or anxiety. For some people, this theory can offer essential insights into the roots of their problems, and it can also offer a pathway to overcome SUDs because addressing the underlying problems that contributed to their drug use can help them to get better. It is also important to remember that, although the theory may apply to a portion of people, not everyone with a SUD necessarily self-medicates.

Many who participate in Alcoholics Anonymous and Narcotics Anonymous believe that people with SUDs have a spiritual disease. They believe a lack of spiritual grounding makes them prone to drug problems. Prominent figures in recovery, treatment, and religious settings promote the spiritual disease theory.[2] Despite the lack of evidence, the connection between spirituality and addiction resonates intuitively for some people. The widespread institutionalized support for this model has made it appealing to others. Proponents of this theory believe that if one develops a spiritual foundation for their lives, they will no longer use drugs, and they will eventually overcome their problems.

Meanwhile, the National Institute of Drug Abuse (NIDA) promotes the theory that addiction is a chronic relapsing brain disease. Proponents of the theory point to research suggesting that drugs affect specific reward centers in the brain and impact the wiring of some critical neural pathways. They also point to genetic research showing that addiction often runs in families. The brain disease theory resonates with many researchers, and some believe that it can help counteract social stigma by medicalizing addiction as a disease rather than affirming that it is a moral failing. However, critics find that a focus on biology and brains neglects the role of social and policy environments on why some people use drugs and develop problems or how experiences can change one's biology.[3] It is also difficult to reconcile concepts of free will and choice against the brain disease theory.

Other theories focus on the role that one's social environment, such as immediate family, friends, and community, can play in drug-related behaviors and choices. Some argue that societal factors like inequality, oppression, poverty, despair, and disconnection impact problematic drug use. Meanwhile, others think problematic drug use is a learned behavior that grows more reinforcing over time as one repeatedly seeks the same pleasurable high. There are theories that certain personality traits like impulsivity and sensation-seeking place people at a high risk of addiction. And there are many more. Such diverse theories illustrate the complexity of addiction and drug use – how much we understand, and how much more we have to learn.

When we find theories that resonate with us, they can help us to make sense of our own experiences or the people around us. Perhaps you find that one or more of these theories applies to you or a loved one while others do not. They can offer explanations for what has happened and why; they can help answer our questions. Sometimes, they can guide us toward a solution or a way to overcome our problems. But although these theories can help understand people's drug use, each is often relatively narrow in scope – no one theory can explain all experiences. This is because most theories either focus on the individual factors that drive one's relationship with drugs or because they explain social- or environmental-level factors that influence drug use. Few bring all these factors together.

For instance, Alex is a middle-aged man who has recently developed a drinking problem but has no family history of addiction. He started drinking more frequently after the stress of his recent divorce. Even though Alex has consistently found that marijuana calms him down, he stopped smoking when he got this job a few years ago because his employer subjects staff to random drug tests. Over the past few months, his drinking escalated as he spent more time at local bars with his college buddies and work friends to avoid being home alone at night. He sometimes goes to work hungover but is still managing his responsibilities for the most part. He is noticing recent weight gain from drinking beers multiple nights a week and eating greasy bar food regularly. These factors and their dynamic interaction can help explain why Alex has developed a particular pattern of alcohol use. Several of the theories I mentioned played a role in his problematic drinking patterns because no single one captured the complexity of his experience.

The Drug, Set, and Setting Model

Whenever asked about addiction, I often return to Dr. Norman Zinberg's seminal 1984 book, *Drug, Set, and Setting*. Zinberg's research found that one's drug experiences cannot be viewed apart from individual and social circumstances (see Figure 5.1). Instead, drug use must be understood within the context of three factors and their interactions:

1 The *drug* itself (i.e., its unique pharmacology, its effects, its risk factors, the route of administration, etc.)
2 The *set*, or the person who used the drug (i.e., age, mindset and emotional state, expectations, personality, preferences, prior experiences, etc.)
3 The social *setting* and environment where the drug use occurs (i.e., who else is present, where it occurs, social norms, cultural context, legality, etc.)

Zinberg's work built upon the "set and setting" concept coined in the early 1960s by Harvard psychology professor and controversial counterculture figure Dr. Timothy Leary. Leary's research suggested that experiences with psychedelic drugs can vary significantly based on one's mindset and the settings in which these drugs are consumed. Zinberg expanded Leary's model

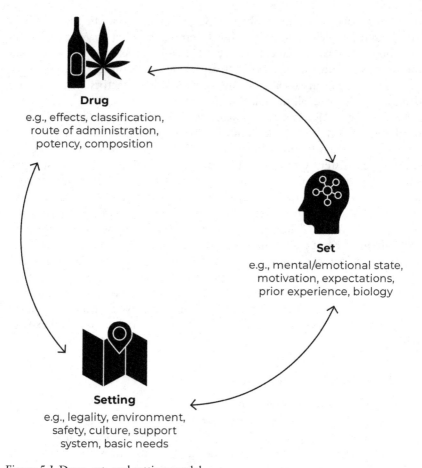

Figure 5.1 Drug, set, and setting model.

Source: Zinberg, Norman. *Drug, Set, and Setting*. New Haven, CT: Yale University Press, 1984.

to include a range of drugs beyond psychedelics and explored how the drug, set, and setting factors interact throughout a person's life to explain one's drug use patterns or habits.

Zinberg's book summarizes his research from the 1960s and 1970s with people who used marijuana, psychedelics, and opiates such as heroin. His early research focused on people who identified any drug in these categories as their primary drug or "drug of choice." He conducted in-depth individual interviews with his research subjects to explore their family history, their past drug use, their immediate social context (including their partners, friends, employment, and education), their current drug use patterns and circumstances, and their general perspective on drugs, culture, and drug policy. He recruited equal numbers of interviewees per drug type who used these drugs in different frequencies and patterns.

He classified his subjects into three categories based on how frequently they used their primary drug. "Marginal" users used the drug occasionally in the past two years but had periods of daily or frequent use in the past; "controlled" users had a few recent periods of daily or frequent use in the past two years but otherwise used occasionally; and "compulsive" users had many recent periods of daily or frequent use in the past two years. In stratifying his sample by drug type and frequency of use, he hoped to understand how his subjects developed their use patterns. Zinberg's later work built on this and focused on controlled opiate users – mainly heroin – to explore how people managed their use of drugs commonly believed to be more addictive than others.

Zinberg and his co-investigators identified the factors in his interviewees' lives that guided their drug-related decision-making. Many marginal and controlled users made drug choices based on their values and life circumstances to minimize the likelihood of experiencing harmful effects while maximizing positive effects. These interviewees considered when, why, and with whom they used drugs, and they set personal rules or guidelines to control the conditions under which they used drugs. A controlled heroin user might, for example, use heroin only on the weekend to have ample time for recovery before weekday responsibilities. Zinberg's interviewees talked about how their social circles had various rituals, norms, and practices that encouraged controlled or managed drug use and safer injection practices. And some circles discouraged risky practices like regular binge use. Through these types of informal social controls, certain risky practices or behaviors were discouraged by group members, while other patterns were sanctioned or encouraged. Throughout their interviews, subjects also described changes in their drug use patterns over their lives, often attributing them to various drug, set, and setting-related factors that led to increased, decreased, controlled, or problematic use.

Zinberg's work can help to explain why some people do not develop drug problems, and why some do. The framework is helpful because it is not deterministic – it recognizes that people, their circumstances, and their behaviors change. It does not presume that their relationships with drugs will stay the same. It challenges dominant ideas that drug use always escalates into problematic use or that once one experiences drug-related problems, the only solution is lifelong abstinence.

I appreciate that the framework is broad enough to hold space for the individual and social theories of addiction described earlier. Multiple individual- and social-level theories can complement one another within the drug, set, and setting categories. In the example that I described of Alex at the top of the chapter, one can see how alcohol was his drug of choice due to its unique psychoactive effects and because it was readily available. He was distressed and regretful about his divorce and had few coping strategies to manage his feelings. Together, the drug and its impact on his mindset made it more likely that he would continue drinking to self-medicate.

Meanwhile, his setting and day-to-day life started to include more frequent happy hours with friends who liked to drink and to avoid being alone. And although he might have otherwise chosen to use marijuana, drug testing policies deterred him from using it to cope with his circumstances. Alex's example shows how the drug, set, and setting framework does not require us to write off any theories but allows us to see how multiple theories and factors can affect someone's circumstances. And that these factors together can dictate the kinds of drug-related choices we make.

Let us explore the framework and how each factor can be addressed with a harm reduction approach to help people to stay safe and reduce drug-related adverse effects.

The Drug

A key takeaway from Zinberg's work is that whether it is experimentation, social use, or more frequent use, we must first look at the qualities and characteristics of the drug itself. In his book, Zinberg noted that each drug used by his study's participants had distinct psychological and physical effects on the body. Since these drugs can vary significantly from one another, people's preferences can vary from drug to drug depending on the effects they seek. Some people prefer using stimulants to be awake and alert, while others may prefer benzodiazepines to help them calm down and relax. Not all drugs appeal equally to everyone because they can serve different functions.

Here are some important questions one may ask to understand the drug factors that can influence one's drug-related choices and how one's drug use patterns may develop over time:

- Which drug effects can be expected (i.e., calm, pain relief, heightened energy, etc.)?
- How long will the drug's effects last – a few minutes, or a few hours?
- Are there different effects if the drug is taken in small doses versus larger amounts?
- How is the drug consumed? Can it be swallowed, smoked, or injected?
- If someone changes their route of administration, how might it alter the drug's effects?
- Can someone expect side effects or adverse effects such as dizziness, nausea, itching, or paranoia?
- What happens if it is taken in combination with other drugs? Which combinations are the riskiest? Can certain combinations be lethal?

- Can someone become more tolerant of this drug and need more over time to achieve the same effect?
- Can someone experience withdrawal symptoms after taking this drug repeatedly or regularly?
- Can this drug be life-threatening in specific doses, combinations, or circumstances?
- Was this drug legally produced and tested for its contents and purity, or was it made in the underground market? Is it possible that someone may not know what they have taken or how much active ingredient is present?

Since each drug differs in its composition and effects, a person's use of heroin has to be viewed independently from their use of other drugs, like psilocybin mushrooms, because one would be motivated to use each drug for unique reasons and different intoxicating effects. Heroin creates comforting, pain-relieving, and euphoric feelings, while psilocybin shifts one's perceptions of themselves and their surroundings, including what one sees, hears, smells, tastes, or feels. Given these fundamental differences, one would likely use them at different times, for different reasons, and under different conditions.

In addition, these drugs do share some characteristics and considerations that can affect one's drug experience. For example, heroin and psilocybin both have effects that can last several hours, cause nausea as a potential side effect, and have dose-dependent effects (because consuming more of each drug can lead to stronger effects). Their route of administration or how they are consumed can also play a significant role in their effects. Heroin is typically smoked or injected, so its effects are felt rapidly, while psilocybin, commonly eaten or swallowed, can take upwards of half an hour or longer to kick in. Together, all these drug-specific characteristics can mean some may enjoy the effects while others may dislike them. Some will seek out the drug again, and others may not.

Interviewees also described their different precautions when using specific drugs because they recognized that each carried risks. Zinberg found that people in his study who used heroin or other opiates took careful measures to space out the frequency and quantity of their use. They did this because they understood the risk of developing physiological dependence if they consumed heroin several times a day for a few days in a row. When someone develops physiological dependence on an opiate, they experience uncomfortable withdrawal symptoms if they go several hours without using the drug. They also develop a higher tolerance for the drug and need to use more to experience the same effects as they once got from a smaller amount of a drug. By intermittently using measured amounts of heroin, Zinberg's occasional opiate-using participants developed strategies to allow them to enjoy heroin's effects while avoiding the risk of physiological dependence.

Zinberg's findings remind us that no two drugs are alike, and we must examine unique drug-specific factors individually for their specific characteristics and effects. The inclusion of drugs as a distinct factor in his model recognizes the role of the drug itself in people's preferences. Many of us have witnessed this by experimenting with various drugs or by hearing the experiences of others. Someone may love the rush of cocaine and enjoy a cigarette occasionally but had a terrible time when they tried LSD, so they never used it again.

While this may sound commonsensical and obvious to many of you, this is a relatively controversial statement in traditional addiction treatment and recovery settings. There are abstinence-only treatment settings and self-help groups across the country where someone says, "A drug is a drug is a drug," to a newcomer. This statement is commonly made by therapists and self-help "old timers" as a warning to new members to explain that even though a person may be seeking help for their drinking, they should not occasionally smoke marijuana or take MDMA the next time they go to a music festival. This statement is grounded in the belief that all psychoactive drugs carry similar risks of addiction for people with existing addictions or drug-related problems. This phenomenon is called "cross-addiction." Essentially, it's thought that a person's addiction to one drug places them at risk of being potentially addicted to all drugs due to an underlying addictive tendency that makes self-control and moderation challenging, if not impossible. There is a small minority of people who may develop a new addiction after resolving a previous one. Still, it is possible that other set and environmental or situational factors in their lives made them vulnerable to this pattern.

The Set or Person's Mindset

Drug effects do not occur in a vacuum, and neither do addictions. For instance, similar quantities of alcohol can sometimes make you the chatty life of the party, and there are times when a few drinks might make you irritable and easily provoked to anger. Cocaine can enhance a fun night out with friends and give you a boost, but on another occasion could make you obsessively reorganize the bookshelf while everyone else at the party dances in the living room. This is because your mental and emotional state can play a significant role in your experience of a drug. Drug effects can vary significantly from person to person, but the same person may experience different effects every time they use a drug. These differences are not explainable by pharmacology alone. A positive mindset and a good mood can increase the chances of having a positive experience with a drug after taking the appropriate dose and precautions. In the same way, feeling anxious or upset before taking a drug can intensify those feelings too.

One's values also play an essential role in deciding whether to try substances or experience certain forms of intoxication. People may be less likely to use a drug if they feel that its use goes against their values or morals. Most religions and cultures had parameters around the types of use that were acceptable and those that were not, long before we wrote laws to regulate or prohibit them. And these norms can affect someone's willingness to use those drugs. For instance, one person may be curious to try a taboo drug to see what all the fuss is about, while a drug's taboo status may deter others altogether. After all, not everyone wants to engage in illegal or stigmatized behaviors, such as certain forms of drug use.

Personality traits can influence drug-related behaviors too. One of the Big Five personality traits is "openness to experience," so some people are more curious and adventurous while others are more cautious. Experimenting with a new drug and altering one's consciousness may be appealing to some and not others. For some, being intoxicated or impaired may be unappealing if they fear losing control or lowering their guard. These individual-level factors play a prominent role in whether one person chooses to use drugs, while another may abstain in the same circumstance.

One's prior experience or exposure to a substance can also guide future drug-related decisions. Often, a first positive experience with a drug can make a person more willing to use it again. In contrast, a negative or neutral experience may not. A person thinking back on their father's harmful use of crack cocaine might make them reluctant to try any drugs. Meanwhile, growing up in a family where it was customary to see an adult drink a glass of wine with dinner and a beer while watching the game may normalize moderate alcohol use. A person with such a background might drink similarly when they get older. Television shows, documentaries, and movies can also impact choices about whether they want to try various drugs.

One's expectations can also influence how someone may experience a drug's effects. If one is already nervous about becoming paranoid when using marijuana, they may become paranoid and worry, "Am I acting weird? Why is she looking at me like that?" This is a well-known phenomenon, regardless of drug or drug class. In addition, the "placebo effect" is a commonly recognized part of medical research and practice; countless studies have taught us that if we expect a drug to work, it may work, even if we haven't consumed a psychoactive substance. Our expectations and beliefs can be powerful enough to impact how we experience anything we consume, whether it is a sugar pill or MDMA.

Underlying mental health conditions or diagnoses, including past trauma, can also impact how one experiences a drug. If a drug's effects help to alleviate or quell one's symptoms, a person may be more interested in trying it again or using it more often. For some people, drugs are an effective tool to help manage negative emotions or symptoms, which is why many say they self-medicate with drugs. However, in some cases, these negative emotions may be only temporarily masked or seem to be alleviated until the drug effects wear off. Unfortunately, for other people, certain drugs can intensify undesirable feelings or bring up other suppressed emotions rather than making them feel better. For instance, research suggests that some types of psychedelic drugs, like psilocybin, can help one achieve important insights while under the influence. These experiences can sometimes be painful or scary as they work through their trauma. In cases like this, being surrounded by people who can support and care for you through the process is essential.

To identify the role of mindset and other individual-level factors that influence drug experiences and drug-related behavior, one can ask these types of questions:

- How might this drug's effects affect their current emotional or mental state?
- Do they like the drug's effects, or does the drug make them feel uncomfortable or afraid?
- Do they expect to have a positive experience with this drug because of their past experiences or from what they have been told about this drug by others?
- Have they had a good day leading up to the moment when they took the drug? Are they in a good mood?
- Do they use this drug regularly enough so that they have some degree of tolerance and need to consume more to feel an effect?
- Have they consumed this drug frequently enough to experience withdrawal when they go without using it for too long?
- Does the person already struggle with impulse control? Are they a risk taker? Do they like seeking out new experiences?
- Does using this drug make them feel more confident, attractive, calm, social, or interesting than when they are sober?

By exploring the individual set-level factors in addition to the characteristics of the drug itself, we can begin to get a clearer picture of what is driving a person's drug use, what might sustain or deter someone's ongoing drug use, and which factors could be increasing or decreasing their drug-related risk behaviors. This can also help make people who intend to use drugs more aware of how their mindset can play a role in how they experience a drug and the steps they can take to maximize benefits while avoiding adverse effects. For instance, they become aware of mental or emotional states in which drug use may not be the optimal or the best decision.

The Setting and Environment

One's immediate environment, location, and circumstances can play a significant role in how one may experience substances. Some key questions one can ask to identify influential setting factors include:

- What message(s) was one given about various drugs at home, school, work, or other contexts? What were they taught about these different drugs?
- Which drugs are legal in their culture, and which are not? Which drugs are stigmatized, and which are sanctioned?
- Do they fear arrest or incarceration if caught using this drug?
- Is this drug acceptable to members of their social, work, and/or family network?
- Do their peers use this drug? If so, what are their use patterns, and do they promote safer use strategies?
- Were they exposed to parental or familial drug use while growing up? What patterns of use were normalized?
- Are their basic needs for food, shelter, safety, stability, and human connection met?
- Do they have access to tools and resources to help them make informed decisions about drug use?
- Do they typically use drugs alone or in social settings? If something were to go wrong, would they have anyone safe whom they could rely on to help?

Drugs play essential social and interpersonal functions for many of us. One's social or peer group, including workplace culture, can significantly impact drug-related experiences and decisions. The presence of others can also dictate whether someone is more likely or less likely to use, and how much they might use when they do. For instance, one may be part of a group of friends that spend their weekends getting high and smoking marijuana while playing video games or watching movies. While this pattern might be relatively harmless for a few weekends a semester, it may not be the best habit during midterms and finals. And if this use pattern starts creeping into weekdays, one may miss class and lose track of homework assignments that count toward one's final grades.

One's social environment and peers can dictate the risks or precautions one might take when using a drug for the first time. How someone is initiated into drug use can play a major role in whether they continue to use or which precautions they will continue to take. During freshman orientation week at college, your roommate may discourage you from taking a shot of vodka on top of the three beers you already drank. Your friends may take you to a harm reduction drug checking stand at a music festival to get your MDMA tested for adulterants before you take it. When one is fortunate enough to have these environmental facilitators for safety, one may internalize the importance of such practices and pay it forward by teaching others how to stay safe.

While these are examples of positive influences, one's peers also have the potential to initiate them into high-risk practices from the beginning or pressure them to push personal tolerance or comfort limits to go along with the group. With this understanding, one can zoom out from viewing an individual's drug use as a personal failing or disease, toward viewing it as a pattern developed and maintained in interaction with their environments. It is crucial to understand who people are using with, where they developed their patterns, and how their drug use is part of their socialization with their peer groups. And when we think about promoting safety or harm reduction, we can better tailor our advice to help people to make the best choices for themselves within their unique circumstances.

The illegality of drug use can often drive people to hide their use to avoid detection or arrest, such as teenagers who throw parties where they drink and use other drugs without parental supervision or when people secretly use stigmatized illegal drugs. The secrecy surrounding drug use can lead people to quickly consume all the drugs they have on hand to "destroy the evidence" so they don't get caught by a police officer, roommate, or parent. This can lead to binge behavior or rushed behavior that lacks adequate precautions. In these situations, an underage person experiencing alcohol poisoning or someone overdosing on illegal drugs may fear calling for help because they do not want to get in trouble or arrested. Beyond this, when drug use remains hidden or underground, people risk developing drug-related problems or habits in isolation and without support, because the closest people in their lives do not know what is happening and cannot offer strategies to help them stay safe. And they may be too ashamed to seek help.

In addition, one's environment can also contribute to "bad trips," or bad experiences with drugs that can deter or discourage them from using drugs again. Many people report having negative experiences when they've used drugs with strangers or when they've used drugs in public settings or new environments. Although setting factors have primarily been discussed for psychedelic drug experiences, research suggests that environmental or setting factors are just as important for other non-psychedelic drugs. Setting and environmental factors can drive overdose risk among people who use opioids and other drugs, such as their recent release from incarceration.[4]

Food insecurity, housing instability, financial challenges, and lack of opportunity can also dictate drug-related choices, but the relationship between drug use and poverty is complicated.[5] Contrary to popular belief, most low-income people and those experiencing homelessness do not have significantly higher rates of drug use than other demographics. People experiencing homelessness and housing instability are a large and diverse group in many different circumstances, not only the visibly unhoused people in crisis who many of us see on the corner. People experiencing homelessness and those who are unstably housed include the 20-year-old who transitioned out of foster care and is crashing on a friend's couch, a waitress living out of her minivan, and a family living in a shelter. While some people's drug use led them on a downward spiral, most people are poor because of low wages, job loss, lack of affordable housing options, lack of insurance, medical and other debt, lack of social support or a safety net, and other reasons.

While groups may not have significantly different rates of drug use, access to stable housing, suitable employment, and other resources can insulate privileged people from experiencing harmful consequences associated with the same drug use patterns. For instance, a white-collar worker's weekend bender on cocaine, pills, and alcohol could lead them to call off from work on Monday morning and take a sick day to recover; an under-the-table restaurant worker may be forced to either go without a day's pay or potentially lose their job for missing work. Although both missed a day of their job due to substance use, one will have far more negative ripple effects in their life than the other. And if both hypothetical drug users develop substance use disorders (SUDs), their ability to access quality treatment may differ dramatically. So while lower-income people may not necessarily engage in more problematic forms of drug use, they likely have fewer buffers to protect them from the consequences of their drug use when it is risky.

Policy factors can also motivate drug use decisions, including whether one's basic needs are met. For instance, a working mother with good insurance coverage can afford a doctor's visit to check her knee injury and receive physical therapy for several weeks while using her sick or flex time at work. Physical therapy can strengthen her knee so that she does not experience pain or damage in the future. In contrast, an uninsured working mom in the same situation might buy some spare Percocet from a friend to get through the week and continue to work in pain until she saves up enough to see a doctor. In her case, her illegal drug use is to cope with inadequate healthcare access, and her knee could sustain further painful damage with lasting effects the longer she goes without treatment.

I've learned that methamphetamine can be used to manage the chaos and unpredictability of housing instability. Taking methamphetamine at night is a strategy that can help someone stay vigilant while on the streets at night to avoid being victimized, robbed, or assaulted in public places in the dark. Methamphetamine could shift the sleep cycles of some users so they can rest in a public place during the day and be visible to witnesses if anything were to happen to them. For those on a limited budget, a drug like methamphetamine is far more cost-effective than buying a meal because it can suppress your appetite while keeping you functional for hours, whereas buying fast food with that money will leave you hungry a couple of hours later and worrying about your next meal again (and eating a meal almost guarantees you will need to find a public bathroom in the next several hours, which is not a luxury that many people have). However, people experiencing food or housing insecurity aren't the only ones who use methamphetamine to skip meals or stay awake. Methamphetamine and other stimulant drugs have long been marketed to middle-class and upper-class housewives as appetite suppressants for weight loss and tools to help them have it all – keeping them energized to cook and clean while caring for their kids. Hence, their husbands come home to a hot meal, an immaculate home, and well-behaved children.

The role of the setting in one's drug use is just as valuable to understand as individual and drug-specific factors because it has the potential to encourage or deter use, as well as to facilitate safe practices or increase risks. In so many cases, the ongoing use of a drug is a response to social, structural, and environmental factors so people can manage impossible situations or unrealistic expectations. When we look at drug use in a bubble and apart from these factors, we miss opportunities to think of the social, interpersonal, and structural changes that would create safer and healthier communities.

Taking Drug, Set, and Setting Together

Zinberg's framework helps harm reductionists explain why most people who have tried drugs do not ultimately develop drug-related problems and it provides a guide for helping people to make better choices surrounding their drug use. It helps us find critical intervention points at the drug, set, or setting level to help people who use drugs stay safe and reduce risk.[6] One can first pinpoint the area(s) that have contributed to harmful or adverse effects in one's life and then discuss potential changes one can make in the area(s) to reduce these risks and increase safety. This approach is in direct contrast to traditional treatment approaches that require one to stop all drug use without exploring other potential ways to change or modify it or their circumstances to see improvements in their life. I appreciate how the framework allows us to explore not only abstinence as one way to reduce risk but also other ways to reduce risk, such as by focusing on various drug, set, and setting-related factors in a person's life that they could adjust or change.

Zinberg's research subjects engaged in occasional or controlled use discussed how they considered each factor – drug, set, and setting – when figuring out how to maximize the pleasurable and positive drug effects while avoiding patterns that could harm or negatively impact their lives. They provided invaluable lessons on how people can ensure their drug use does not hinder achieving their goals and meeting their responsibilities. Most of his research subjects managed to use highly stigmatized and illegal drugs while still achieving milestones, making them otherwise indistinguishable from their peers who did not use them. They completed advanced degrees, maintained important family and social relationships, secured stable employment, and more. Many of these marginal or controlled users reported using these drugs off and on for an average of seven to eight years, roughly the same length of time as compulsive users. By determining that not all controlled users ultimately begin to use more frequently or heavily, his research challenged the idea that there was a clear or direct trajectory of drug use for interviewees in his studies.

Zinberg's research findings challenged dominant conceptions that drugs like marijuana, psychedelics, and opiates were instantly addictive, that people who used these drugs could not manage life responsibilities, and that these drugs rendered people incapable of caring for themselves. His findings added complexity and nuance to the conversation about drugs because they suggested that people who use these drugs are autonomous and complex people who make drug-related decisions for themselves. His interviewees talked about their choice to use drugs in the same way they talked about other choices they made in their lives – choices made within the contexts of their current circumstances while considering their values and priorities. His research also defied misconceptions that certain drugs were used only by the so-called deviant and the "maladjusted" because the people he studied in his research were everyday people from all walks of life.

Harm Reduction and Drug Factors

We must first discuss various factors associated with the drugs to consider how people can stay safe within the Drug, Set, and Setting model. Fortunately, we have learned a lot about drug safety precautions from our experience with medications, which can also apply to all other drugs. Zinberg's subjects talked about how they made these drug-related decisions. Dose, potency, route of administration, and interaction effects are just a few examples of considerations for drug use. Harm reductionists do their best to educate people about how to consider these factors for both legal and illegal drugs so they can stay safe.

Potency and Dosage

"The dose makes the poison." The potency of a drug is the amount of a drug that can cause an effect so that a high-potency drug can cause effects in relatively small quantities or doses. The potency of a drug is an important consideration so that one can get the optimal effects they seek while also taking adequate precautions to reduce the risk of adverse effects from taking too much. Drug dosage is an essential consideration for all forms of drug use, including high- and low-potency drugs. People who use legal drugs benefit from more information, tools, and strategies to manage dose and potency than those who use illegal drugs.

We must know the difference between an effective dose versus a dangerous dose to maximize benefits and avoid harm. Doses can vary dramatically from drug to drug, so a standard dose for one drug could be measured in milligrams, while the standard dose for another drug may be measured in micrograms. Most, but not all, commonly used psychoactive drugs (legal and illegal) have dose-dependent effects, meaning that different doses can lead to different effects. Sometimes, higher doses can produce more substantial effects than lower doses. In other cases, the difference between a small and lethal dose is dangerously narrow. Meanwhile, several drugs have ceiling effects, meaning that there is a level at which drug effects hit a plateau, so increasing the dose may not be worthwhile because they do not increase the effect or lead to more intoxication.

People who use other legal and illegal drugs must be armed with information about the potency and dose-dependent effects of drugs to stay safe. For instance, legally regulated alcoholic beverages have a broad range in potency. Liquors are often measured in shot glasses up to 1.5 ounces to account for their relatively high potency. Meanwhile, a serving size for wine is typically 5 ounces since wine is less potent, and beer servings are 12 ounces because it is the least potent of the three. These standard serving sizes can help calculate someone's Blood Alcohol Content (BAC) over time based on how quickly they may metabolize alcohol.

Harm reduction for alcohol often includes advice to consider diluting higher-potency liquors, counting the number of drinks per hour to estimate BAC and impairment, and measuring one's drinks to track consumption accurately (it can be very easy to accidentally pour oneself more than a standard serving in a drink). Since alcohol also can affect the GI system and cause dehydration, harm reduction advice also includes the guidance to drink more water and to avoid drinking on an empty stomach.

However, this information is virtually impossible to provide for illegal drugs, which often have unknown composition and are mixed with various additives or adulterants. People who use illegal drugs often must rely on the anecdotal experience of others or learn these things through trial and error. Unfortunately, this means that most people who consume illegal drugs typically do not know how much of the active drug they have consumed, whether it was a standard dose, or which other psychoactive drugs or adulterants may have been added. Given the significant role that dose can play in the safer use of medications and other legal drugs, it is clear that illegal drugs are not inherently any more dangerous than most legal medications. However, the policy context of criminalization deprives users of vital information.

Within this context, harm reductionists and more experienced drug users often recommend that people "start slow" when using a drug that they purchased illegally and not use everything all at once immediately. By starting slowly, one can determine whether they can get the effects they seek with a smaller dose. Remember, you can always take more, but you cannot do much after a drug has already been consumed. This is essential advice, especially for those who may have bought the drug from a new source, although it is still a good idea even if you get your drugs from the same person as usual. This is because drug supply chains are constantly shifting and changing (often due to being intercepted by law enforcement), so different manufacturers and distributors could have added different adulterants or contaminants along the way.

Until people who use illegal drugs are offered a safe supply, advanced drug-checking technologies beyond fentanyl test strips can also provide vital information to reduce harm. Running illegal drug samples through a machine using the analytical method of Gas Chromatography-Mass Spectrometry (GC-MS) can help to identify which drugs are present in a sample, so people who use those drugs can make better decisions and take precautions when using drugs. But these machines cost thousands of dollars and require trained staff to run and maintain them and interpret the results accurately. In addition, drug checkers must be exempt from local drug paraphernalia and possession charges to process and test samples on site. A growing number of programs offer these services in parts of the country – both in person and via mail – but we need more access to keep people informed.[7]

Route of Administration

How a drug is consumed can significantly affect how quickly its effects are felt, how long they may last, and which precautions must be taken to stay safe. Some routes of administration can help reduce drug-related risks and harms, while others can potentially make drug use more risky or harmful. The most common routes of administration, or modes of ingestion, include oral consumption (i.e., eating, drinking, or swallowing), smoking, snorting, and injection. Though less common, people also take drugs that can be absorbed through mucous membranes in the nose, mouth, or anus (such as chewing tobacco or suppositories). Each route allows drugs to enter our bloodstream, yet they are associated with different tradeoffs and considerations. Some drugs can be consumed through several routes of administration and still cause effects, while others may not be psychoactive through all methods.

Different routes of drug administration are used in medical treatment and scientific research every day, many of which are also the same routes of administration for illegal drugs. Yet the stigma and scorn for these routes are very different, as are the real-world risks. Consuming a drug orally by eating, swallowing, or drinking leads to the slowest onset of drug effects since it must first pass through the stomach and liver before entering the bloodstream, and much of the drug can be lost to metabolism before someone can feel the effects. Intravenous injection is one of the fastest ways to feel a drug's effects since it directly enters the bloodstream. Yet, injections also expose people to the risk of infection and other injection-related harms.

From a harm reduction perspective, it is essential to educate and inform people who use drugs of the possible routes of administration for each drug they may use, along with the pros and cons of each, and then to teach strategies to reduce the risk of harm with their preferred route. One of the reasons why injection, smoking, and snorting are common routes of administration for many people who use illegal drugs is because they tend to be more efficient and cost-effective ways to consume your drug of choice, since you can literally "get more bang for your buck," so to speak. This is because illegal drugs can often be expensive and of fluctuating quality, so many users want to ensure they get all they paid for. Unfortunately, this can also end up incentivizing some of the riskier routes of administration to maximize effects.

Considering these various factors is essential when discussing safety, yet our current models of care do not create contexts where people can safely or comfortably have these conversations. However, these are ordinary conversations among harm reductionists. They often educate people about how switching from a higher-risk route of administration to a lower-risk route of administration can reduce risks of blood-borne diseases, skin and soft tissue infections, and damage to the lungs or nasal cavities (i.e., switching from injecting to smoking, transitioning from smoking to swallowing, etc.). In addition, harm reductionists advocate for policy changes to reduce the risk of various routes of administration – such as decriminalizing the possession of syringes, crack pipes, and other drug-using equipment, legalizing SSPs and other modalities where sterile drug-using equipment and supplies can be freely distributed (e.g., vending machines, via mail order).

Polysubstance Use and Interaction Effects

It is common for many people to use multiple drugs together simultaneously or in sequence, also known as polysubstance use. This is because certain drugs have synergistic effects. Other drugs can complement each other's effects, intensify their effects, substitute for other drugs, or even offset one another's effects. For instance, many people enjoy smoking cigarettes while drinking alcohol because of the interplay of their stimulating and relaxing effects. Certain drug combinations may come with fewer risks due to the class of drugs involved. In contrast, other drug combinations can be harmful and potentially life-threatening, such as when people consume multiple "downers" together, like heroin, alcohol, and benzodiazepines. The effects of mixing illegal and unregulated drugs can be riskier, since these supplies are of unknown composition.

Harm reductionists acknowledge that polysubstance use already occurs among significant percentages of the population – whether under medical supervision or involving drugs of various legal statuses. Yet the ultimate tool in keeping people safe when they use any drug is information and tips for minimizing risk, such as considering dose, potency, route of administration, and the drug classes involved. Many harm reductionists discuss these considerations with people who use drugs to help them understand what might happen in their bodies when they take several drugs together or soon after one another so they can understand how to avoid adverse or even lethal effects. If and when possible, harm reductionists recommend avoiding polysubstance use, especially multiple central nervous system depressants and/ or opioids, since they can contribute to a fatal overdose.

How Harm Reduction Can Address Set-Related Harms

Harm reductionists help people develop the skills to manage set or mindset-related factors that can help make drug-using experiences both less risky and safer. They also advance policies to make this knowledge more accessible and make it easier to provide the support people need.

As noted earlier in the book, harm reductionists believe that everyone should be more educated drug consumers to have as much information as possible to keep themselves and others safe. When people are armed with facts and accurate information about drugs, they can be better prepared and know what to expect. This includes knowing which precautions to take and how to manage potential feelings of discomfort or distress in the case of a "bad trip."

In addition, ensuring that people have adequate access to effective, affordable, and trauma-informed mental health and medical treatment is another harm reduction priority. And promoting positive community and mutual aid ties through one's harm-reduction community can foster stronger self-esteem and improve one's outlook on life. When people feel alone, sick, depressed, and hopeless, controlling or managing their drug use can be difficult. By ensuring people are in the best possible mental and physical health, we can ensure that they are better equipped to use drugs in ways that provide them with positive effects and reduce the likelihood of engaging in harmful or damaging practices.

How Harm Reduction Can Address Setting-Related Harms

We can do many things to reduce drug setting-related harms and make people safe. For instance, it is essential to consider how the social, legal, and policy environments that people live in can affect their drug-related decisions. Once these are understood, harm reductionists can offer strategies to reduce these risks so people can be safer.

Understanding the interpersonal or social functions of drug use can be a crucial part of identifying the factors contributing to someone's increased risk-taking, which can help harm reductionists offer them practical strategies to stay safe in specific environments and with others. They may suggest that a person could avoid using drugs with certain people or, if they do, they could plan to practice safer use strategies. A harm reductionist may suggest that someone brings along a friend to support them in using less or abstaining, or that they come to certain events prepared with an escape plan, including the phone number of a safe person to pick them up. Alternately, a person concerned about problematic or risky drug use in their social circle may also be the best person to promote harm reduction by bringing sterile drug-using equipment to the next event or encouraging people to take breaks or slow down.

As I've mentioned earlier, harm reductionists also believe that people need to be in safer environments when they use drugs – including safe and secure housing and the option to use in Overdose Prevention Centers or other legally sanctioned places. When people have the stability and resources to make safer decisions about where and with whom they use drugs, it reduces the likelihood of adverse or harmful effects.

Lastly, we must acknowledge that policies can increase drug-related risks and harm in our communities in ways that affect us all. When people do not have their basic needs met, fear arrest or incarceration, or are forced to navigate an unpredictable drug supply, it can make drug use riskier and put people in harm's way. Our policies must prioritize public health, community investment, build a social safety net, and legally regulate our access to substances to ensure that people have all the resources and tools they need for their safety and well-being.

Conclusion

This chapter covered the pros and cons of various explanatory theories for addiction. It highlighted how the drug, set, and setting model offers a more comprehensive view of the factors contributing to people's drug use patterns and risk-taking. It also helps us to understand why some people develop problems and others do not. When harm reductionists use information gained about people's drug, set, and setting factors, they can tailor messaging and interventions, as well as policies, to help keep people safe.

Notes

1 Han, Beth, Wilson M. Compton, Carlos Blanco, and Lisa J. Colpe. "Prevalence, Treatment, and Unmet Treatment Needs of US Adults with Mental Health and Substance Use Disorders." *Health Affairs* 36, no. 10 (2017): 1739–47. https://doi.org/10.1377/hlthaff.2017.0584.

2 Grant Weinandy, T. Jennifer, and Joshua B. Grubbs. "Religious and Spiritual Beliefs and Attitudes towards Addiction and Addiction Treatment: A Scoping Review." *Addictive Behaviors Reports* 14 (December 2021): 100393. https://doi.org/10.1016/j.abrep.2021.100393.

3 Heather, Nick, Matt Field, Antony C. Moss, and Sally Satel (eds.) *Evaluating the Brain Disease Model of Addiction*. New York: Routledge. 2022.

4 Ataiants, Janna, Alexis M. Roth, Silvana Mazzella, and Stephen E. Lankenau. "Circumstances of Overdose among Street-Involved, Opioid-Injecting Women: Drug, Set, and Setting." *International Journal of Drug Policy* 78 (April 2020): 102691. https://doi.org/10.1016/j.drugpo.2020.102691.

5 Chen, Ruijia, Ronald C. Kessler, Ekaterina Sadikova, Amanda NeMoyer, Nancy A. Sampson, Kiara Alvarez, Corrie L. Vilsaint, et al. "Racial and Ethnic Differences in Individual-Level and Area-Based Socioeconomic Status and 12-Month DSM-IV Mental Disorders." *Journal of Psychiatric Research* 119 (December 2019): 48–59. https://doi.org/10.1016/j.jpsychires.2019.09.006.

6 Denning, Patt, and Jeannie Little. *Over the Influence: The Harm Reduction Guide to Controlling Your Drug and Alcohol Use* (2nd ed.). New York: Guilford Press, 2017.

7 The New York City Department of Health has hired a staff person who visits local Syringe Service Programs (SSPs) throughout the city and checks drugs on site for participants. People in Massachusetts and partnering organizations in several states nationwide can drop off their samples at participating sites and get their drug-checking results through https://www.info.streetcheck.org/. Meanwhile, several innovative community- and email-based drug-checking programs, including https://www.drugsdata.org, run by Erowid, and UNC Street Drug Analysis Lab's program https://www.streetsafe.supply/.

6 Treatment and the Harm Reduction Gap

What about treatment?

I'm commonly asked this question by well-intentioned folks when I say I am a harm reduction advocate, or whenever it is suggested that we need more access to harm reduction services in the community.

The people who ask me this are diverse and come from all races, genders, ages, socioeconomic backgrounds, and political leanings. They are parents, community members, journalists, healthcare providers, recovery advocates, students, and just about everyone else. They ask this question with sincere curiosity and good intentions. They care. After all, one of the more notable recent shifts in public opinion is that more people than ever now view addiction as a treatable health condition. And this is a good thing. It is progress.

The issue is that now many people see treatment as the *only* solution. So in their minds, if treatment is the ultimate solution and end goal, why would we need more harm reduction, or even need harm reduction at all?

I try to approach these conversations as teachable moments. And I start by telling them I am a former treatment provider myself.

I explain that I know how life-changing treatment could be, because I saw firsthand how it helped my former clients to achieve stability in their lives. But then I also talk about how working in treatment also made it clear to me how difficult it is for the average person to find, access, afford, and complete treatment in its current state. And that the treatments that are the easiest to access are not always the ones that are evidence-based and proven to work. I also clarify that while some people are helped by traditional addiction treatment, there are others whose needs are far greater or complex than what our treatment system can address, but they are still sent to treatment because there is nowhere else to go. I explain how most people who start treatment in any given year do not successfully complete it, and that then there are few options for support once they are discharged from services. Finally, I talk about how over 90% of people who have addictions do not

DOI: 10.4324/9781003301745-7

receive any treatment each year, so that they are left without any other options for support or safety in the community.

All these factors mean that while treatment is a needed support for many people, it will never meet all the needs of everyone who uses drugs, even those with addictions. And when treatment does not or cannot meet people's drug-related needs, they will need more options in the community for help. I want people to understand that being a harm reduction advocate means that I want people to have an even larger safety net to fill the gap. I want people to have a broader range of available services in the community in addition to and beyond treatment.

That's it.

* * *

My first job after completing my master's in social work was at an outpatient substance use treatment facility in my hometown in rural upstate New York. I had just completed a 10-month student internship there as part of my social work degree and was excited to continue working and learning at the facility. I was hired to conduct several intake evaluations a week for new clients, to do some individual counseling, and to facilitate aftercare groups for clients living with co-occurring substance use disorders (SUD) and mental health diagnoses who were phasing out of our intensive outpatient program or rehab program. Eventually I also became our agency representative at the local drug court, but I will tell you more about that later in the book.

Conducting intake evaluations on new potential clients was an important part of my job since our agency first had to determine whether the client met criteria for a diagnosable SUD and then, based on the severity of their problems and other considerations, which level of care or type of treatment would best meet their needs. This is important because not everyone who uses substances experiences problems, and even if they do, not all those problems are at the level of severity where they require addiction treatment to address them. Additionally, since such a range of services are available at different types of treatment settings, it was my job to figure out which setting was best suited for the client's unique circumstances and needs. A portion of the clients I met with were not appropriate for the types of services we provided at our facility, so I sometimes made referrals to other facilities better suited to meet their needs.

I used the *Diagnostic and Statistical Manual of Mental Disorders'* Fourth Edition Text Revision (DSM-IV-TR) to assess whether each client's substance use patterns and related problems met criteria to be diagnosed with a SUD. (Providers today now use the DSM-5 to make these diagnoses since the manual was updated in 2013.) During these evaluations, I would ask the client detailed questions about their substance use patterns and history, any prior substance use treatment, any current or past health (including mental health) diagnoses or treatment, current housing status, family medical history, current or past involvement with the criminal legal system, current relationship status and their social support system, and much more. After collecting all of this information in a 45- to 60-minute interview and conducting an on-site urine drug test, I would determine whether the person met the criteria for one or more SUDs. One could potentially be diagnosed with an SUD for any drug they used, although often people had a primary drug that was the most problematic.

If the client met the criteria for a SUD diagnosis, I then had to determine which level of care was best suited for each client's needs using the American Society of Addiction Medicine (ASAM) standardized criteria. According to the ASAM, individual client needs and circumstances should be considered when determining which level of treatment intensity would be most beneficial.[1] Considerations should be made based on many factors including but not limited to the severity of their SUD, withdrawal risk, any co-occurring mental health diagnoses, and all the factors I listed above such as housing and support system. The standardized ASAM criteria are meant to ensure that the treatment recommendation was matched to the client's needs so they were not unnecessarily referred to an intensive treatment setting when a less intensive, community-based option would have been successful, or vice versa.

Addiction Treatment in the United States

According to recent estimates, the addiction treatment system in the United States is comprised of over 16,000 publicly funded addiction treatment facilities.[2] This number has remained relatively stable for the past decade.[3] Some treatment facilities are stand-alone specialty addiction-only treatment programs while others are integrated into hospitals, community health centers, and facilities that provide mental health and other services. While enrolled in treatment, clients may receive a wide range of services, including individual or group therapy, medications, psychiatric or medical treatment for other health issues, and/or case management. These services and many more may be a part of the client's individualized treatment plan to help them to achieve stability and work toward their recovery. There are several different types of treatment programs available in the United States, and they fall along a continuum that ranges from less intensive treatment options all the way to much more intensive and restrictive treatment to meet varying client needs.

Outpatient treatment and office-based buprenorphine prescribing are two examples of less intensive treatment types because clients travel to treatment several times a week, month, or year while still living at home. According to the ASAM criteria, these options are best for people with some degree of stability in their lives because they can remain at home to manage life responsibilities, including family, work, and/or school, while getting support to address their substance-related treatment needs. Outpatient treatment can vary in intensity, so someone may come to treatment for only one or two individual or group sessions a week; or receive intensive outpatient treatment for four hours a day, three days a week; all the way up to outpatient rehab for six hours a day, five days a week.

However, not everyone in outpatient treatment lives at home or has a home. Some may be advised to stay in sober housing or in supportive drug-free housing while attending outpatient treatment because these settings can provide much-needed support and structure outside of treatment hours. Supportive housing may be recommended if someone lives in a situation that could place them at risk of returning to use – for instance, if they live with family members or roommates who also have substance-related problems. Someone may also be advised to live in supportive housing for the duration of treatment if they are currently homeless or unstably housed. When someone travels to outpatient treatment while living in supportive housing, this is viewed as a higher level of care due to the additional structure it provides.

Then there are more intensive treatment settings such as inpatient treatment, detoxification, and residential treatment. While someone might stay in detoxification for up to a week, inpatient treatment could last for up to 28 days, and residential treatment could last several months. In these settings, clients stay on site at a hospital or treatment facility for the entirety of their treatment. Clients qualify for these levels of care because they may have complex withdrawal symptoms or other psychiatric or medical needs that also require attention and stabilization, and their immediate housing situation may be unstable or not conducive to managing these needs in early recovery. Program policies in these intensive settings are typically very strict; they often do not allow clients to go off site, or they restrict departures to specific circumstances. Outside visitors and phone calls may also be limited. After completing these more intensive levels of care, clients are usually referred to outpatient treatment to continue to build on the stability they achieved as they reintegrate into the community.

It was my job to apply the ASAM criteria to each client's unique circumstances to see which of these levels of care were most appropriate for the person and to make the treatment recommendation that would help them on their path to recovery. Sounds pretty straightforward, right? Even though the ASAM criteria may seem like a helpful and systematic way to make sure that people get matched with the treatment they need, I learned early on that it is not that simple in the real world.

There are a number of outside factors that can also dictate the type of treatment any individual may receive, or whether they receive treatment at all, and these can sometimes have little to nothing to do with the ASAM criteria or treatment need. As I did more of these intake evaluations on clients, I quickly learned that the type of treatment that someone may receive could be impacted by factors like geography, referral sources, mandates, waitlists, cost, and insurance companies. For some of my clients, any of these factors, or several factors combined, could override ASAM recommendations so that clients would end up in different places from what might be clinically indicated. I also learned that even after a client started their recommended treatment, there was a significant chance that they would not complete it, meaning that if they were terminated from treatment for noncompliance or dropped out, they would be left with no alternatives for support. And it wasn't until years later that I came to know that for every one person in treatment, there were nine people in the community who had SUDs and were not receiving services at all.

Limited and Inaccessible Treatment Options

Unfortunately, our treatment system is not robust or accessible enough to meet the needs of our communities, and this can create both a treatment *and* a harm reduction gap where many of us live. Treatment facilities along the continuum of care are not evenly distributed across the nation. In fact, where one lives dictates which types of treatment may be accessible, affordable, or available.

I worked at one of the two addiction treatment facilities in my hometown and together these two served our community and the neighboring rural communities for miles. We provided outpatient treatment while the other facility in town provided both inpatient and outpatient services. There was one main recovery housing program where some of our clients stayed and traveled to our facility for the duration of treatment. However, there were a limited number of beds at any given time for men and fewer for women, so sometimes people had to travel to treatment from one of the local homeless shelters. For clients who were at risk of experiencing opioid, alcohol, or benzodiazepine withdrawal, there was one addiction crisis center with minimal medical staffing that provided people with a temporary place to stabilize for several hours or days, and more formal medicalized detox units in one of the community hospitals. We had relationships with some longer-term inpatient and residential treatment programs in neighboring counties, and sometimes we had to refer clients to them since they were often the closest options when beds weren't available locally. I have come to realize that, even though we faced barriers to getting people the help they needed, we had a decent range of services at the time compared to many other parts of the country.

The fewer treatment options in a community, the more challenging it can be to find services to meet the diverse needs or preferences of clients. For instance, someone who would prefer to receive counseling using a Cognitive Behavioral Therapy (CBT) approach may find that the only treatment program in town predominantly uses Twelve Step Facilitation (TSF), a therapy approach with a spiritual orientation, grounded in the principles of Alcoholics Anonymous (AA). Someone with private health insurance from their full-time job may need evening and/or weekend treatment options but may find that neither of the treatment centers in their community have openings for new clients in their evening groups. In these scenarios and many more, people are often forced to accept whatever services are available or go without any treatment at all.

Waitlists are common at many facilities around the country due to limited capacity, particularly in small towns and rural communities that have only a few agencies with a limited number of treatment slots. But waitlists are also becoming a common problem in major cities, since demand is outpacing the supply in many parts of the country. This can mean that people must wait for days or weeks before they can start treatment, with no options for support in the meantime. Sometimes clients could get referred to a lower level of care in the hope that it could tide them over or keep them connected to some sort of services, but this approach did not always work because clients weren't always able to comply with abstinence requirements in less intense services without the additional support or structure. This could result in termination of services for noncompliance, leaving them with nowhere to go for help afterwards. But in other cases, there are simply no other options to turn to for services, meaning that even highly motivated people may be forced to wait for a treatment slot to become available. And while they wait, they may slip back into engaging in high-risk drug using practices with no other options for help.

Another factor that complicates treatment engagement is transportation. Outpatient programs like where I worked require clients to come to the program in person on a daily or weekly basis. Frequent attendance can also be required at methadone treatment settings and when someone is first started on buprenorphine. If one does not have a reliable car or decent public transportation options in the community, it can be really challenging to comply with strict attendance requirements to get services. We had public buses in my hometown, but they did not run very frequently or cover all neighborhoods, so getting to and from outpatient treatment could take over the better part of someone's day because they may have to walk long distances to the nearest bus stop to then transfer several routes back and forth to treatment every day. Fortunately, New York State Medicaid paid for cabs to bring patients from distant parts of our county and the surrounding counties to treatment, but this was also time-consuming and required a lot of planning in advance, since clients were coming from long distances. And inclement weather could lead to treatment noncompliance – buses and cabs could be difficult to secure during the snowy winters of upstate New York. Even for those who had cars, it could be challenging to monopolize the family car for several hours every day, multiple days a week, for months on end. And many programs have very strict rules about attendance and being on time – too many late or missed sessions can be a problem. In fact, most insurance plans will pay for treatment sessions only if the client received a minimum number of minutes or hours of treatment that day, so if a client missed enough of a session, the treatment agency may not get paid for services that day. Chronic lateness or missing too many sessions can eventually lead to termination due to noncompliance.

Taken together, limited local options and difficulty accessing them can make it challenging to get services and support when people need them the most. And while much-needed efforts are underway to expand access to treatment across the nation, including via telehealth, there is actually a lot we can do *right now* to ensure people remain connected to community alternatives that are flexible, accommodating, and health promoting. These changes can help the tens of thousands of people who fall into the harm reduction gap this way every year. Harm reduction programs and support groups can easily fill that gap by providing support to reduce isolation and ensure people have a sense of community, both in person and virtually. Tools and support such as sterile drug-using equipment, drop-in groups, harm reduction psychotherapy, naloxone, or an Overdose Prevention Center (OPC) can be a lifeline for those disconnected from care or terminated from traditional treatment. Since harm reduction services do not have strict attendance requirements for engagement and are not beholden to insurance plans, they can provide in-person, virtual, or mail-based support to those who need them the most. They are also designed and often implemented by people with lived or living experiences of drug use, and so accessibility is often a key priority in program design and implementation.

The Most Effective Treatments Are Often Out of Reach

In 2020, almost 27% of the nation's 1.4 million treatment admissions were for a primary opioid use disorder (OUD), second only to alcohol use disorder.[4] Methadone and buprenorphine are both FDA-approved medications for treating OUDs. Both have decades of data to support their use, and they are often referred to as medications for opioid use disorder (MOUD). Research shows they help people to cut down on street opioids like heroin and fentanyl, they reduce opioid overdose risk by over 50%, and they lead to better health outcomes for patients.[5] Since the 1970s, methadone has been internationally known as the "gold standard" treatment for OUDs, and has even been approved for the treatment of OUD among pregnant people. Buprenorphine, often known by the brand name

Suboxone, is a newer medication with the same health benefits and outcomes as methadone with a similar mechanism of action in the brain. Despite their positive effects, these two highly effective and lifesaving medications are incredibly difficult to access in most of the United States. In fact, a recent study found that only roughly one out of four people with a past-year OUD received a medication like methadone or buprenorphine.[6]

Why are methadone and buprenorphine such transformative treatments for people with OUD who use street opioids? And why do so few people have access to them?

Opioids like heroin and fentanyl wear off after several hours, leaving people with OUD or those who have developed physiological dependence to opioids to experience withdrawal symptoms like nausea, diarrhea, sweats, chills, and body aches multiple times a day, every day. This means that people with OUD will spend much of their time seeking and using opioids to feel better and alleviate withdrawal. And this quickly becomes a cycle that occurs every four or five hours, every single day, and which can go on for weeks, months, and years on end. Along the way, the person's tolerance can also increase so that they need more opioids to alleviate withdrawal and achieve any of the euphoric or pain-relieving effects they seek. Many people grow tired after years of the cycle of opioid use followed predictably by withdrawal. It can be exhausting to hustle all day long to scrape together enough money to get high and try to stave off withdrawal all day, every day. It makes it hard to plan for anything or make commitments, because they are always trying to calculate how long before they go into withdrawal again, and it ends up taking priority over just about everything else.

This is where MOUD can be lifechanging – when people with OUD are given the proper dose of either of these medications, opioid cravings and withdrawal symptoms can be alleviated for *a full 24 hours*. This is a long time! It is a dramatic change for people who are accustomed to the cycle of opioid use and withdrawal who are ready for a change. When prescribed the correct dose, patients can suddenly do things they were otherwise unable to do – they can reclaim their time and energy, they can make plans, they can keep appointments, they can live their lives again. Countless people credit methadone and buprenorphine with giving them their lives back since they can better care for themselves and their families, go back to school, keep a stable job, attend medical appointments, explore hobbies and interests, and so much more.

Despite their unparalleled success rate and immediate beneficial effects, these incredible medications are inaccessible for the average person with OUD in the United States, as illustrated by the statistic I mentioned earlier. Case in point: my home county still has only one methadone clinic, or Opioid Treatment Program (OTP), and it serves the entire county and most of the surrounding counties in the area for hours in each direction. And this is common; several studies have calculated drive times to OTPs in small towns and rural communities across the country and found that people travel, on average, upwards of an hour each way every day for their medication.[7,8,9] Unfortunately, this is because methadone in the United States can be dispensed only at OTPs, even though other nations treat it like any other medication and dispense it to patients at pharmacies. Most new patients in methadone treatment are expected to come to the OTP on a daily basis and are subjected to random urine drug testing to monitor compliance and abstinence from other drugs. In many clinics, compliant patients can eventually earn the privilege of take-home doses for a few days, then eventually a few weeks at a time. Unfortunately, fear of diversion (i.e., sharing or selling the medication) or medication misuse can motivate these very tight restrictions. Because methadone is a highly controlled medication, OTPs must be licensed with the Drug Enforcement Agency (DEA) and comply with very strict regulations to operate. Between the difficult federal regulations placed on OTPs and the disruptive efforts of NIMBY (not in my backyard) activists to keep OTPs from opening in their communities, it is challenging to open and operate OTPs even though they are needed in communities across the nation. Despite these issues, as of this writing, more OTPs are operating in the nation than even a few years before. However, for far too many, they remain unavailable or out of reach.[10]

Additionally, the ambiance at OTPs can make them feel more like a jail than a medical treatment program – many have bulletproof glass at the dispensing counter, for example. Far too many people find the expectation of daily pickups to be burdensome, combined with the embarrassment of having to open one's mouth after taking their methadone to show the staff person that they have not "cheeked" it to spit out and sell to someone else. The feeling that many patients have is summarized by the title of this article in the online magazine *Filter*: "I chose fentanyl over the humiliation of methadone treatment."[11] It is deeply upsetting to think about how strict policies and a shaming approach to treatment deter many from choosing this lifesaving option.

Meanwhile, buprenorphine has its own unique barriers to prescribing and access on the ground. On the one hand, policies were passed to make it more accessible in traditional medical settings and to allow for take-home doses that could be picked up at the pharmacy. But fears that patients would divert and misuse the medication, combined with concerns that physicians would overprescribe the medication, led to a problematic policy compromise. Starting in the early 2000s, physicians could prescribe buprenorphine for only up to 30 patients at any given time, and only then if they had completed an eight-hour training and registered for a special X waiver with the DEA. On the other hand, other healthcare professionals who can otherwise prescribe medications (e.g., Physician Assistants, Nurse Practitioners) had to complete a 24-hour training to initially prescribe to 30 patients. If X-waivered physicians or the other professionals wanted to prescribe to more patients, they would have to apply for another waiver to treat up to 100, and then apply again to treat up to 275 patients. Buprenorphine could be dispensed in take-home doses for up to a month at a time as long as patients were also receiving some form of counseling, which made it far more convenient and appealing to patients compared to the daily dispensing of methadone. But given the strict regulations on buprenorphine prescribing, the vast majority of prescribers decided that jumping through so many hoops to prescribe the medication was not worth the trouble, because it would mean that they would have more patients with OUDs in their practice (an otherwise undesirable and highly stigmatized patient population).

Over the years, more medical and other professional programs tried to incentivize X waiver training, with many incorporating the training into their curricula and doing more to destigmatize patients with OUD. Some restrictions were loosened due to the COVID-19 pandemic, waiving in-person evaluations and allowing telehealth prescriptions. Combined with these efforts to expand the waiver training, thousands of patients across the country gained access to the medication. In 2021, the X-waiver requirement was loosened for physicians so that they could file a Notice of Intent with the government to prescribe to 30 patients. In 2023, the X-waiver requirement was finally lifted, and patient limits were also eliminated for prescribers who already met certain training criteria. All of these policy changes are a tremendous step forward, and there is evidence to show that buprenorphine prescribing more than doubled between 2009 and 2018 and continued to increase through 2021.[12,13] Though the availability has not increased enough to fully meet demand, this is progress.

No other medications in the United States ever required this type of approval process for prescribers or had such tight prescribing restrictions. I hope that the most recent policy changes continue to increase access to lifesaving medication, because prior to the pandemic-related policy changes, patients had a difficult time trying to find any X-waivered buprenorphine prescribers in most parts of the country other than by using an unreliable online database that was run by the Substance Abuse and Mental Health Services Administration (SAMHSA). In 2019, a team of researchers attempted to use the database to identify buprenorphine prescribers in the ten states with the highest overdose rates to see how helpful the tool could be to find a provider and get access to this medication.[14] The researchers found that only 60% of prescribers had their correct telephone numbers on the database; 38% said they prescribed buprenorphine; most accepted only a few insurance plans; and only 27% had available appointments for new patients. This study highlighted the unnecessary and devastating barriers that patients faced to find potential providers while also revealing how patient prescribing caps limited the number of available appointments among pre-scribers in most communities. It also showed how difficult it was to find providers who accepted certain types of insurance, especially since signifi-cant numbers preferred to treat self-pay patients at average costs of over $200 a session.[15]

Although prescribing policies have changed, barriers to patients may still persist. For one, for years there have been tremendous racial disparities in who is prescribed buprenorphine: white patients are far more likely to receive a prescription than racial or ethnic minority patients. In addition, many may still face barriers at the pharmacy level, particularly in rural com-munities and southern states. For years, buprenorphine patients have talked about being unable to fill their prescriptions at pharmacies in their commu-nities because many do not stock it or because they are placed under scru-tiny for filling the prescription, since it is an opioid. In a recent study, researchers found that when they called over 5,000 pharmacies across the country asking if they could fill a buprenorphine prescription, only 57.9% reported that they had any in stock.[16]

It is a tragedy that as the overdose crisis has raged on for over two decades and claimed over a million lives, access to these two lifesaving medications has remained so limited. Part of this is due to tight policy restrictions, but another is stigma toward the medications themselves. Since both medica-tions work as opioids, there are misconceptions that these medications "replace one addiction with another," which deters many abstinence-ori-ented and TSF programs from encouraging clients to use these medications. In one study, researchers called over 600 residential treatment programs across the country and found that fewer than one-third provided buprenor-phine; another third provided it only as a short-term detox medication; and nearly 40% of programs did not offer it at all.[17] In fact, a significant number of programs tried to deter the callers from pursuing buprenorphine treat-ment, perpetuating false and stigmatizing messages about the medication to callers. However, as we discussed in an earlier chapter, addiction is charac-terized by ongoing use of a substance despite negative consequences. Tak-ing medications like methadone or buprenorphine can lead to reduced street opioid use, which reduces the drug-related negative consequences in patients' lives and enables them to build the lives they want. These out-comes are the exact opposite of an addiction – these are positive improve-ments resulting from receiving an effective treatment.

Yet, without easy access to MOUD, many people who seek treatment are set up to return to opioid use again, since experiencing withdrawal symp-toms during psychosocial or talk therapy can be challenging to the most motivated clients. When people drop out of treatment because they've been given less effective treatments that are not tailored to their specialized needs, too often we blame the client rather than the system that is failing them.

And then they have nowhere to turn. In recent years, harm reduction programs and other healthcare systems have tried to integrate a low-threshold approach to maintaining clients on buprenorphine in an attempt to make it easier for them to start and stay on it. We need more systems to do this and to find ways to make methadone available outside of the tightly structured and rigid OTP system as well.

Treatment Is Often Expensive and Unaffordable

Cost and affordability remain challenges for people seeking addiction treatment, affecting both those with insurance and the millions who remain uninsured or underinsured in the United States. Many insurance plans, private and public alike, require prior authorization before the company will agree to pay for services, and they may decide that they will pay only for certain services or medications and not others. They may even state that they will authorize payment for only a certain portion of the cost or for only a certain period of time. When prior authorization is required, the treatment provider or physician must first provide documentation to justify why the patient needs certain treatment so that the insurer will agree to pay for it. This additional step can become a barrier for those who could not afford treatment otherwise, and especially for those who are in urgent need of care.

When I conducted intake assessments and made treatment recommendations for certain clients with private insurance, I would have to fax them a copy of the full initial diagnostic assessment to show how the treatment recommendation was made based on the ASAM criteria to show clinical need and justify why the level of care was indicated. Even then, sometimes the insurance plan might approve only a limited number of sessions to start, requiring us to resubmit paperwork weeks later to attempt to get approval to complete the full course of treatment. If we did not get approval, it could mean that we would simply have to end services based on the last session the insurance company would pay for. At the time, intensive outpatient services would entail roughly 10–12 hours of group therapy sessions per week for approximately 12 weeks. I remember conducting an assessment on a client whose alcohol use disorder was disrupting his life and affecting his ability to manage his work and life responsibilities, but whose private insurance plan was willing to pay for only six weeks, about a month and a half of treatment. Ultimately, I resubmitted paperwork and documentation after the six weeks to see if we could extend it longer and only got them to agree to pay for two more weeks. After that, we had to stop services because he couldn't afford to pay out of pocket for any more sessions.

Waiting for insurance approval or prior authorization before starting or continuing services could end up delaying or disrupting access to lifesaving services. For example, prior authorization requirements can frequently delay getting a buprenorphine prescription filled, on top of the fact that many insurance policies do not allow patients to receive early refills of this medication. Missing even a single dose of buprenorphine can lead to uncomfortable and distressing withdrawal symptoms that place the patient at risk of returning to street opioids to alleviate withdrawal. In these situations, prior authorization can become a demoralizing and time-consuming hassle that both prescribers and patients may not want to deal with on a monthly basis or several times a year. And the effects can be lethal for people who are otherwise currently in treatment and trying to stay off drugs for their recovery. A study found that when prior authorization for buprenorphine was removed as a requirement of Medicare, it was associated with a significantly higher number of filled prescriptions among patients with OUD. This policy change also dramatically reduced instances of various other negative health effects, including all-cause inpatient hospital admissions, SUD-related inpatient admissions, and emergency department visits.[18] As shown in this example, restrictive insurance policies can often act as an obstacle to receiving services even though being insured should theoretically increase access to healthcare and treatment.

Patients can be harmed or shortchanged when insurance plans have tight restrictions on reimbursement, coverage, and eligibility, even when a healthcare provider deems the treatment necessary. As I noted earlier, a patient may be approved to get coverage only for a shorter course of treatment than is typical for the setting; for example, 14 days in inpatient rather than the recommended 28 days. Alternatively, certain levels of care may not be covered by the plan, which is commonly the case for residential treatment, or patients may be approved for services only at certain types of facilities that are within network, despite another level of care being indicated by the ASAM criteria.[19] In far too many cases, insurance plans will pay for some treatment but still require patients to cover costly co-pays or deductibles, which can vary greatly across different insurance companies, across levels of care, and from state to state.[20] High co-pays and deductibles, in addition to the money that many people already pay into their private insurance plans on a monthly basis, can quickly add up. In sum, cost can still present obstacles and barriers to treatment *even when clients are motivated for care and insured*. So what options remain?

The growing number of for-profit addiction treatment facilities that do not accept any public or private insurance plans has only exacerbated disparities in treatment access between high-income people and everyone else. A wealthy person can afford to leave their city, state, or even time zone to travel to a luxurious spa-like rehab while using their allotted sick days or medical leave time from their white-collar job and can afford to pay entirely out of pocket without going bankrupt. They can still provide for their family and make their car, mortgage, or rent payments because either they are still receiving their salary or they have ample savings that allow them to focus on their recovery. Meanwhile, a working-class person may be stuck on a waitlist for the local outpatient program that accepts their insurance because they cannot afford to miss work. These class differences further disadvantage people with limited funds, leaving them with few options in our current system where they have to choose between treatment and their livelihoods.

Sadly, the uninsured and underinsured struggle to find any affordable options for their care compared to all other groups. This is an especially harsh reality for those who live in states with strict income limits on Medicaid eligibility that exclude low-income working individuals. But it also affects people who do not have adequate savings, paid medical leave, or time off, or who cannot afford to stop working while receiving services because they receive an hourly wage. It also affects families with members who are undocumented and work off the books with no insurance plan at all. Though some facilities offer sliding fee options or payment plans, costs can still be prohibitive for people who already struggle to make ends meet. In the absence of any other affordable options, many of these people may attempt to pay for some treatment until it becomes unsustainable or forego care altogether despite their desire to receive services.[21]

The National Survey on Drug Use and Health (NSDUH) is a large annual nationally representative survey conducted annually in the United States to estimate the prevalence of various mental health and substance use diagnoses, including access to and utilization of treatment.[22] One consistent finding of the study at least since 2013 has been that treatment cost prevents people with SUDs who know they need treatment from getting it. In their 2021 survey, they found that a lack of health insurance coverage and an inability to pay for treatment was the reason why nearly 25% of people with diagnosable SUDs who knew they needed treatment did not receive it. An additional 12% with SUDs who knew they needed treatment did not receive treatment because their insurance plans would not pay for treatment or would not cover the full cost of treatment. Combined, this means that *over one-third* of people surveyed with SUDs who thought they needed treatment were deterred from getting treatment due to cost in 2021. Although people with SUDs often spend a lot of money to maintain their habits, our treatment system can often end up costing them more per session (or per refill) than it did to use alcohol or street drugs. (Not to mention that one can barter and trade various services with their drug sellers to fund their habit, but these activities will not pay your treatment bill!) Many methadone programs require patients to pay upwards of $25 per day when they pick up their dose; a significant number of buprenorphine prescribers prefer self-pay clients who may pay over $200 per visit (not including the cost of the medication itself at the pharmacy).

All of this is to say that while treatment can be helpful and lifesaving, a significant number of people with SUDs cannot afford treatment and will not receive it. Being priced out of treatment as a potential pathway to recovery is still a reality in much of the United States. This is why universal healthcare must be at the forefront of efforts to truly address health inequities and improve access to treatment. Interim steps can be to ensure that we are enacting behavioral health parity in reimbursement for addiction treatment, expanding Medicaid eligibility in all states, and ensuring that our state insurance marketplaces provide competitive affordable options for people who seek out their own coverage.

Where are people supposed to turn for help in the meantime? Our current system of care offers no alternatives. Harm reduction services can be the primary community support grounded in mutual aid that keeps people safe in lieu of treatment or when treatment is out of reach.

"Abstinence-Only" Expectations Are a Deterrent

Some people fall into the harm reduction gap because they are deterred from seeking treatment to begin with. Rigid treatment expectations (or the perception of them) can contribute to low treatment uptake among those who could potentially benefit from care. Most addiction treatment in the United States is abstinence-based, which means that you have to be willing to give up all drugs, including the ones you may only use occasionally, in order to start treatment. Typically, it is also expected that you commit to abstinence from all drugs for the duration of treatment. Although a growing number of individual facilities or private therapists may have more flexible policies around drug use during treatment, the abstinence-only expectation of treatment is often presumed since it is so widespread and entrenched in the status quo. This "one-size-fits-all" approach to delivering services overlooks the fact that people who use substances and people with SUDs are a diverse and heterogeneous group of people who may have varying goals surrounding their substance use and that many may indeed be capable of moderating their use of some drugs.

The disconnect between abstinence-only treatment goals and the goals of people who use substances was also affirmed by a 2021 report based on surveys and focus groups with over 800 people who had current or past substance use problems, and family members of people with substance-related problems.[23] Respondents were asked to identify which treatment outcomes were most important for them and their loved ones, and the results were tabulated and sorted by race/ethnicity. The researchers found that "staying alive" was chosen by nearly one-third of respondents, making it the top overall response. "Staying alive" was even more commonly chosen by racial and ethnic minorities: 39% of Black respondents, 41% of Latinx respondents, and 33% of multiracial respondents prioritized this outcome. "Improved quality of life" was the second-most popular response, and "stop all drug and alcohol use" was chosen by less than a quarter of all respondents. Other top responses included "address issues that come up in daily life," and "improve mental health," which were ranked highest among minority respondents. These responses reveal that the shared priority of keeping a loved one alive so that they can work to improve their daily functioning can be at odds with traditional treatment that requires abstinence before any other goals can even be discussed. Meanwhile, harm reduction programs and supports prioritize engaging with people to first keep them alive and then find other ways to support them to make other healthier and safer choices along the way. Starting with this priority opens the door to a host of other possibilities.

In fact, the reluctance to stop using drugs is a leading reason that people with SUDs who thought they needed treatment did not seek it in the past year. The NSDUH, the study I just mentioned in the previous section, found that 36% of people with SUDs who believed they needed treatment did not seek it out in 2021 because they did not want to stop using drugs at the time, and they presumed treatment would require abstinence.[24] This statistic has remained relatively stable for several years and suggests that the common assumption that most treatment is abstinence-based is in itself a barrier to seek any help at these facilities. The belief that receiving any help or support is contingent upon abstinence directly leads these people to fall into the harm reduction gap because they are left with no other options in our current continuum of care. And many people who seek out treatment to pursue moderation or reduced-use goals see this firsthand when they are terminated from treatment for continued drug use because they do not want to maintain abstinence.

The assumption that abstinence will be required in treatment can discourage people from seeking services because they do not think they could pursue moderation or reduced use, let alone take their time to work toward abstinence while in treatment. The fact that our treatment system has implicitly or explicitly conveyed this message means that they hold some responsibility for why so many are not in care. We are currently in a situation where far too many people with diagnosable SUDs who recognize that they have a problem have nowhere to go because they believe that addiction treatment facilities will turn them away for not committing to abstinence from the start. So where do they go? What do they do? What are their options? Unfortunately, it can mean that they continue to use drugs in risky and problematic patterns, without support and the tools to stay safe or alive. This increases their risk of infectious disease, overdose, and countless other preventable or avoidable drug-related harms.

Meanwhile, harm reduction programs welcome people engaging in the highest-risk behaviors without any requirements or expectations. There, people can learn about safer strategies and the importance of using sterile equipment and keeping naloxone on hand. In addition, OPCs welcome any and all people who use drugs to ensure they are using safely on site and can get immediate help when needed. Harm Reduction Psychotherapy practitioners can work with people to address their substance-related goals in addition to their broader needs for mental health support in their day-to-day lives. Harm reduction programs help people stay alive and connected to a community built upon mutual aid and support. They ensure people can stay as safe as possible as they continue to use drugs and help people to explore safer usage practices and patterns without the expectation that they must be able to change overnight. Clients can explore different strategies that work best for them on an individualized basis, rather than presuming that the only way to be safer or healthier is via abstinence.

Enforcing Abstinence in Treatment Creates Challenges

For those who end up in treatment, abstinence is monitored regularly. Routine random urine drug tests are a well-known practice to monitor abstinence while in treatment because most facilities do not simply take a client's word about whether or not they have recently used drugs. It is common for a staff person to observe clients while they are urinating to prevent deception or tampering with their samples. At least, this was the explanation given to me as a young social worker when I was first instructed to follow my clients into the bathroom to observe them.

At best, having your social worker or drug counselor watch you pee is an awkward and uncomfortable experience. But for most people, this repeated event is humiliating, damaging, and triggering, especially among those who have histories of abuse and trauma. I myself felt such a cognitive dissonance every time I had to observe my patients in the bathroom. On the one hand, my social work training taught me the importance of unconditional positive regard for my clients and how I should build a strong therapeutic alliance with them based on respect, trust, and safety so that we could really uncover their issues and work on solutions together. But on the other hand, my job required me to invade their privacy by watching them pee every few days, which conveyed to my clients that I did not trust them. It felt like an ethical conflict between my training and agency policy.[25] Client comfort was not a consideration when such policies were developed, and there was no room for debate; these were the rules, and we were the authority figures there to enforce them.

Outpatient programs like the one where I worked had policies dictating that multiple positive drug test results would eventually lead to a client being transferred to an even more intensive treatment setting such as detox or inpatient. Ongoing use was interpreted as an indication that the client needed more structure than we could offer. In any given year, roughly one in five clients (22%) in any treatment setting across the country are discharged because they are transferred to another treatment facility, and these rates are highest from intensive outpatient settings.[26] From my experience, continued or ongoing drug use is a common justification for many of these transfers to more intensive care. Again, cost can emerge as a barrier when it comes to these transfers, since more intensive programs can also be more expensive for both insured and uninsured people. These referrals can also end up putting someone in the challenging position of having to spend a few days or weeks at a detox or inpatient program away from home, forcing them to neglect family and work responsibilities. This presents an impossible choice for many working people, especially breadwinners and caregivers, who are forced to choose between their own treatment, their livelihoods, and/or their families. When these referrals are not followed through, the client can end up being discharged from the current treatment setting because they cannot remain compliant with policy requirements for abstinence. These scenarios can be demoralizing to clients, who can then feel like failures for not meeting the narrow definition of treatment success. While it is easy to tell people struggling with their substance use to "go get treatment," it doesn't recognize that many who seek treatment are often rejected or turned away for noncompliance with strict abstinence-based policies. We then leave them with no other options when treatment does not work out.

Not All Treatments Deliver Results

The most common type of treatment in the United States is what we call psychosocial treatment, or "talk therapy," in the form of individual, couple, family, and group counseling sessions. In addiction treatment specifically, group therapy is the most common modality of psychosocial treatment. Within these groups, therapists can use various clinical approaches to engage clients toward change. They each involve different strategies for helping clients to address their life challenges. For instance, they may use a very common approach called Cognitive Behavioral Therapy (CBT), in which they engage group members in discussions and various exercises to reflect upon the thoughts, expectations, biases, and deeply ingrained beliefs they hold (i.e., cognitions), and how those are connected to their behaviors and actions, including their drug use. It is believed that by identifying and challenging misconceptions, negative thought patterns, and false beliefs, people can develop new ways of thinking about themselves and others, view their experiences differently, and explore new behaviors and responses in their day-to-day lives. Another common approach is Twelve-Step Facilitation (TSF), which incorporates the philosophy of Alcoholics Anonymous (AA) and Narcotics Anonymous (NA), wherein clients are supported in working toward the 12 steps of recovery as defined by AA and NA, read AA and NA literature, and are required to attend AA and NA meetings in the community throughout treatment as well. Another common approach is Motivational Interviewing, where therapists use strategies to engage clients in conversations about their motivation for behavioral change and use various techniques to strengthen their commitment to change.

While there is some evidence to support the use of these psychosocial treatments for SUDs, their effectiveness on the ground can vary because the conditions under which they were studied are very different from the real-world conditions in which they are delivered. In most studies, they were typically delivered in a standardized manner for a set number of total sessions with trained therapists who used formal curricula and manuals to deliver treatment in the same exact way in sessions. But in the real world, therapists often are a bit more eclectic in their use of these approaches and rarely stick to manuals from week to week, meaning that it is difficult to say that they are truly adhering to a single approach or are remaining consistent to the approach in practice. In addition, research suggests that some approaches (e.g., TSF vs. CBT) are more effective for some drug use disorders but not others (e.g., alcohol versus marijuana), or they have better outcomes for certain subpopulations of people who use drugs and not others (e.g., pregnant people versus older adults).[27,28,29,30] When different treatment approaches have strong evidence only to support their use with certain SUDs and/or with certain client populations but we then implement the approaches indiscriminately with clients who have other complex needs and characteristics, it can actually set the client up to "fail."

Beyond this, there are also treatment centers where people are provided with approaches that have never been studied for their efficacy or that have minimal evidence for their efficacy, like equine therapy (horse therapy), art therapy, wilderness therapies, confrontational approaches, shaming approaches, and more. Since there is often minimal or no regulatory oversight of the types of treatment approaches provided at facilities, it can mean that people seek out and often receive psychosocial treatments in their community that may not have strong evidence to address their unique issues. Or it can mean that treatment is not delivered in ways that have been studied and shown to work. And sometimes these approaches can border on abuse and malpractice. A 2023 secret shopper study focused on identifying residential treatment facilities that prescribed buprenorphine for a hypothetical 16-year-old who recently survived a nonfatal fentanyl overdose.[31] They found that only roughly a quarter of facilities offered this FDA-approved medication. The researchers also found that 25% of programs offered equine therapy and 25% provided art therapy. It is remarkable that at a time when teen overdose deaths are at historic highs, treatment programs across the country offered two approaches that have not been proved to work at the same rate as the gold-standard medication that could cut the risk of fatal overdose in half.

Yet for far too many people seeking treatment, these may be the only options they may have, or they have been misled to think these approaches will help them. And we can end up blaming the client for not maintaining abstinence or for dropping out of treatment when it may really be the case that the psychosocial treatment approach that was offered was not well-suited for their needs or was unlikely to be helpful anyway.

For many people on the outside, treatment is a mysterious black box, where people with SUDs are sent away and then return home magically cured or better. However, in many cases much of what happens behind closed doors may not in fact set clients up for success and can instead set them back. Moreover, when they return home with as many problems as before, or more than when they started, it can make it even more difficult to convince them to try treatment again. Andrew Tatarsky, a prominent harm reduction psychotherapist, often calls this "treatment trauma." This trauma can be a strong deterrent for some people to ever go back, since many do not want to be subjected to the intrusiveness and shaming that is characteristic of some settings. This is another reason that the harm reduction gap exists, because when people do not have access to high-quality effective services, they may not have the intended outcome of abstinence or recovery and be left with no other source of support. They should have harm reduction support to help them stay safe until they find another program that is better suited for them or until they find another way to meet their goals.

Most People Do Not Complete Treatment

One key observation I made when I worked at the outpatient treatment facility was how few of our clients who started treatment ended up completing it. As the intake coordinator, I saw most of our clients the first day they came to the facility for their initial assessment. But the other part of my job was to facilitate one of the aftercare groups for clients who were phasing down and transitioning out of our intensive outpatient program or daytime rehab program. I soon noticed that only a small portion of our clients actually made it from intake all the way to aftercare at our facility. Where did they go? What happened?

I believe they fell into the harm reduction gap.

Data from the Treatment Episode Data Set (TEDS), an annual survey of publicly funded treatment programs, finds that most clients do not finish the treatment episode they start any given year (see Figure 6.1). Over 40% of treatment admissions in 2020 resulted in clients successfully completing the treatment episode. This number was consistent with previous years

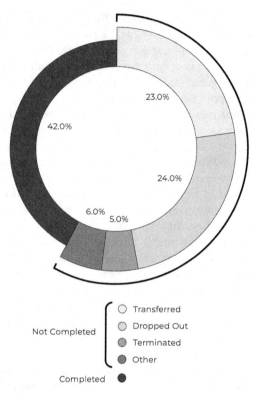

Figure 6.1 Reasons for treatment discharge: 2020.

Source: Substance Abuse and Mental Health Services Administration, Center for Behavioral Health Statistics and Quality, *Treatment Episode Data Set (TEDS): 2020. Admissions to and Discharges from Publicly Funded Substance Use Treatment Facilities.* Rockville, MD: Substance Abuse and Mental Health Services Administration, 2022.

despite the COVID-19 pandemic.[32] Intensive outpatient treatment programs like the one where I worked typically see less than 25% of people who start treatment complete it in any given year. Meanwhile, hospital residential treatment and detoxification settings boast higher-than-average treatment completion rates, at 70% and over 60%, respectively. These ranges show that different levels of care retain clients at different rates, and that noncompletion is more common than many may think.

Nearly one out of every four treatment discharges in 2020 was due to client dropout. People drop out of treatment for many reasons such as cost, scheduling conflicts, or dissatisfaction with services provided. Far too often, when treatment policies create barriers for people to stay engaged in services, clients may walk away from services that could otherwise improve their health and well-being. Dropout rates vary by treatment setting, with the highest number being at outpatient MOUD treatment settings where *one-third* of discharges in 2020 were due to client dropout. Based on what I described of how MOUD treatment is provided in this country, it is easy to see why many who start treatment decide to leave: the strict rules at OTPs and difficulty maintaining perfect daily on-time attendance could challenge the most committed clients, but also the difficulty associated with securing a buprenorphine prescriber and getting refills. And, tragically, dropping out of treatment can have lethal consequences. A study found that fatal overdose death risk was nearly six times higher for patients who left MOUD treatment often because their opioid tolerance can decline and they soon return to illicit opioid use.[33]

Administrative discharge, also known as termination, is another reason why about 5% of discharges occur every year – this is when the treatment program discharges the client due to policy infractions, behavioral issues, or other reasons. Though that may seem like a small portion of overall discharges, it totaled over 66,700 discharges in 2020. This number is troublingly large, especially when one considers what can happen when tens of thousands of clients with diagnosable SUDs per year stop receiving treatment that could be helpful and stabilizing. In their 2020 paper, Williams and Bonner reframe administrative discharge as clinical abandonment because, while sometimes clients are discharged because of safety concerns, in many cases the subjective and biased opinions of staff can lead them to terminate patients they see as being defiant, noncompliant, and unmotivated. They wrote:

> Patient termination is the ostensible course of action only in extreme circumstances (e.g., physical assault causing severe bodily injury). In most cases, however, the decision whether to administratively discharge a patient from addition services is not as clear-cut, and its complexities make for one of the most morally vexing and ethically complicated experiences practitioners face. This is in large part because, despite the known repercussions of termination (which include premature death), the decision to terminate patient care is [a] largely unregulated administrative practice.[33]

Administrative discharge is hard to justify, especially when clients have been participating in treatment for a while but then are abruptly told to leave. According to the 2020 TEDS, patients who were administratively discharged from outpatient MOUD treatment spent a median number of *124 days in treatment before getting terminated.*[34] Clinical abandonment feels like an accurate term for the act of cutting patients off of from medications that, when taken regularly, can cut their risk of fatal overdose in half. When this happens, patients have no recourse or other options for support.

Between dropouts, terminations, and other reasons for discharge, it is estimated that *60% of all people who start treatment at an addiction program in a given year will not even complete that treatment episode.* A message consistently given at many facilities when someone drops out or is terminated from treatment is, "Come back when you're ready." My colleagues often said this at our outpatient facility. This statement can be interpreted in a few ways. It could be taken as a sincere and open invitation to return at any time, "Come back when you're ready! We'll be here waiting for you!" Or it could imply that it is the client's fault that treatment didn't work out for them, and they are expected to come back when they are willing to stick with it and comply with program rules. Either way, it simply means that when they leave treatment, they are out on their own. Although a growing number of treatment settings have been discharging clients with naloxone in hand, there is still a long way to go to ensure that people who prematurely leave treatment are offered additional harm reduction support as a backup.

It can be especially difficult to complete treatment while someone is in a period of housing instability, financial precarity, or lacking a support system. Yet, too often, people are mandated to complete treatment or are sent to treatment before they have the necessities in their lives for stability. Treatment will not cure homelessness, hunger, or poverty, but we send unhoused, hungry, and low-income people to treatment and expect them to be able to focus on giving up drugs when they have so many other challenges they are trying to address. In fact, we often make public benefits such as housing, cash, and food assistance, contingent upon treatment enrollment and completion every day. This can mean that people who do not change fast enough or comply with treatment rules can place their housing, nutritional, and financial status at risk – and then they lose benefits and are made to feel like failures.

Because of the barriers to treatment and the obstacles faced while in treatment, many facilities end up losing clients who could still benefit from some sort of support or connection. These clients fall into the harm reduction gap because most of our current systems of care have nothing else to offer them if they don't comply or follow through on a referral for more services. Meanwhile, there is often little examination of how treatment policies or structures might have contributed why someone could no longer remain in care.

This harsh reality should concern us all, because it is possible that these clients could have still been helped and supported. What if we could give them the tools to stay safe in programs that were less rigid and demanding so they could stay connected and get help? In our current system, a lucky few may be fortunate enough to have harm reduction programs available where they live so they can get tools and skills to minimize their risks, like safer injecting or smoking equipment and naloxone. Meanwhile, others may only have the option of attending free self-help groups like AA or NA in their communities on an ad hoc basis, but even those groups require one to strive toward an abstinence-based recovery. Far too many do not even know what options, if any, are available where they live. Expanding access to harm reduction programs in states across the country is one way to ensure that there is a safety net of services and tools available to most people who attempted treatment but did not complete it in a given year.

Multiple Treatment and Recovery Attempts Are Common

There are people who successfully complete treatment and will maintain abstinence, both in the short and long term. But a significant portion of people who have been to treatment will return to substance use in some way, often within the first year. Studies suggest that up to 75% of people who complete treatment will use again in the year following treatment.[35] Some will return to problematic levels of use soon after treatment, while others may phase in and out of drug use and abstinence, and a number may go on to lower-risk use. For these people, few options exist for staying safe during these episodes beyond making the decision to immediately return to treatment to pursue abstinence again.

Returning to alcohol or drug use after any period of abstinence can increase the risk of unintentional alcohol poisoning, harmful drug effects, or overdose, since one's tolerance can dramatically and unpredictably drop. Assuming one can resume old usage patterns with similar quantities of drugs can be risky, especially if one was accustomed to binge use.

The shame of returning to substance use after pursuing abstinence can also increase the risk of drug-related harms. There is a concept in the drug literature called the "abstinence violation effect," which has been used to describe the guilt and shame that someone might experience if they use a drug after a period of abstinence and how such an experience can affect one's self-confidence in their ability to get back on track.[36] For some people, these negative feelings and the decreased confidence can send them on a self-destructive spiral because they feel like they messed up and blew it, so to speak. The abstinence violation effect can turn a single drink into a weekend-long bender because one may feel as though they have already relapsed and "failed." Anyone who has ever been on a diet could relate to the extreme thinking that occurs after one violation by eating an "unhealthy" or "bad" food or meal, which can lead to going overboard since the diet has already been ruined. For some, the feeling that they broke their streak of abstinence by a single violation can make it easy to justify extreme use since they believe they will have to start all over from scratch again anyway.

This is particularly devastating for people who track their abstinence days as part of their participation in AA or NA, where members are given a "chip" or token to celebrate the number of months or years they have remained abstinent. For instance, someone may receive a chip to commemorate six months of abstinence or get one on their one-year anniversary. These can be helpful reinforcers for people in their early days of abstinence, especially since the first chip one can earn is to mark their first 24 hours drug-free. Yet, the hazard of participating in this type of system is that the rigidness means that a single return to use resets the person's recovery clock to zero, and they must start counting their days again from the beginning. It doesn't matter if they were five years abstinent and went on one weekend bender but were able to restrain themselves and stopped on Monday morning in time to go to work. They must start again with their one-day chip. While there are those who see these restarts as an essential part of their recovery journey, others may find that this can make it feel like they have erased their prior progress and gains over a single instance of use.

Harm reduction support and strategies are especially important for people who return to any type of use because it can help them to ensure they have sterile equipment, the tools to check their drugs for adulterants, and naloxone on hand in case of overdose. It can also mean that they may choose to use at an OPC where help can be provided as needed. But additionally, harm reduction support may be useful to help prompt them to consider not mixing drugs, remind them to not rush and to go slowly, not to use alone, and to take other precautions to stay as safe as possible. They may also get tips like counting the number of drinks they consume, never driving after use, staying hydrated, and taking breaks. Most importantly, these programs do not convey disappointment, shame, or guilt associated with ongoing use or because someone has returned to use after a period of abstinence. This can be lifesaving and can prevent some people from disconnecting from their support network, self-destructing, or engaging in harmful practices in isolation.

For those whose usage patterns become harmful and problematic again, treatment may be an appealing option to get back on track eventually. In any given year, about 60% of people who go to treatment have been to treatment at least once before, including people who successfully completed it, dropped out, were terminated, or did not follow through on transfers to other services. In fact, one-third of people admitted to treatment in 2020 had been to treatment three or more times in the past (see Figure 6.2). Decades of long-term studies suggest that multiple recovery attempts (with or without treatment) are the norm. Change is hard, and most people need time and support until they achieve their goals. For those pursuing abstinence, it can be unrealistic to expect that it will all "click" the first time. In these situations and in so many more, the most important role harm reduction can play is keeping people alive long enough to figure out what their

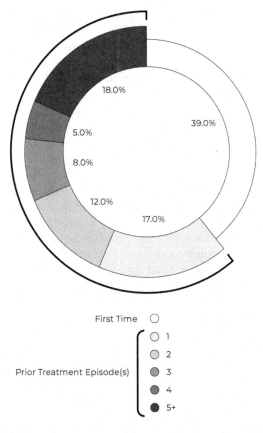

Figure 6.2 Number of prior treatment episodes: 2020.

Source: Substance Abuse and Mental Health Services Administration, Center for Behavioral Health Statistics and Quality, *Treatment Episode Data Set (TEDS): 2020. Admissions to and Discharges from Publicly Funded Substance Use Treatment Facilities.* Rockville, MD: Substance Abuse and Mental Health Services Administration, 2022.

drug-related goals are, how they would like to achieve those goals, and whether it could be through treatment or by making other lifestyle changes. All the while, harm reduction programs ensure that they are grounded in a community that unconditionally supports them in the ups and downs of this journey while they figure out what it is they want.

Most People with SUDs Do Not Receive Treatment

Lastly, 90% of people with diagnosable SUDs, 38.4 million people, did not receive any treatment in the past year. The reality is that only a small fraction of people with addictions will receive treatment at any time, let alone over the course of their lives.

As I have noted elsewhere, someone can be diagnosed with a SUD only if they meet a minimum of 2 out of 11 possible criteria within a one-year timeframe, such as: the continued use of a substance despite repeated negative consequences in various aspects of their life (e.g., health effects, family troubles, relationship problems, educational or employment issues, etc.); difficulty managing role responsibilities; experiencing withdrawal symptoms or cravings; developing a higher tolerance for the substance; or spending a lot of time using the substance or recovering from its effects.[37]

By definition, these are individuals who could benefit from support to ensure they stay safe because they are experiencing substance-related problems; yet the majority are not connected to our treatment system. Their ongoing use keeps them at risk of experiencing even greater harm and negative effects, many of which might be preventable or avoidable if they could be given access to the proper tools, support, and strategies.

People with SUDs are a significant portion of the millions of people across the United States who fall into the harm reduction gap every year. Many Gen Xers and millennials completed abstinence-based drug prevention programs in school (like I did), and previous generations barely received any drug-related education, if at all. Either way, the majority of us eventually went on to use substances, legal and illegal alike. And regardless of drug type, few had access to the knowledge and tools to stay safe when they started experimenting, or even after they began to use these drugs more frequently. For the subset of people who went on to develop SUDs or experience drug-related harmful effects, treatment is portrayed as the only option. But in reality, treatment is an option for only a select few, for the many reasons I have covered in this chapter. Not everyone will make it to treatment, get effective services, or successfully complete treatment and remain abstinent forever. Our current broader approach to drugs just presumes that people will simply figure out how to stay safe, comply with treatment, or just have to live with the consequences (if they are so lucky to survive them).

The Majority of People with SUDs Do Not Want Treatment

The truth of the matter is that most people with SUDs, 37.5 million of the over 38 million people with addictions who did not receive treatment, *did not even want treatment.*[38] It could be because they do not want to stop using drugs, it could be that they don't think the severity of their problems rises to the level of needing services, or it could be because they think they can handle it on their own. It could be that some had negative experiences with treatment and do not want to return. There are countless reasons why someone may not want treatment. Unfortunately, many people look at this as evidence that these people are "in denial" about the substance-related problems in their lives, when the truth may be far more complicated.

But it shouldn't mean that they are left on their own with nowhere to turn. It doesn't have to be this way. A greater availability of community-driven harm reduction programs, developed by and for people who use drugs, could help provide a source of support outside of the formal treatment system, for these people have their own reasons for not engaging in services. Most will never walk into a treatment program but may be more willing to access resources on a website and order harm reduction supplies to be delivered to their home; or they may walk through the doors of a local Syringe Service Program (SSP), where they are made to feel welcome. Considering the tens of millions of people who fall into the harm reduction gap this way, we should want to build and support the development of a more robust continuum of services and programs in our community that include the range of harm reduction services so people can find the options they want when they are ready to get help. This includes providing grant funding to harm reduction programs that develop innovative, accessible programs to target this otherwise-disconnected population of people who use drugs.

Treatment Will Not Fill the Harm Reduction Gap

The way that our current treatment system is set up and structured has helped to create the harm reduction gap. Our current addiction treatment system is intended for people who want it, can afford it, can access it, can adjust their lives around it, and can comply with its many rules. Even those who complete treatment may have multiple treatment episodes. Change does not happen overnight, and substance-related patterns can take time to adjust; as a result, they often return to problematic use again after leaving. Rather than seeing these realities as signs that their services could be improved, adjusted, or revised to keep clients connected to support, many treatment facilities justify their approach by placing sole responsibility on the client population for their inability to comply. And for those who ultimately drop out or are terminated from treatment, few other alternatives exist. There is no safety net to catch them. We should be most concerned that most people with diagnosable SUDs do not receive treatment because most of them do not want it, and they are left to fend for themselves.

The formal treatment infrastructure should be viewed as an extension of a broader healthcare system that is largely inaccessible, unaffordable, and stigmatizing toward people who are seen as undesirable or undeserving. This can include the people who use the most stigmatized illegal drugs, low-income and homeless people, people with complex mental health and medical needs, queer communities, and racial and ethnic minorities who have had negative experiences in these settings. Meanwhile, community-based and community-driven harm reduction programs where these services are integrated can be a safe and appealing touchpoint for care. In states across the country, SSP are becoming sites where clients can receive buprenorphine in a setting that is accommodating to their needs and literally "meet them where they're at" and where they already receive services. In addition, SSP are integrating more health services on site, with New York State's model of Drug User Health Hubs being a great example of showing that harm reduction sites staffed by caring and knowledgeable staff can better meet community health and harm reduction needs in the same place. These sites where people can get both harm reduction and treatment on site can help people to seamlessly transition between both without every being disconnected from support.

Our unprecedented overdose crisis, combined with the fact that alcohol- and tobacco-related health harms claim lives every day, show that we must do more for people who are otherwise not connected to the formal treatment system. It is naïve and unrealistic to assume that over 30 million people could somehow receive services in our formal, costly, highly structured, one-size-fits-all treatment system comprised of just over 16,000 facilities. In any given year, these facilities conduct about 1.5 million admissions for services. The current system is not equipped for a sudden influx of this population into services, and is likely not appropriate for all of them anyway. Many of the people who I speak to talk about how we need more treatment in our communities, and that is a completely valid point. We do need more treatment along the continuum of care in all parts of the country, including online and via telehealth options for people who could benefit from that accessibility. And these options should be affordable and available to the people who want them. But we must acknowledge that our current system currently does not have much to offer the millions who will never set foot in one.

What if they had more options for help to choose from, such as services with few requirements and that were easily accessible on their terms? What if the education and tools to engage in safer or less risky drug use were more readily available to them, in their communities, at SSPs, via mail order, and in other settings? What if they could go to an OPC or a safe location to use when they are worried about adverse effects or a potential overdose? What if they knew there were harm reduction psychotherapy providers who were willing to work with them on staying safe and who would not impose abstinence on them to be able to get help?

This is how we fill the harm reduction gap.

Notes

1 Mee-Lee, David, Gerald D. Shulman, Marc J. Fishman, David R. Gastfriend, Michael M. Miller, and Scott M. Provence (Eds.). *The ASAM Criteria: Treatment Criteria for Addictive, Substance-Related, and Co-Occurring Conditions* (3rd ed.). Carson City, NV: The Change Companies, 2013.

2 This data is from an annual survey conducted by the Department of Health and Human Services of "publicly funded" addiction treatment programs, meaning those that are certified in their states or by the federal government to provide services so they are required to report their admissions and discharges to relevant entities. Many of these programs receive various state funds or grants to help fund their operations, in addition to accepting private and/or public insurance. This survey does not collect data from treatment programs that are not certified by the state or those that may not receive government funding. This means that there are significantly more than 16,000 operating facilities in the United States, including those that are not formally licensed or credentialed but may represent themselves as treatment facilities or wellness centers.

3 Substance Abuse and Mental Health Services Administration. *National Survey of Substance Abuse Treatment Services (N-SSATS): 2019. Data on Substance Abuse Treatment Facilities.* Rockville, MD: Substance Abuse and Mental Health Services Administration, 2020.

4 Substance Abuse and Mental Health Services Administration, Center for Behavioral Health Statistics and Quality. *Treatment Episode Data Set (TEDS): 2020. Admissions to and Discharges from Publicly Funded Substance Use Treatment Facilities.* Rockville, MD: Substance Abuse and Mental Health Services Administration, 2022.

5 Santo, Thomas, Brodie Clark, Matt Hickman, Jason Grebely, Gabrielle Campbell, Luis Sordo, Aileen Chen, et al. "Association of Opioid Agonist Treatment with All-Cause Mortality and Specific Causes of Death among People with Opioid Dependence: A Systematic Review and Meta-Analysis." *JAMA Psychiatry* 78, no. 9 (2021): 979–93. https://doi.org/10.1001/jamapsychiatry.2021.0976.

6 Mauro, Pia M., Sarah Gutkind, Erin M. Annunziato, and Hillary Samples. "Use of Medication for Opioid Use Disorder among US Adolescents and Adults with Need for Opioid Treatment, 2019." *JAMA Network Open* 5, no. 3 (2022): e223821. https://doi.org/10.1001/jamanetworkopen.2022.3821.

7 Joudrey, Paul J., E. Jennifer Edelman, and Emily A. Wang. "Drive Times to Opioid Treatment Programs in Urban and Rural Counties in 5 US States." *JAMA* 322, no. 13 (2019): 1310–12. https://doi.org/10.1001/jama.2019.12562.

8 Iloglu, Suzan, Paul J. Joudrey, Emily A. Wang, Thomas A. Thornhill, and Gregg Gonsalves. "Expanding Access to Methadone Treatment in Ohio through Federally Qualified Health Centers and a Chain Pharmacy: A Geospatial Modeling Analysis." *Drug and Alcohol Dependence* 220 (March 2021): 108534. https://doi.org/10.1016/j.drugalcdep.2021.108534.

9 Ibid.

10 Furst, John A., Nicholas J. Mynarski, Kenneth L. McCall, and Brian J. Piper. "Pronounced Regional Disparities in United States Methadone Distribution." *Annals of Pharmacotherapy* 56, no. 3 (2021): 271–79. https://doi.org.10.1177/10600280211028262.

11 Hawes, Ethan. "I Chose Fentanyl over the Humiliation of Methadone Treatment." *Filter*, June 15, 2023. https://filtermag.org/methadone-clinic-fentanyl/.

12 Olfson, Mark, Victoria Zhang (Shu), Michael Schoenbaum, and Marissa King. "Trends in Buprenorphine Treatment in the United States, 2009–2018." *JAMA* 323, no. 3 (2020): 276–77. https://doi.org/10.1001/jama.2019.18913.

13 Larochelle, Marc R., Christopher M. Jones, and Kun Zhang. 2023. "Change in Opioid and Buprenorphine Prescribers and Prescriptions by Specialty, 2016–2021." *Drug and Alcohol Dependence* 248 (2023). https://doi.org/10.1016/j.drugalcdep.2023.109933.

14 Flavin, Lila, Monica Malowney, Patel Nikhil, Michael D. Alpert, Elisa Cheng, Gaddy Do Noy, Sarah Samuelson, Nina Sreshta, and J. Wesley Boyd. "Availability of Bu-prenorphine Treatment in the 10 States with the Highest Drug Overdose Death Rates in the United States." *Journal of Psychiatry Practice* 26, no. 1 (2020): 17–22.
15 Patrick, Stephen W., Michael R. Richards, William D. Dupont, Elizabeth Mc-Neer, Melinda B. Buntin, Peter R. Martin, Matthew M. Davis, et al. "Associa-tion of Pregnancy and Insurance Status with Treatment Access for Opioid Use Disorder." *JAMA Network Open* 3, no. 8 (2020): e2013456. https://doi.org/10.1001/jamanetworkopen.2020.13456.
16 Weiner, Scott G., Dima M. Qato, Jeremy Samuel Faust, and Brian Clear. "Phar-macy Availability of Buprenorphine for Opioid Use Disorder Treatment in the US." *JAMA Network Open* 6, no. 5 (2023): e2316089. https://doi.org/10.1001/jamanetworkopen.2023.16089.
17 Beetham, Tamara, Brendan Saloner, Marema Gaye, Sarah E. Wakeman, Richard G. Frank, and Michael L. Barnett. "Therapies Offered at Residential Addiction Treatment Programs in the United States." *JAMA* 324, no. 8 (2020): 804–6. https://doi.org/10.1001/jama.2020.8969.
18 Mark, Tami L., William J. Parish, and Gary A. Zarkin. "Association of Formulary Prior Authorization Policies with Buprenorphine-Naloxone Prescriptions and Hospital and Emergency Department Use among Medicare Beneficiaries." *JAMA Network Open* 3, no. 4 (2020): e203132. https://doi.org/10.1001/jamanetworkopen.2020.3132.
19 Grogan, Colleen M., Christina Andrews, Amanda Abraham, Keith Humphreys, Harold A. Pollack, Bikki Tran Smith, and Peter D. Friedmann. "Survey High-lights Differences in Medicaid Coverage for Substance Use Treatment and Opi-oid Use Disorder Medications." *Health Affairs* 35, no. 12 (2016): 2289–96. https://doi.org/10.1377/hlthaff.2016.0623.
20 Peters, Rebecca, and Erik Wengle. *Coverage of Substance-Use Disorder Treat-ments in Marketplace Plans in Six Cities.* New York and Washington, DC: Rob-ert Wood Johnson Foundation and Urban Institute, 2016.
21 Ali, Mir M., Judith L. Teich, and Ryan Mutter. "Reasons for Not Seeking Sub-stance Use Disorder Treatment: Variations by Health Insurance Coverage." *The Journal of Behavioral Health Services & Research* 44, no. 1 (2017): 63–74. https://doi.org/10.1007/s11414-016-9538-3.
22 Substance Abuse and Mental Health Services Administration. *Key Substance Use and Mental Health Indicators in the United States: Results from the 2021 National Survey on Drug Use and Health* (HHS Publication No. PEP22-07-01-005, NS-DUH Series H-57). Rockville, MD: Center for Behavioral Health Statistics and Quality, Substance Abuse and Mental Health Services Administration, 2022.
23 The National Peer Council. *Peers Speak Out: Priority Outcomes for Substance Use Treatment and Services.* 2021. https://communitycatalyst.org/wp-content/uploads/2023/02/Peers-Speak-Out.pdf
24 Substance Abuse and Mental Health Services Administration. *Key Substance Use and Mental Health Indicators in the United States: Results from the 2021 Na-tional Survey on Drug Use and Health* (HHS Publication No. PEP22-07-01-005, NSDUH Series H-57). Rockville, MD: Center for Behavioral Health Statistics and Quality, Substance Abuse and Mental Health Services Administra-tion, 2022.
25 Lee, Heather Sophia. "The Ethical Dilemma of Abstinence-only Service Deliv-ery in the United States." *Journal of Social Work Values and Ethics* 12, no. 1 (2015): 61–66.

26 Substance Abuse and Mental Health Services Administration, Center for Behavioral Health Statistics and Quality. *Treatment Episode Data Set (TEDS): 2020. Admissions to and Discharges from Publicly Funded Substance Use Treatment Facilities.* Rockville, MD: Substance Abuse and Mental Health Services Administration, 2020. https://www.samhsa.gov/data/sites/default/files/reports/rpt38665/2020_TEDS%20Annual%20Report-508%20compliant_1182023_FINAL.pdf.

27 Gates, Peter J., Pamela Sabioni, Jan Copeland, Bernard Le Foll, and Linda Gowing. "Psychosocial Interventions for Cannabis Use Disorder." *Cochrane Database of Systematic Reviews* 2016, no. 5 (2016): CD005336. https://doi.org/10.1002/14651858.CD005336.pub4.

28 Minozzi, Silvia, Rosella Saulle, Frank De Crescenzo, and Laura Amato. "Psychosocial Interventions for Psychostimulant Misuse." *Cochrane Database of Systematic Reviews* 2016, no. 9 (2016): CD011866. https://doi.org/10.1002/14651858.CD011866.pub2.

29 Klimas, Jan, Christopher Fairgrieve, Helen Tobin, Catherine-Anne Field, Clodagh S. M. O'Gorman, Liam G. Glynn, Eamon Keenan, Jean Saunders, Gerard Bury, Colum Dunne, and Walter Cullen. "Psychosocial Interventions to Reduce Alcohol Consumption in Concurrent Problem Alcohol and Illicit Drug Users." *Cochrane Database of Systematic Reviews* 2018, no. 12 (2018): CD009269. https://doi.org/10.1002/14651858.CD009269.pub4.

30 Kelly, John F., Keith Humphreys, and Marica Ferri. "Alcoholics Anonymous and Other 12-Step Programs for Alcohol Use Disorder." *Cochrane Database of Systematic Reviews* 2020, no. 3. (2020): CD012880. https://doi.org/10.1002/14651858.CD012880.pub2.

31 King, Caroline, Tamara Beetham, Natashia Smith, Honora Englander, Scott E. Hadland, Sarah M. Bagley, and P. Todd Korthuis. "Treatments Used among Adolescent Residential Addiction Treatment Facilities in the US, 2022." *JAMA* 329, no. 22 (2023): 1983–85. https://doi.org/10.1001/jama.2023.6266.

32 Substance Abuse and Mental Health Services Administration, Center for Behavioral Health Statistics and Quality. *Treatment Episode Data Set (TEDS): 2020. Admissions to and Discharges from Publicly Funded Substance Use Treatment Facilities.* Rockville, MD: Substance Abuse and Mental Health Services Administration, 2022. https://www.samhsa.gov/data/sites/default/files/reports/rpt38665/2020_TEDS%20Annual%20Report-508%20compliant_1182023_FINAL.pdf.

33 Krawczyk, Noa, Ramin Mojtabai, Elizabeth A. Stuart, Michael Fingerhood, Deborah Agus, B. Casey Lyons, Jonathan P. Weiner, and Brendan Saloner. "Opioid Agonist Treatment and Fatal Overdose Risk in a State-Wide US Population Receiving Opioid Use Disorder Services." *Addiction* 115, no. 9 (2020): 1683–94. https://doi.org/10.1111/add.14991.

34 The median is the middle number in a series of data points. So when we say that the median number of days is 124 days in treatment, that means that exactly half of the people who were administratively discharged from MOUD treatment were enrolled in treatment for *more than 124 days, or four months.*

35 Maisto, Stephen A., Kevin A. Hallgren, Corey R. Roos, and Katie Witkiewitz. "Course of Remission from and Relapse to Heavy Drinking Following Outpatient Treatment of Alcohol Use Disorder." *Drug and Alcohol Dependence* 187, (June 2018): 319–26. https://doi.org/10.1016/j.drugalcdep.2018.03.011.

36 Collins, Susan E., and Katie Witkiewitz. "Abstinence Violation Effect." In *Encyclopedia of Behavioral Medicine,* edited by Marc D. Gellman and J. Rick Turner, 8–9. New York: Springer, 2013. https://doi.org/10.1007/978-1-4419-1005-9_623.

37 American Psychiatric Association. *Desk Reference to the Diagnostic Criteria from DSM-5*. Arlington, VA: APA, 2016.

38 Substance Abuse and Mental Health Services Administration. *Key Substance Use and Mental Health Indicators: Results from the 2021 National Survey on Drug Use and Health* (HHS Publication No. PEP22-07-01-005, NSDUH Series H-57). Rockville, MD: Center for Behavioral Health Statistics and Quality, Substance Abuse and Mental Health Services Administration, 2022.

7   What Harm Reduction Is Not

Certain characteristics distinguish harm reduction from other types of community programs, services, and policies. As I described elsewhere, harm reduction is grounded in several key foundational principles. In this chapter, I will contrast what distinguishes grassroots-driven mutual aid harm reduction from entities that may provide harm reduction interventions while still embedded in other systems or institutions. While these institutions may claim that they "do" harm reduction, they may still participate in (or be complicit in) harmful policies and structures. Unfortunately, this is part of the "professionalization" or "cooptation" of harm reduction that has grown more commonplace in recent years as more public funds have been allocated to the approach. I will also talk about other programs and policies that have incorrectly been deemed "harm reduction" that do not align with the values of harm reduction.

Harm Reduction Is More Than Its Tools

Since harm reduction's roots are in mutual aid, people who currently or formerly used drugs run most programs. Many know how to create a safe and welcoming environment for other people who use drugs – either because someone did the same for them or because they want to create a space they wished they had when they needed it the most. It is understood that participants must feel invited to and welcome in programs so they can take advantage of the services available, whether it is safer drug-using equipment, counseling or support groups, acupuncture, referrals to other services, naloxone, supervised consumption, or something else. This characteristic distinguishes harm reduction settings from other settings where harm reduction services and tools may be provided.

In recent years, several harm reduction interventions have been outsourced and integrated into the day-to-day work of various professions outside of harm reduction settings. One example includes police officers trained to administer naloxone to opioid overdose victims, since they are often the

DOI: 10.4324/9781003301745-8

first on the scene after 911 is called. However, research suggests that police officer views about people who use drugs are generally negative, and studies show that prior experience administering naloxone to an overdose victim is *not* associated with more positive views about this aspect of their jobs.[1,2] Expecting a police officer to respond to an overdose may present a conflict for him within the broader context of the war on drugs. Law enforcement officers have been taught to see an overdose victim as a criminal who illegally acquired and used drugs from the underground market for half a century. Rather than viewing an overdose as a medical emergency, many have been trained to see it as evidence of criminal activity. Yet we now instruct officers to intervene at the overdose victim as needing medical assistance and intervene with naloxone. And at the same time, we expect people who use illegal drugs to be willing to call 911 for help with the full knowledge that officers with the power to arrest them may be the first to respond. As I mentioned in an earlier chapter, 911 Good Samaritan Laws were passed to protect overdose victims and bystanders from arrest when police officers respond to overdose calls. However, these laws have not significantly reduced overdose deaths because many people still fear arrest due to the limitations of state-specific protections in the Good Samaritan Laws and because many people still fear arrest.

The disconnect between the criminalization of drug use and our desire to promote a public health approach to the overdose crisis plays out in these situations every day. While it is important to ensure that any potential first responder, including a police officer, is prepared to help save a life and armed with naloxone, we must question whether police officers should be dispatched to overdose 911 calls at all. Why *are* police officers the first to the scene of a medical emergency rather than an EMT or another first responder with training in crisis response? What else could an emergency response look like?

Many harm reductionists support alternative crisis response hotlines which dispatch people trained in mental health and crisis response, like social workers and paramedics, to overdoses rather than police. More of these alternative hotlines are popping up in communities across the country, since it is clear how these trained responders would be better equipped to save lives, and vulnerable people may feel safer when calling for help. Harm reductionists also want public funds to prioritize buying and distributing naloxone for community distribution in higher quantities because families and friends respond to far more overdoses in our neighborhoods than law enforcement. Beyond this, harm reductionists continue to advocate for Overdose Prevention Centers so people can avoid calling 911 and get the help they need on site.

A second example that comes to mind is the provision of sterile syringes outside Syringe Service Programs (SSPs). Some states have passed laws so that you can legally buy syringes at the pharmacy without a prescription to increase access to sterile syringes for people who may not have an SSP nearby. For instance, in New York State – where most counties do not have an operational SSP – you can buy ten syringes without a prescription at any pharmacy through the Expanded Syringe Exchange Program (ESAP). By offering these services, pharmacies can fill this harm reduction gap in more parts of the state.

However, there are limits to how much these programs can increase access to sterile syringes for the most marginalized people who use drugs. As you will see, there's often a large difference between what is legal and what happens in practice. Just because someone can legally sell syringes does not make their program a harm reduction program. And just because you *can* sell syringes to people who use drugs does not mean you *will*. Studies with pharmacists in several US states suggest that only a small percentage of them are willing to sell syringes without prescriptions and that many pharmacists hold negative and stigmatizing views of people who inject drugs.[3,4]

I learned this firsthand.

I once guest lectured on harm reduction to a class of pharmacy students enrolled in the university's PharmD program when I was an Assistant Professor of Social Work. Almost all of the students had current internships for school credit at community pharmacies across New York City and Long Island, so I asked them if they knew about the state's ESAP law. Most of the students had no idea what I was talking about. One student raised his hand and told me he recently had a customer come up to the counter to purchase syringes without a prescription. When he asked the managing pharmacist on shift whether he was allowed to sell the syringes, the pharmacist told him to lie and say they had no syringes in stock. Another student then raised her hand and said she had a similar experience; however, the managing pharmacist told her to tell the customer they only had large gauge syringes (intended for intramuscular injections) in stock, not the smaller hypodermic syringes the person had requested. The student observed that it seemed strange to deny the request by offering them a product they did not ask for. In both cases, the customers left without the syringes they wanted.

I wish I could say I was surprised.

I asked the class why they thought their classmates were discouraged from selling syringes. Some described a phenomenon known in the research as the "honeypot effect." They believed that the managing pharmacists worried that selling syringes to people who used drugs would attract more of them to their pharmacies, particularly from other communities. The students hypothesized that the pharmacists wanted to avoid serving these so-called undesirable customers and did not want to gain a reputation as a pharmacy that sold syringes to drug users because they wrongly believed it would invite more criminal activity to their neighborhood. Other students talked about how perhaps the pharmacists were worried about "enabling" or "encouraging" injection drug use by selling syringes.

When these pharmacists then conveyed this value judgment to their students, they promoted the same stigma and misconceptions to the next generation of pharmacists.

I used these anecdotes as an opportunity for further discussion. First, I dispelled the honeypot theory by discussing existing research both in the United States and internationally that found that harm reduction programs of all types typically draw in only existing members of the neighborhood and do not increase crime in the vicinity of the program.[5] I also encouraged them to think about how hard it must have been for these customers to walk through the door in the first place, given the stigma toward injection drug use and the fact that they "outed" themselves by making such a request. I asked them how these customers must have felt when they were treated this way – did the students think the customers believed the staff when they said they had no syringes or only had certain ones, or did they know the pharmacy staff simply did not want to serve them?

I asked them to imagine what happened when the customers left the pharmacy after being unable to buy those syringes. Would they try another pharmacy? Would they wake up the next day and simply stop injecting drugs because they had no new syringes? Would they reuse or share a syringe with someone else the next time, since they did not have sterile syringes of their own?

I also reminded the students that these customers came to the pharmacy fully intending to pay for these syringes. After all, SSPs give them out for free. So, if someone is coming to a pharmacy, they either have no nearby program or prefer the setting. By refusing to serve them, the pharmacists made it hard for these customers to engage in health-promoting behavior. And they may have just discouraged these people from seeking syringes at a pharmacy ever again.

I encouraged the students to think about what they would do if they were in this situation in the future. Would they behave differently? Many raised their hands when I asked whether they would consider selling syringes to customers.

I left that presentation thinking about the pervasiveness of drug-related stigma in our society and how much work it will take to get people to challenge their deep-seated thoughts and beliefs about people who use drugs. But it also reminded me that we cannot simply expect systems and institutions to be effective substitutes for harm reduction programs without adequate training and monitoring for compliance. While it's important to have alternative sources of sterile syringes, especially given how prevalent pharmacies are in communities across the country, how useful are such laws if pharmacists will not comply with them in practice? And if they will only perpetuate greater stigma?

This is why many harm reductionists want to allow for even more alternative sources where this equipment can be acquired. Programs like NEXT-Distro are a great example because they provide online and mail-based harm reduction services for people in several states nationwide to ensure people get their supplies easily and with no stigma or shame. And a growing number of SSPs have also added mail-order supplies to their local services. In addition, communities across the country are allowing syringe and harm reduction vending machines so that people can get their supplies in their neighborhoods any hour of the day. The more options we provide to our communities, the better the chance that the people who need these supplies will get them.

These two examples of police officers and pharmacists suggest that some who can legally provide harm reduction interventions but who may avoid doing so or may not believe in the deservingness of these individuals to get help. As such, the provision of harm reduction interventions alone should not be used to credit various individuals or professions as so-called harm reduction practitioners. Of course, ESAP programs are reducing the spread of blood-borne infections, and police officers are reversing overdoses every day, and there are well-intentioned people who want to do it. But reviewing the research and reflecting on conversations like the one in my classroom also highlight exactly why harm reduction programs are still so essential and can never truly be replaced (at best, they could be supplemented by such approaches.) Harm reduction programs clearly fill a gap in our communities because, unlike many parts of our healthcare system and criminal legal system, they not only welcome the highest-risk and most marginalized people in the door but also *want them to be there*. Harm reduction has always been a mutual aid movement by and for those that society has deemed disposable.

Harm Reduction and the Nonprofit Industrial Complex

In recent years, harm reduction has become more professionalized and institutionalized outside of grassroots peer-to-peer service delivery, mutual aid, and advocacy. Programs have become a part of the broader nonprofit industrial complex and often have lost their radical and activist orientation and roots. Some community SSPs are in local public health departments. At the same time, a growing number of healthcare and treatment settings claim they have integrated harm reduction into their work by expanding access to buprenorphine or naloxone. However, we must recognize that many of these settings have values and practices that conflict with a harm reduction approach or make it harder for grassroots programs to do their work.

Limiting the Role of Lived and Living Experience

There is a growing recognition that peers with lived experiences of drug use can be valuable to healthcare and other service delivery because they can relate to people who use drugs in ways that professionally credentialed staff cannot. Some programs hire them to help clients navigate the treatment system or to accompany them to medical appointments. While "lived experience" is increasingly required for these peer roles, there is an implicit or explicit expectation that peers should have a *history* of drug use or be in abstinence-based recovery. As more grants or insurance plans pay for "peer-delivered services" or "peer navigators," harm reductionists have challenged policies that disqualify people who use drugs or people receiving MOUD who could support new clients seeking services. Beyond this, many professionalized settings that claim to embrace a harm reduction approach still have exclusionary policies such as mandatory drug testing or background checks that can exclude people who use drugs from being hired for most positions – from janitors to program managers to supervisors. "Nothing about us without us" remains an elusive disability rights and harm reduction principle in settings that were never equipped for true inclusivity for staff or leadership outside the professionalized working class.

When I worked at the SSP, we hired several peers who actively used drugs to work on our team. They helped us with the day-to-day operations of our program – one worked at our reception desk, another two shared the responsibility of providing ear acupuncture, and one helped co-facilitate our healthy eating and cooking class. Other participants saw them as role models and community members who were still entitled to use the SSP services when needed. When a peer's wife died of complications due to AIDS, he returned to chaotic alcohol and crack cocaine use in his grief. He struggled to maintain his acupuncture schedule, so we put his peer responsibilities on hold. He continued to use our drop-in services and process his grief in our support groups. After connecting with a treatment program, he felt ready to resume acupuncture sessions. We gradually added a few sessions to his schedule a week until he eventually returned to his full schedule. The flexible policies at our program allowed us to accommodate his needs, which might not have been possible in a different setting that required more paperwork and documentation before allowing someone to resume work.

Program Policies May Not Be Welcoming

Administrators or higher-level staff may institute organizational policies that are unintentionally exclusive or unwelcoming. It can be incredibly challenging when so-called harm reduction programs are embedded in treatment settings, medical environments, or public health departments. For instance, some programs may provide safe supplies, medication, or naloxone only on weekdays during business hours to accommodate the schedules of the professionalized staff, even though participants may want weekend and evening options. Or programs may be brick-and-mortar locations only in parts of town inaccessible by public transportation. Or these locations may not offer mobile outreach or mail-order options to engage more of the community.

The program environment may not be welcoming for drug users, either. Sometimes, waiting rooms and other communal spaces are designed for the general public's comfort – expecting people to be quiet and orderly and to leave soon after receiving services. Spaces can feel clinical and formal rather than warm and inviting for participants. In addition, many of these settings allow law enforcement officers to pass by or patrol the area, which may make participants feel unsafe accessing services. Without Client Advisory Boards or similar mechanisms for participants to provide feedback, such programs can alienate the populations they intend to serve or fall short of meeting community needs. We cannot bring harm reduction interventions into settings that were not tailored for people who use drugs and expect they will have an impact.

Competing Against Grassroots Harm Reduction for Funds

The professionalization of harm reduction now means that grassroots mutual aid groups are increasingly competing for grants and funds. Sometimes these are more established and experienced institutions from healthcare, treatment, or public health, which may have only nominally integrated harm reduction into their work. In 2021, the federal government, via the Substance Abuse and Mental Health Services Administration (SAMHSA), made a historic $30 million grant program to expand harm reduction services nationally. These grants were made available to 25 programs for $400,000 annually for up to three years – this was a lot of money and promised a huge cash infusion into communities to expand harm reduction efforts. It was worth celebrating.

But most harm reduction programs did not apply for this money. Many groups that applied did not receive funds. Federal grants are notoriously difficult to complete. They require a lot of documentation and paperwork to determine whether organizations qualify for funding. There are strict formatting requirements, and programs must know how to write about their work compellingly to the government bureaucrats reviewing their applications. Harm reduction programs that ran on shoestring budgets of tens of thousands per year via small grants and donations could not compete with multimillion-dollar treatment institutions or public health departments that could hire grant writers. Grassroots harm reduction programs were set up to fail.

In addition, a grant of $400,000 for three years in a row may not seem like a lot of money to an established institution with a big budget – it would be enough to launch some special projects and hire some new staff. And they could return to their regular funding streams after the funding ran out in three years. Meanwhile, $400,000 for a single year of work is more than the operating expenses of most harm reduction programs for several years *combined*. While that amount of money could have been life-changing for three years, most of these programs would simply be left to tighten their budgets immediately after the grants ended. Newly hired staff may need to be laid off, new initiatives may end, and rent may not be paid because it would be difficult to find large funds like that again. Instead, many harm reduction programs would have been happier to get smaller grants over an extended period to gradually build up their programs and eventually sustain them long term.

Harmful State and Local Policies Can Stifle Harm Reduction Programs

As I have mentioned before, decades of research show that SSPs are associated with lower rates of HIV in communities where they operate. They can also reduce participants' risk of contracting hepatitis C and other skin and soft tissue infections. However, policies can greatly impact how SSPs operate and what kind of work they can do in the community.[6] Just as our policies have created the harm reduction gap, they can also make it difficult for programs to narrow it if they cannot do the work.

One way that state policies can impact SSPs is through the types of allowable distribution models. There are three main kinds of syringe exchange models, and their legality varies from state to state, with some states allowing multiple models and some allowing only one type. One model is called "need-based" syringe exchange, wherein SSPs are free to give syringes to people based on their average number of injections per day and the number of days until the participant can return to the program again. In this model, the *need* for syringes is prioritized when deciding how many syringes to give to the participant, and this is the model supported by the Centers for Disease Control (CDC) to control the spread of blood-borne infections and disease transmission.[7] For instance, if Joe injects five times a day and does not think he will be able to return for a few days, I may give him 30 syringes to tide him over until he returns. When he returns next time, it is okay to return 25 since he explained that he gave two to friends and safely disposed of three syringes in a sealed laundry detergent bottle, as I taught him. I can still give him another 30 syringes or more during that visit if it may be some time before he can return to the SSP.

Another structure for SSPs allowable in some states is "secondary exchange," where some participants can collect more syringes than they individually use. They also exchange for those who cannot attend the SSP themselves. This model prioritizes *expanding the reach* of the SSP to as many participants as possible. For instance, maybe Mario drives to the SSP in the neighboring community since there isn't one in his county. At this program, he is allowed to pick up syringes for himself and the four friends he injects with because not all of them can manage to come by and pick up syringes regularly. He then returns as many syringes as possible every time he returns to the SSP.

The third model in some other states only allows "1:1," or one-to-one exchange, which means that programs are allowed only to give one syringe for every syringe returned. In this model, syringe *return* is a priority when deciding how many syringes to give. If I was serving Joe from the earlier example, I could only send him home with 25 syringes – he would have to return all 30 syringes if he wanted to receive 30 syringes again this time.

As you can imagine, these three different models can have dramatically different impacts on their surrounding communities due to the scale of distribution and exchange allowable at the sites.

Another consideration is that policies can directly or indirectly dictate who runs SSPs. Not all states have SSPs led by people who use drugs, sometimes due to tight state restrictions or limited funding for community groups. In some US states, a significant number of the SSPs are run by the county's public health departments and are housed inside their offices. In these cases, most of the staff at the program are public health administrators and professionals, often with few or no people who use drugs on staff.

The spirit of harm reduction can be lost in the day-to-day bureaucracies of a government institution. These institutional programs cannot engage in the often-necessary subversive acts of civil disobedience when unjust policies restrict their work. Remember, the first operating SSPs in this country and many parts of the world were underground and illegal, run by people who used drugs, many of whom risked arrest and incarceration to deliver lifesaving services to their community. Public health departments and their staff are limited in how much they can push back against restrictive policies or take steps to deliver innovative services without proper permissions.

Two tragic examples come to mind that illustrate what can happen in a community when state policy restricts harm reduction and makes it virtually impossible to provide services with the true spirit of harm reduction at the scale needed to make an impact in the community. Both examples come from communities in West Virginia, which was harder hit by the overdose crisis than most others in the early years. Both were triggered due to key policy changes at the state and local level in 2018, amid that crisis. Both communities had county health department-based SSPs, leading to nationally recognized HIV outbreaks whose effects continue to impact these communities.

Although West Virginia already had some of the strictest SSP policies in the country, such as only allowing 1:1 exchange, in 2018, those programs faced some tough challenges from the community and policymakers due to stigma and misinformation. Without any credible evidence, there was a misconception that SSPs were encouraging and promoting drug use and increasing syringe litter and crime in the community. There were several operating SSPs across the state at the time, and many of them were housed within county public health departments. All along, they helped injection drug use-related cases of HIV to remain relatively low and stable for years, and communities experienced fewer hepatitis C cases as well.

In 2018, the Kanawha-Charleston Health Department-operated SSP that served the capital city of Charleston was suspended and ultimately closed. This was because they were unable to comply with the new rules proposed by the police chief, which included a requirement that participants provide government-issued identification upon enrollment, required participants to receive HIV and HCV tests, expected them to receive drug counseling, and only allowed the distribution of retractable syringes.[8] Programs were told they "must submit monthly reports listing participants, including those who have entered a rehabilitation program and who have tested positive for HIV or hepatitis infections."[9] The chief and his supporters claimed that these policies would ensure that only local community members were using the programs and that people were using harm reduction as a pathway to treatment. However, these policies violated the confidentiality and privacy of participants in an already small and tight-knit community, and they presumed that participants could rapidly transition to treatment (or that treatment was easily accessible).

Between the closing of the program in 2019 and late 2021, at least 55 new HIV cases attributable to injection drug use were identified in the county. In late 2020, when a new nonprofit SSP opened in the community to fill the harm reduction gap left by the closure of the health department SSP, it was subjected to an undercover police investigation due to their outreach efforts and the false belief that they were engaging in illegal activity during their street outreach activities. The police investigation ultimately determined that "no laws were broken during their distribution process." Yet, it was clear that community hostility could threaten their operations and continue to be challenging for them or anyone else attempting to do this work in the community.[10]

Meanwhile, the CDC responded to an HIV outbreak between 2018 and 2020 in Cabell County, West Virginia, where the midsized city of Huntington is located.[11] The outbreak included 82 people, and the CDC discovered that their infections were directly attributable to injection drug use or sexual activity with people who injected drugs. Notably, this outbreak occurred *even though the county had an operational public health department-based SSP for years.* The CDC investigation found that this outbreak was closely tied to newly instituted policies at the SSP due to pressures from the local government and the sheriff. According to their report, these new policies "required near 1:1 exchange, discontinued secondary exchange and limited the maximum number of syringes dispensed to 40 per visit. As a result, SSP visits fell from *1,553* [emphases are mine] in January 2018 to a monthly average of *510* during July 2018–December 2018, and syringes distributed fell from *62,120* to *17,681* per month."[12] This shocking drop in SSP utilization did not mean that people stopped injecting drugs; it just meant they stopped coming to the SSP for sterile supplies.

This is why harm reductionists often urge caution when people claim that their states are doing "enough" harm reduction (or whether they are truly doing harm reduction at all). Just because SSPs legally operate in your state does not mean they are legally allowed to provide all the services and equipment they can. State policies can harshly restrict what harm reductionists can do and how they can do it. In this sense, we should be critical of those who point to harm reduction programs alone as evidence that enough is being done to improve the health of people who use drugs. If SSPs are overly restricted by stigmatizing policies, struggling with financial instability, or at constant threat of shutdown due to community hostility, these programs may be unable to operate to the fullest extent possible. And if anything, it means that there is likely an even *greater* need for harm reduction-based services because the current programs are limited in their capacity and scope.

Harm Reduction and Coerced Treatment

As more Americans view drug use as a health issue, fewer are willing to support a punitive approach that includes incarceration. This is a good thing. People on both sides of the aisle recognize that we cannot arrest our way out of our drug-related problems. The growing nationwide consensus has helped reduce incarceration rates for drug possession from historic highs in the 1980s and 1990s. But even though fewer people are in jail or prison for low-level drug charges, drug-related arrests remain high nationally. So what happens when someone is arrested on drug charges? In most of the United States, courts have begun to sentence people to "alternatives to incarceration" for drug-related and other low-level and nonviolent charges. There are several alternatives, and they vary in their availability and eligibility criteria. These include forms of community supervision such as probation and parole and drug courts.

Probation is a form of community supervision wherein someone convicted of a crime can remain in the community instead of being sent to jail or prison. Probation may last for several months or years. During this time, the person on probation must frequently check in with a probation officer (PO) responsible for always knowing their whereabouts and ensuring they do not commit any new crimes. People on probation must maintain stable housing and gainful employment, and POs conduct unannounced visits to someone's home or workplace to make sure they are where they say they are. POs can also require random drug tests and impose curfews on people to closely monitor and restrict their movements.

Parole shares many similarities with probation, and parole officers (also called POs) can place the same restrictions on people on their caseloads. A key difference is that people on parole have already served several years in prison as part of their sentence for a crime, but the judge decided that they could be eligible to return to the community to serve the rest of their sentence after good behavior while incarcerated. Parole can be an important opportunity for people to transition back to "civilian" life after being in prison for years, and many people want this chance to get their lives back.

POs often require new people on their caseload to complete a diagnostic substance use assessment at a treatment facility to determine whether they need addiction treatment. Research suggests that roughly 25% of people on probation or parole are convicted of drug-related crimes,[13] so treatment is often seen as a way to prevent recidivism. They may also recommend an assessment for someone who tested positive on a routine drug test so they can get help. If the person is diagnosed with SUD, the PO can make treatment completion one of the conditions of their compliance with parole or probation.

Drug courts are another alternative to incarceration that has grown in popularity in many parts of the country and has strong bipartisan support. Proponents of drug courts claim that they are a more humane alternative to the otherwise punitive criminal legal system. In theory, they aim to expand access to treatment for people with SUDs and prevent future criminal activity by helping to address the underlying behaviors that led to their arrest. In most jurisdictions, there are restrictive criteria to determine who is eligible for drug court, and these criteria can vary from community to community. Some allow only first-time offenders, while others exclude people with felonies. Some allow people with complex co-occurring mental health and health disorders, and others do not.

In most jurisdictions, drug court participants must first plead guilty to their crime. If the participant completes drug court, the court will drop their charge. If they do not complete drug court, the court can charge them with their crime and hand down a sentence that could include incarceration. Drug court participants must comply with all treatment requirements and work toward abstinence. Drug court participants may also stay in recovery housing and be involved in other programs in the community. Participants are expected to appear in court to meet with the judge and drug court team regularly to discuss their progress and to show that they are taking steps toward a productive life in recovery. Drug court enrollment can be for an average of 12 months or longer, depending on a participant's treatment progress and ability to achieve stability in their lives.

The criminal legal system is not the only one that can mandate or coerce people into treatment. Institutions like the Department of Social Services and Child Protective Services (CPS) often flag people for substance use. In many states, receipt of public benefits may be contingent upon enrollment in treatment for people who admit to using illegal drugs or who have SUDs. Meanwhile, a parent can be mandated to treatment if their CPS caseworker deems their drug use has contributed to child abuse or neglect.

Between the criminal legal system and other civil systems, roughly 50% of substance use treatment facility admissions in any given year are for clients mandated to receive services. When I worked at the outpatient treatment facility, many of my clients were also mandated to treatment. These clients enrolled in treatment with the threat of jail or prison hanging over their heads and the threat of losing custody of their children or various government benefits like cash or food assistance. Clients were required to sign release forms so that I could speak about their treatment engagement and progress with their PO or DSS, or CPS case worker. The release form also allowed me to report whether the client tested positive on a drug test that we conducted as part of treatment. Sometimes I was asked to send a letter or submit quarterly paperwork to provide updates on the client and their progress. Most POs and caseworkers seemed to want what was best for the people they worked with; they were not trained mental health professionals. They varied a lot in how they interacted with our clients – some were very strict and did not tolerate my clients being late to appointments or testing positive on a drug test. Meanwhile, others were more understanding and tried to work with people on their caseloads to give them a chance to succeed at treatment.

After a few months of working at the treatment program, I became the drug court representative. Although the drug court coordinator would call periodically to check in on the status of the participants, I had to visit our courthouse a few times a month to report back to the judge about how they were doing. We usually had two to four clients involved in drug court at any given time. On these days, participants would be brought to the front of the courtroom one at a time. The judge and drug court team members would question them about their progress. If the client was doing well in treatment and had other positive things to report, such as a good visit with their children or getting a job interview, the judge and team would publicly praise them or give them a round of applause, or the judge might even come down and hug the participant. But if the client tested positive on a drug test or got into a fight at the recovery home where they were staying, the judge might ask them to explain their actions. In these situations, the team may express disappointment in the person and ask them what they will do differently next time. Sometimes the judge would sanction the participants by giving them a curfew, asking them to write a letter of apology to the court, or even requiring them to spend the weekend in jail to reflect on their actions.

Maintaining confidentiality with my clients was almost impossible because I often owed various referral sources periodic updates about their progress in treatment. What they said and how they behaved in treatment could be used against them by their PO or caseworker. And if our clients do not successfully stay abstinent and complete treatment, bad things could happen. I always found it strange that clients were simply expected to talk openly about their deeply personal challenges in group therapy with me just moments after I had followed them into the bathroom to watch them pee into a cup for a random drug test. And if they tested positive, I would betray my client's trust because I was required to call their PO, caseworker, or drug court coordinator to tell them about the test results. In the case of probation or parole, it was then up to the PO to decide if my client violated the terms of their probation/parole by using an illegal drug and if the client should be sent to jail and sentenced to even more time. Sometimes a PO or drug court may impose a sanction, and sometimes they would give the client another chance. Similarly, caseworkers could decide that the client was not making adequate progress in treatment. They could use the positive drug test result to make the case that my client was an unfit parent or should be denied certain government assistance (even though they qualified for the help because they lived at or below the poverty line).

I often felt like I was ratting out my clients. At times all I could do was try to persuade these entities that my clients were still benefiting from treatment and needed another chance. Sometimes this strategy worked. Sometimes it didn't. Either way, I hated having to argue to justify why someone needed help and not punishment.

Meanwhile, my colleagues implicitly encouraged me to keep positive relationships with POs and caseworkers since these people played an important role at the agency. We wouldn't have much work to do if they didn't send us clients! After a few years at the treatment facility, I felt ineffective and like I was hurting my clients. These were not the conditions for a collaborative therapeutic relationship. This was not why I became a therapist.

Many people wrongly say that alternatives to incarceration and other mandated treatment are a form of "harm reduction." Some argue that alternatives to incarceration are more therapeutic and rehabilitative than jail or prison. And they believe that the threat of incarceration or harsher penalties can finally get people motivated to stop using drugs. Similarly, others claim that requiring treatment to receive benefits or keep custody of their children is good because the threat of a negative consequence properly motivates someone to finally comply with treatment. And they all think these mandates help to provide access to treatment for people who would otherwise not receive it.

However, I would disagree, and most harm reductionists would too. This is because those systems – the criminal legal system, DSS, or CPS – do not understand that behavior change is difficult and often slow. Instead, they expect a person to change a lifetime of drug use patterns within a few weeks because they have a big negative consequence hanging over their heads. These systems are not built to recognize "any positive change," and they are not usually willing to understand that there are many parts of their lives where clients can show improvement, such as maintaining a new job and attending counseling sessions, even if they are not fully abstinent. Even clients motivated to achieve abstinence can take multiple attempts over several years to make necessary changes and could have times when they may return to use in the process. In addition, the drug, set, and setting model shows us that people's drug use occurs within the broader context of their lives and circumstances. The use of mandates and coercion places a lot of pressure on a person. Someone trying to get a job, attend treatment, and manage the stress of being monitored by their PO may get high to cope with the stress because the pressure is overwhelming, and that person hasn't yet developed new coping strategies.

The use of these mandates highlights a fundamental tension in our culture – that while people are increasingly willing to view SUDs as a treatable health issue, this conceptualization will always conflict with our drug war that views people who use drugs as criminals who deserve punishment. While we make exemptions for some people to get access to treatment, our criminal legal system limits how flexible and patient they are willing to be, and we will still default to punishment if someone does not change fast enough. As long as the threat of punishment remains, alternatives to incarceration are not harm reduction. Instead, these so-called alternatives to incarceration can end up simply delaying incarceration and becoming a pathway to incarceration and even harsher penalties.

The treatment requirement for public benefits is problematic. Harm reductionists believe it is cruel to make a person living in poverty comply with treatment requirements just so they can eat and have a little cash to buy tampons and toilet paper. What is the logic behind cutting someone off food or cash benefits if they cannot stay abstinent? *How will someone who cannot afford to eat or buy basic necessities stay sober?* There is no logic to this; there is only cruelty. Policies like this reveal that our society believes that only certain people are worthy of the dignity of having a full stomach and shoes on their feet. This is incompatible with harm reduction values. Harm reductionists believe that all people deserve food and enough money to survive, including people who use illegal drugs and those with SUDs who may not currently be involved in treatment.

Using child custody as leverage to coerce someone into treatment is also unethical. The expectation that a parent must "earn" custody of their children by completing treatment presumes that the only reason some may have parenting challenges is due to their substance use and that once a parent stops using substances, they will be a more effective parent. However, this fixation on the parent's substance use can overlook the fact that structural, financial, and social challenges could impact their parenting abilities. For instance, these parents may also need assistance with childcare, more skills-building and support, stable housing, access to transportation, stable employment, or better mental health support. And if these needs were met, it is possible that more parents would be better equipped to care for their families, and it could help prevent future challenges. Harm reductionists and advocates for family preservation believe that we should reallocate funds from entities like CPS into community groups that can help support families to stay together, and more resources should be provided directly to families to help them thrive since the families largely targeted by CPS are low income.[14] Advocates also believe that when parents are offered treatment, their inability to pursue abstinence immediately should not be used to keep their children away from them since even those with SUDs may take time to make changes. The temporary or permanent removal of children from their parent's custody for not completing treatment is a traumatizing event for both parents and their children. It can set the parent up to fail if they feel like they are facing insurmountable challenges to reunite with their children or if there is no pathway to be reunited.

Harm reductionists do not believe drug test results can tell whether someone is a loving parent or capable of raising their children. Yet drug testing is commonly used by CPS to determine whether a child should be temporarily or permanently removed from a parent's custody every day. *In fact, entire cases have been built against parents based on the results of a single drug test and without any other evidence of harm to the child.* Due to many states' so-called chemical endangerment laws, pregnant people can be routinely drug tested during their prenatal visits and at delivery without their consent to determine whether they have "endangered" the fetus. Drug testing rates show healthcare providers' biases in who they imagine these parents are – research shows that Black patients are twice as likely to get tested as white patients even though they do not test positive at higher rates.[15] A recent *New York Times* article highlighted the traumatizing experience of an Arizona mother who had her newborn taken from her at the hospital because she tested positive for taking her prescribed buprenorphine.[16] (As a reminder, this is an FDA-approved medication to treat opioid use disorder that is safe to use during pregnancy and, when taken as prescribed, can cut the risk of lethal opioid overdose in half.)

Rather than using harsh punitive measures to coerce and mandate people into SUD treatment, harm reductionists believe we should make our treatment system more affordable and accessible so those who want it can get it voluntarily. And we should ensure that the services are trauma-informed, culturally relevant, and backed by the best available evidence so people can benefit most. In addition, treatment goals and outcomes should be flexible and include harm reduction support so that people are more easily retained in care to stay safe. Our communities must also make treatment and harm reduction services available on demand so people can get services when they are most interested and motivated. Waiting lists, limited hours, and delays due to insurance's prior authorization can leave people in a holding pattern until they can get the services they want, so we must consider how to expand service capacity and ensure that their services are paid for with no delay. Our current system is far too invested in forcing people into treatment because it presumes that the problem lies with people with SUDs – they are wrongly viewed as unmotivated and unwilling to improve their well-being. Instead, harm reductionists would suggest that until our treatment is functional, effective, affordable, and accessible for those who want them, we cannot keep forcing people to receive services.

Harm Reduction and Corporate Money and Influence

Just as the involvement of non-harm reduction institutions in the delivery of services can pose challenges, so can the involvement of for-profit corporate entities. It is a fine line to walk, since forming alliances or relationships with these industries is often the only way most nonprofit programs, including harm reduction programs, can sustain themselves.

Harm reductionists promote positive change, mutual aid, and collectivism, while corporate cultures are often harm-producing, alienating, and profit-driven. Yet even though the values that drive for-profit industries and structures are antithetical to those that fuel harm reduction and mutual aid, many harm reductionists are reliant upon these very industries to be able to do their work. They must seek private grants and donations, often from corporate-backed foundations or philanthropists. They need these funds because federal, state, and local funding for harm reduction programs is not always consistent or feasible. In this sense, harm reductionists, like nonprofits from other fields, compromise to keep doing their work within the capitalist corporate system. Sometimes this money comes with no strings attached, but sometimes these funds can feel like some must compromise their values.

For instance, the multimillion-dollar HepConnect initiative funded by pharmaceutical company Gilead has expanded access to much-needed harm reduction services and linkages to hepatitis C treatments for people who use drugs in Appalachia.[17] It is already saving lives and building valuable healthcare infrastructure. Still, you can't ignore that it is also funded by the company that makes the hepatitis C treatment that patients will likely be prescribed. The medication can be pretty expensive, and although their motives may be altruistic to cure the disease, they are also likely to profit from this.

Similarly, the pharmaceutical maker of a well-known high-dose naloxone formulation has negotiated discounts and free donations to harm reduction programs nationwide since their product hit the market. We are all desperate to saturate our communities with naloxone, and many people have accepted these donations and discounts because more naloxone means more lives saved. We need more affordable options. However, many harm reductionists have expressed concern that the quantity of naloxone in this high-dose formulation could unnecessarily put people into severe withdrawal when a smaller dose could have revived them. Of course, we must ensure that anyone responding to an overdose is prepared with a second dose if needed. But it's better to administer more naloxone after waiting a few moments rather than to overwhelm an overdose victim's system all at once with more than what might be necessary to revive them. This is another example of the types of compromises that programs must make because of financial need and how corporate actors are still ultimately trying to push their products. In contrast, it has been exciting to see the launch of Remedy Alliance/For The People, a nonprofit organization that has negotiated its contract with a generic naloxone manufacturer to provide low-cost naloxone directly to SSPs and other programs at fair prices that consider program budgets and what they can afford. More of these innovative models could be helpful as we ensure that we get the right supplies to help our communities stay safe.

Meanwhile, the role of Big Pharma in our current overdose crisis is widely recognized. Certain actors engaged in unscrupulous practices and advocated for policies that bolstered their profits while harming communities and claiming hundreds of thousands of lives. And now opioid settlement funds in several states have been earmarked for lifesaving harm reduction programs in parts of the country that desperately need this funding. While it is important to receive this financial support, it is unfortunate that our programs must rely on funds from a devastating and avoidable tragedy.

For decades, harm reduction advocates have engaged in backroom negotiations with Big Pharma and other corporations, which helped to bring down prices for syringes, naloxone, and other harm reduction supplies. These negotiations were often the only reason many harm reduction programs could afford to distribute lifesaving supplies in their communities. It is complicated when the materials needed to sustain harm reduction programs are from industries that have sometimes engaged in troubling practices. Yet, these entities are the only ones with tax incentives or other means to offset these discounts. Though it may seem strange, some of these corporations have often become better and more consistent supporters of the work than other traditional public health funding streams. And many of our programs will continue to need corporate backing, as our work remains politicized and publicly unfunded or underfunded.

But just because a major industry or corporation supports harm reduction work doesn't necessarily mean they are harm reductionists. This is an important point to remember, and it is no different from when companies donate to or support other causes, such as LGBTQIA+ rights, cancer research, HIV/AIDS, or reproductive justice. We should always remember that although some of these institutions have well-intentioned decision-makers who funded various causes (or negotiated discounts), these entities are still predominantly motivated by profits. They may still engage in questionable practices in other parts of their work, have problematic policies about drug use among their staff, or support elected officials who promote harmful public policies.

A Case Study: Tobacco Harm Reduction

According to the CDC, "tobacco use is the leading preventable cause of death" in the nation.[18] Estimates suggest that 20% of deaths in any year can be attributed to tobacco use. This is because of decades of poor regulation and oversight of Big Tobacco, widespread commercialization, and the suppression of research on health harms for far too long. These combined factors normalized and increased cigarette smoking, exposing generations to health risks. Fortunately, decades of lawsuits, settlements, and stronger tobacco regulations have contributed to such low rates of smoking in younger generations that many fail to realize that we are still living with extensive tobacco-related harms today. This public health crisis is no longer the topic of media headlines or public outrage as it once was, even though tobacco claims over 1,000 lives a day in this country. Most would be shocked to see that the scale of the current overdose crisis is relatively small compared to the annual deaths driven by tobacco.

Abstinence is the safest strategy to reduce tobacco-related harms, and countless people successfully quit by simply waking up one day and stopping "cold turkey" with no treatment. Others may take several attempts but eventually stop for good. Some might seek counseling for support or use one of the two FDA-approved medications to help them quit.

However, abstinence can be challenging for many tobacco consumers, and some will continue to struggle. This is why tobacco harm reduction (THR) is so essential. THR proponents aim to reduce the health harms associated with tobacco use by helping people to reduce their use or to switch to safer alternatives. People who support THR understand that many will struggle to stop using tobacco products because they are addicted to nicotine. Nicotine is the psychoactive drug found in tobacco, and it provides the high that people seek when they smoke or chew tobacco. Nicotine is a relatively safe and mild stimulant on its own and in moderate quantities. Nicotine can be calming or energizing, depending on how much is consumed and how frequently. Many people also use nicotine to improve focus and concentration, aid with digestion, suppress appetite, boost mood, and much more.

Most of the public health harm in our communities is due to tobacco consumption, not nicotine itself. Different forms of tobacco consumption carry different risks, and the two most prevalent ways that people consume it are through either combustible (i.e., smoked) tobacco, as in cigarettes or cigars, or smokeless tobacco, like chewing tobacco. Smoking tobacco is the fastest way to release nicotine into the bloodstream, so it is an appealing option for many people. However, tobacco smoke contains over 7,000 chemical constituents that can harm smokers and bystanders. And chewing tobacco can put users at risk of oral and throat cancers. People who practice THR recognize that those who use tobacco have reasons to want to continue using nicotine but may also be worried about their health. Harm reduction strategies can include switching one's route of nicotine consumption from a risky one to a safer alternative and reducing or moderating one's use.

Nicotine replacement therapy (NRT) is a popular option for many, and it can include the use of FDA-approved nicotine gums, lozenges, patches, or the lesser-known nicotine nasal spray or inhaler options. Some forms of NRT are available over the counter, while others are prescription only. NRT is appealing because people can still get the nicotine boost while taking steps to improve their health. Some people use NRT to reduce tobacco use, while others use it to manage nicotine cravings to achieve abstinence. For instance, somebody can use a piece of gum or a lozenge during the day instead of smoking a cigarette or apply a patch for a steady dose of nicotine for hours.

Other alternative products are more widely used abroad than in the United States. For instance, Japan and several other countries allow heat-not-burn tobacco cigarettes that do not raise the temperature of the tobacco high enough to cause combustion. Some research suggests they may release fewer chemicals than traditional cigarettes while providing the user with nicotine and a tobacco flavor. Snus is a Swedish form of smokeless tobacco in a small pouch that can be held in the upper lip and releases nicotine for several hours. It is also associated with fewer harms than cigarette smoking and is safer than some chewing tobacco because of the manufacturing process.

Beyond these options, smokers have yet another harm reduction alternative product, and a report by the British Royal College of Physicians found they were 95% less harmful than cigarettes.[19] Estimates suggest that there are nearly 100 million current users around the world who are using them to cut down or stop smoking. Yet, they are stigmatized, scapegoated, and viewed with suspicion by some experts and the public in the United States. They are not an FDA-approved smoking cessation tool, even though a 2022 systematic review by the internationally renowned health research network Cochrane found that this option helps people to stop smoking and is even more effective than NRT.[20]

If you haven't already guessed, I'm talking about e-cigarettes.

While more countries worldwide see the benefits of e-cigarettes on public health, the American public has good reason to be skeptical of anything coming from Big Tobacco. It is hard to overlook that this lifesaving THR option is primarily made available by industry and helps them get richer every day. After all, the same for-profit and unscrupulous actors who contributed to widespread tobacco use and related public health harms are now the ones who stand to profit off our most vital tools to help people to transition away from them. It's a win–win for Big Tobacco because people can keep buying harmful tobacco products or switch to e-cigarettes as the safer alternative. The industry makes money in any case.

Many today may understandably question the validity of claims that e-cigarettes are relatively safer than traditional cigarettes, since Big Tobacco did not disclose the harmful research on cigarettes for decades. Their past behavior makes them an unreliable source of information, even though their claims today are, in fact, correct. And though most of the research on e-cigarettes is funded by governments and other sources, many have noticed that the industry has directly or indirectly funded a significant amount of the research.[21]

Lastly, while e-cigarette brand JUUL claims their products are only intended for the "one billion adult smokers" of the world, there are valid reasons for the public to be skeptical about the degree to which the company (and the rest of the industry) is genuinely motivated by public health. A study of JUUL advertisements found that their first several years of product marketing used predominantly young models and influencers to promote their products on social media platforms frequented by youth.[22] Many of these advertisements are reminiscent of the imagery used just a few decades ago to make smoking seem cool and appealing to young people. These targeted tactics likely led some youth to experiment with e-cigarettes, and some tried cigarettes too. However, adults continue to comprise the majority of e-cigarette consumers.

These factors together have all affected public opinion about Big Tobacco and e-cigarettes, and rightfully so. These reasons are all valid. And we should continue to hold these corporations accountable, demand transparency, and ensure proper regulation and oversight.

The challenges we face due to widespread tobacco-related harm directly result from our troubling history of corporate interests harming public health. But this current moment shows how sometimes our relationships can change when these interests suddenly (and quite narrowly) align. We desperately need e-cigarettes and THR. Millions of Americans may not succeed at abstinence, and NRT may not be an effective option for all. Despite historically low smoking levels in the country, some at-risk groups continue to face tobacco-related harms disproportionately. Research suggests that smoking rates remain highest for low-income and working-class people, Indigenous communities, LGBTQIA+ people, people without advanced degrees, and people with co-occurring mental health and/or substance use disorders.[23] Tobacco-related harms are unevenly experienced across our society, and we need all options to be available for those who need help. Access to THR is both a health equity issue and a racial and social justice issue.

Conclusion

The greater provision of harm reduction resources and tools is a significant win that cannot be understated. Expanding access through various disciplines and models, including via police and pharmacists, has likely helped to save lives and reduce the spread of infectious diseases. In addition, the greater expansion of services in treatment, medical, and public health departments has helped to engage people in harm reduction who may not have otherwise been able to access those tools. However, we must remain aware that expanded acceptance and access can come at a cost if it compromises the delivery of services and if those tasked with doing the work are reluctant participants. Lastly, as "harm reduction" gains greater recognition as a concept, we must be wary of those who misuse the term to justify harmful practices they claim are "reforms" or improvements to systems that cause real damage to our communities.

Notes

1 Kruis, Nathan E., Katherine McLean, Payton Perry, and Marielle K. Nackley. "First Responders' Views of Naloxone: Does Stigma Matter?" *Substance Use & Misuse* 57, no. 10 (2022): 1534–44. https://doi.org/10.1080/10826084.202 2.2092150.

2 Murphy, Jennifer, and Brenda Russell. "Police Officers' Views of Naloxone and Drug Treatment: Does Greater Overdose Response Lead to More Negativity?" *Journal of Drug Issues* 50, no. 4 (2020): 455–71. https://doi.org/10.1177/0022042620921363.

3 Syvertsen, Jennifer L., and Robin A. Pollini. "Syringe Access and Health Harms: Characterizing 'Landscapes of Antagonism' in California's Central Valley." *International Journal of Drug Policy* 75 (January 2020): 102594. https://doi.org/10.1016/j.drugpo.2019.10.018.

4 Chiarello, Elizabeth. "Nonprescription Syringe Sales: Resistant Pharmacists' Attitudes and Practices." *Drug and Alcohol Dependence* 166 (September 2016): 45–50. https://doi.org/10.1016/j.drugalcdep.2016.06.023.

5 Day, Carolyn A., Bethany White, and Paul S. Haber. "The Impact of an Automatic Syringe Dispensing Machine in Inner-City Sydney, Australia: No Evidence of a 'Honeypot' Effect." *Drug and Alcohol Review* 35, no. 5 (2016): 637–43. https://doi.org/10.1111/dar.12397.

6 Davis, Corey S., Derek H. Carr, and Elizabeth A. Samuels. "Paraphernalia Laws, Criminalizing Possession and Distribution of Items Used to Consume Illicit Drugs, and Injection-Related Harm." *American Journal of Public Health* 109, no. 11 (2019): 1564–67. https://doi.org/10.2105/AJPH.2019.305268.

7 Centers for Disease Control and Prevention. "Needs-Based Distribution and Syringe Service Programs." December 2020. https://www.cdc.gov/ssp/docs/CDC-SSP-Fact-Sheet-508.pdf (accessed December 5, 2022).

8 Retractable syringes are typically meant to protect against accidental needle stick injuries. However, in the context of SSPs, retractable syringes can create a bind for participants who may be delayed in returning to the SSP to get new ones. Although SSPs encourage a new syringe every time, harm reductionists understand this may not always be possible. If someone absolutely must reuse a syringe, it is better to reuse your own than someone else's to reduce the likelihood of catching hepatitis C or HIV. Retractable syringes do not provide people with that backup option in emergencies.

9 Associated Press. "Needle Exchange Suspended in West Virginia Capital." *WOUB Public Media*. March 27, 2018. https://woub.org/2018/03/27/needle-exchange-suspended-west-virginia-capital/.

10 City of Charleston, West Virginia Police Department. *Investigation into SOAR-Solutions Oriented Addiction Response – Needle Distribution*. Charleston, WV: James A. Hunt, 2021.

11 Atkins, Amy, R. Paul McClung, Michael Kilkenny, Kyle Bernstein, Kara Willenburg, et al. "Notes from the Field: Outbreak of Human Immunodeficiency Virus Infection among Persons Who Inject Drugs — Cabell County, West Virginia, 2018–2019." *MMWR Morb Mortal Wkly Rep* 69 (2020): 499–500. https://doi.org/10.15585/mmwr.mm6916a2.

12 McClung, R. Paul, Amy D. Atkins, Michael Kilkenny, Kyle T. Bernstein, Kara S. Willenburg, Matthew Weimer, Susan Robilotto, et al. "Response to a Large HIV Outbreak, Cabell County, West Virginia, 2018–2019." *American Journal of Preventive Medicine* 61, no. 5 (2021): S143–50. https://doi.org/10.1016/j.amepre.2021.05.039.

13 Ibid.

14 Sangoi, Lisa. "'Whatever They Do, I'm Her Comfort, I'm Her Protector': How the Foster System Has Become Ground Zero for the US Drug War." *Movement for Family Power*. 2020. https://www.movementforfamilypower.org/ground-zero

15 Winchester, Mae-Lan, Parmida Shahiri, Emily Boevers-Solverson, Abigail Hartmann, Meghan Ross, Sharon Fitzgerald, and Marc Parrish. "Racial and Ethnic Differences in Urine Drug Screening on Labor and Delivery." *Maternal and Child Health Journal* 26, no. 1 (2022): 124–30. https://doi.org/10.1007/s10995-021-03258-5.

16 Walter, Shoshana. "They Followed Doctors' Orders. Then Their Children Were Taken Away." *New York Times*. 29 June 2023. https://www.nytimes.com/2023/06/29/magazine/pregnant-women-medication-suboxonbabies.html.

17 HepConnect. https://www.hepconnect.com/ (accessed December 6, 2022).

18 Centers for Disease Control. "Tobacco-Related Mortality." 2020. https://www.cdc.gov/tobacco/data_statistics/fact_sheets/health_effects/tobacco_related_mortality/index.htm (accessed December 7, 2022).

19 Royal College of Physicians. *Nicotine without Smoke: Tobacco Harm Reduction*. London: RCP, 2016. https://www.rcplondon.ac.uk/projects/outputs/nicotine-without-smoke-tobacco-harm-reduction (accessed December 9, 2022).

20 Hartmann-Boyce Jamie, Nicola Lindson, Ailsa R. Butler, Hayden McRobbie, Chris Bullen, Rachna Begh, Annika Theodoulou, Caitlin Notley, Nancy A. Rigotti, Tari Turner, Thomas R. Fanshawe, and Peter Hajek. "Electronic Cigarettes for Smoking Cessation." *Cochrane Database of Systematic Reviews* 2022, no. 11 (2022): CD010216. https://doi.org/10.1002/14651858.CD010216. pub7.

21 Vassey, Julia, Yogi H. Hendlin, Manali Vora, and Pamela Ling. "Influence of Disclosed and Undisclosed Funding Sources in Tobacco Harm Reduction Discourse: A Social Network Analysis." *Nicotine & Tobacco Research: Official Journal of the Society for Research on Nicotine and Tobacco* (October 2022). https://doi.org/10.1093/ntr/ntac250.

22 Jackler, Robert K., Cindy Chau, Brook D. Getachew, Mackenzie M. Whitcomb, et al. 2019. "JUUL Advertising over Its First Three Years on the Market. Stanford Research into the Impact of Tobacco Advertising (SRITA)." https://tobacco.stanford.edu/juulanalysis (accessed December 9, 2022).

23 Drope, Jeffrey, Alex C. Liber, Zachary Cahn, Michal Stoklosa, Rosemary Kennedy, Clifford E. Douglas, Rosemarie Henson, and Jacqui Drope. "Who's Still Smoking? Disparities in Adult Cigarette Smoking Prevalence in the United States." *CA: A Cancer Journal for Clinicians* 68, no. 2 (2018): 106–15. https://doi.org/10.3322/caac.21444.

Conclusion
Moving Beyond Drug (and Drug User) Exceptionalism

For over a century, the United States has categorized drugs to distinguish between those that are acceptable and those that are not. While some of this categorization is formalized through our laws and policies, there are also many informal ways that we continue to stratify the category of "drugs" into what we consider "good" and "bad" drugs. But rarely have these distinctions ever been driven by the unique psychoactive characteristics of the drugs themselves; instead, we have drawn these lines because of the association of certain drugs with various racial, ethnic, and social groups. Over time, some lines blurred. Other lines shifted as the groups associated with certain drugs gradually changed. The new "face" of a drug could persuade us to take a gentler and more open-minded approach to a drug and its users, but a new face could also motivate greater judgment and scorn. Ultimately, even these changes have upheld a system wherein those people who are already entitled to safety and dignity preserve steady access to the drugs they choose, while those on the margins of society remain excluded from that safety and dignity, both in general and in regard to their drug use. And many lose their freedom. Over a million lost their lives in the past two decades alone. All the while, one thing has remained constant: people continue to use drugs.

This book has covered how our nation's policies separated mood-altering drugs into three main categories: those that are legally regulated for adult use, some highly restricted prescription medications that are available only for certain patients, and a variety of banned drugs that cannot be used legally and that lead to arrest and incarceration.

And beyond these legally distinct categories of drugs, there are quite a few other ways our culture thinks of drugs. For instance, some are referred to as "hard" drugs, such as heroin and cocaine, and they are often contrasted with "soft" drugs like marijuana. One group is seen as more problematic or dangerous, while another is seen as less so. Meanwhile, there are those who condone the use of "natural" or plant-derived drugs such as psychedelic mushrooms while disparaging the use of "unnatural" human-made drugs like methamphetamine and other pills and powders. Our

DOI: 10.4324/9781003301745-9

culture also vilifies cheap "street" drugs like crack cocaine, which we have been taught to associate with low-income people and communities of color, in direct contrast to pricier "party" drugs (like MDMA and powder cocaine), which are associated with white upper-class users in social or recreational contexts.

   The creation of these drug binaries of "good" versus "bad" drugs contributes to what many harm reductionists refer to as *drug exceptionalism*. Drug exceptionalism is an ideology that affirms that drugs are generally bad, harmful, or dangerous, but that certain drugs are better or acceptable. When our communities uphold various categories or hierarchies between drugs through drug exceptionalism, we intensify the stigma for the broader category of unacceptable drugs while only carving an exception for the drugs we like. It further stratifies people along the lines of their drug preferences, but it is not intended to help everyone. In fact, it can set others back and keep them stigmatized and punished. (And sometimes that is the point.)

The Effects of Drug Exceptionalism

A Two-Tiered System for the Same Drugs

One of the reasons that harm reductionists reject drug exceptionalism is because there are several examples of similar drugs that have very different policies – in which one can be purchased legally and is culturally normalized, but the other is criminalized and stigmatized. The best example is crystal methamphetamine, an illegal stimulant drug, and Adderall, a legally prescribed medication that is FDA-approved to treat Attention-Deficit/Hyperactivity Disorder (ADHD) and narcolepsy. Both are in the same family of amphetamine drugs. When we smoke crystal methamphetamine or swallow a tablet of Adderall, our bodies have similar reactions, because crystal methamphetamine and Adderall are chemically similar drugs that activate the same neurotransmitters in our brains.

   Our bodies do not distinguish between these drugs just because one was sold on the underground market and the other was dispensed at a pharmacy with a prescription. Our brains don't respond differently because one was manufactured in a clandestine underground laboratory and the other in a pharmaceutical company's laboratory.[1] How they are consumed (one is smoked and the other is swallowed) may affect how quickly and intensely we feel their effects, but our bodies don't distinguish between the drug that could lead to jail time and a lifelong criminal record, and the one that makes you a compliant patient in the eyes of your doctor.

   Since we prescribe amphetamines to children, clearly these drugs can be taken safely. We would not give these drugs to young people around the country unless we knew that it could help them. The problem is not the drugs. Our criminal legal system and medical system take issue with the unsanctioned use of the drug by people who were not deemed to have legitimate medical need for it, and who may use it for unapproved purposes, including self-medication, productivity, or recreational purposes.

As a society, we do not actually have a problem with people experiencing the stimulating effects of amphetamines, if they experience those effects while under the authority of a medical professional, and if the drugs are consumed at the lowest effective dose and are taken for what we deem to be "medical" purposes. Because of this, we only allow some people access to a regulated supply of amphetamines of known quality and potency, while others are forced to use the unpredictable and adulterated underground drug supply. And people who use illegal methamphetamine may face the challenges of criminalization and arrest, which can disrupt their lives and cause more problems, while a patient on Adderall can get their drug safely at a pharmacy and their insurance will pay for it.

Our culture has created two very distinct ideas of the people who use these drugs, and it impacts how we view the drugs themselves. Films, television, and popular news media often depict low-income rural white people as the "face" of crystal methamphetamine, clearly illustrated in shows like *Breaking Bad* and *Cops*, and in local news coverage that prominently features stigmatizing mugshots of people on some of the worst days of their lives. On the other hand, prescription stimulants are depicted as an essential tool for academic success for unfocused and ambitious young kids and college students to get ahead. We think of one group as having squandered their lives. And we see the other as having a bright future. But they all use the same drugs.

There are several problems with this contrasting depiction of people who use stimulants. One is that our public has never been educated that these two drugs are virtually the same, so when they see a stereotypical image of a rural white person with methamphetamine use disorder, they wrongly believe that there must be something so uniquely addictive, dangerous, and harmful about methamphetamine that put this person in that position. For instance, many falsely believe that methamphetamine use causes "meth mouth" but do not realize that college students who use the same drug do not have dental problems. So why do some people who use meth have bad teeth and others don't? In this case, we must consider that set and setting factors, such as access to dental care, poverty, sleep deprivation, dehydration, and high sugar consumption, could also have contributed to teeth problems. Many people who smoke methamphetamine also smoke cigarettes, and we all know that smoking is very damaging to teeth. Perhaps it is important to consider that young people who take Adderall seem healthier because they have access to healthcare and insurance, and probably have a stable home, access to healthy and nutritious food, and regularly visit the dentist. But when we are quick to focus on the drug rather than the other potential explanatory factors, it is easier to justify more stigma.

Another problem is that, despite media telling us that low-income rural white people are the predominant users of methamphetamine, they are not. Many high-functioning people in mainstream life use methamphetamine, and their use goes undetected because they do not experience methamphetamine-related problems and never develop a methamphetamine use disorder. In addition, methamphetamine-related stigma often leads many to hide their use or be secretive so that their loved ones may never know. But the awareness that methamphetamine users are a diverse group could help people dispel myths and stereotypes so that more people understand that the drug itself is not always a problem. According to the National Survey on Drug Use and Health, 2.5 million people across the United States used methamphetamine in 2021.[2] This includes a range of diverse people, such as a middle-aged truck driver who drives long cross-country routes and must stay awake and focused, and a young gay man going clubbing on a Friday night. Why must they risk punishment to use the same drug that others can get with a prescription? And why shouldn't adults be allowed to use methamphetamine if it makes them productive or if it is fun and they do not experience other negative consequences?

Harm reductionists do not endorse drug exceptionalism because they are committed to keeping all people who use drugs safe with no exceptions. Meanwhile, those who ascribe to drug exceptionalism believe that people who use certain drugs deserve to be safe, while others do not. They affirm and uphold that it is acceptable for some people to fall into the harm reduction gap. Harm reductionists believe that people who use any of these drugs should know the risks and how to stay safe. And they recognize how our policies themselves can make any drug more harmful by driving it into the underground market where it is unregulated. Drug exceptionalism contributed to the two-tiered system we live with today, where certain versions of drugs remained medically available for a privileged few, while different versions of them became criminalized and riskier without quality control. But harm reductionists find that the two-tier system affords only some safety while it puts others at risk. Instead, harm reductionists advocate for policies so that all people can have access to a regulated supply, and that all people are equipped with the tools and tips to stay as safe as possible when using these drugs.

Harm reductionists do not deny that people can have drastically different experiences using the same drugs if their set and setting factors differ. Privilege can help prevent drug-related harms, and it can also help one to get help if they ever experience harm. Harm reductionists want all people to live in the conditions that could keep them as safe as possible, whether they use drugs or not. This means having a stable home, adequate healthcare coverage, access to effective mental health and substance use treatment, harm reduction resources, drug education, healthy food, living wages, family supports, and so much more. We should create conditions in our communities so that more people who use any drugs can live fulfilling lives.

Drug Exceptionalism Fuels Stigma and Punishment

When cultures affirm drug binaries and "exceptionalize" certain drugs, they marginalize and stigmatize the people who use other unacceptable drugs. This is because we are often told that only a bad or immoral person would choose to use illegal street drugs like methamphetamine, heroin, or crack cocaine. Since these drugs are not culturally sanctioned for any reason, people who use them are subject to social stigmas which can have varied and often harmful effects on their well-being, such as shame and guilt. Social stigma can often lead everyday people to develop prejudices or biases against people who use other drugs because they are wrongly seen as untrustworthy, deceptive, and deviant. This can then lead to discrimination in settings such as healthcare and employment because they are seen as dishonest patients or unreliable employees. It also leads members of the public to support harsher and punitive policies to address these so-called deviant people's substance use. It can also make the public less understanding of why these people deserve access to harm reduction, housing, and other supports. Taken together, stigma against illegal drug use can lead to compounding harms for people who use drugs because it can negatively impact their ability to meet their basic needs and get the help they may need.

Ultimately, the stigmatization of these drugs also justifies punishing and excluding entire groups of people in society because of their choice of drug. In this way, what many incorrectly view as a moral issue is transformed into a criminal issue. This often makes the public more likely to support tougher drug policies and harsher penalties that they believe will reduce the availability of those drugs. As a result, the people who use those drugs face dire long-term consequences for their use, including years of incarceration and a lifelong criminal record, which carry the modern-day "mark" of stigma. People who have been criminalized for their drug use suffer innumerable lifelong individual, family, and community collateral consequences that can hold them back from progressing in life. For instance, a criminal record can show up on a background check when applying for a new job or as part of a housing application, can impact one's ability to gain a professional license in some fields, and can prevent someone from accessing public benefits such as cash assistance or food stamps to get back on their feet.

Taken together, stigma and drug exceptionalism go hand in hand, creating more harmful circumstances for people who use certain drugs and those with addictions by fueling hostility toward them and relegating them to the margins and the shadows.

Drug Exceptionalism Can Lead to Incremental Reforms

Marijuana and psychedelic drugs have become less stigmatized, and it has led to recent support for policy changes and reduced criminalization. Though there were many points when the "faces" of these drugs shifted, I have a distinct memory of the face of the little white girl Charlotte, who was featured in a 2013 CNN documentary because medical marijuana helped treat her seizures. And the diligent work of researchers and advocates to increase the evidence base for psychedelic-assisted treatment has provided thousands with the hope that their treatment-resistant depression or PTSD could be overcome. Many are now more open to seeing the medical uses of these drugs, especially for health concerns inadequately addressed by our current system.

Marijuana use is far more socially acceptable among adults as of this writing in 2023 than it was even a decade prior, and it started with states first decriminalizing possession, then expanding legal medical access, and a portion of states eventually allowing full adult access. More American adults have legal access to this drug than ever before, and they are using it for a variety of reasons. And now we are seeing new local and state policy reforms to decriminalize psychedelics and advance research into the potential therapeutic uses of these drugs. This is a positive step. Psychedelic policy victories should be celebrated and can help increase access to these drugs for those who could potentially benefit from them.

However, these drug-specific policy reforms are still limited. While marijuana arrests have dramatically decreased in states that enacted policy changes, they remain high nationally, since it is not fully legal in much of the country and police often use legal loopholes to disproportionately target Black people for possession charges. In fact, marijuana is still the top drug for which people are arrested across the country. And while psychedelic policy reforms are good, psychedelic users comprise a small portion of those criminalized for drug use so these policy changes will not reduce the criminal legal impact on the lives of as many people. Harm reductionists would encourage us to see psychedelic policy reform as a starting point to further drug policy reforms, rather than an endpoint. Even after these drugs are decriminalized and become FDA-approved treatments for certain conditions, hundreds of thousands of people will continue to face criminalization for using other drugs like heroin, cocaine, and methamphetamine. And it is those people who will remain at highest risk of overdose, because they will not have a regulated drug supply.

This is why harm reductionists caution us to avoid affirming drug exceptionalism by stopping only at drug-specific reforms, such as marijuana and individual psychedelic drugs, since it still leaves behind hundreds of thousands of people. Harm reductionists pose questions such as, whose interests are we advancing, and who are we neglecting? Who has the most to gain, and who will continue to lose? In what ways will these changes ensure that some get safety and others will continue to experience harm? So while these policy reforms can help some, we cannot stop until others are also protected from criminalization.

Harm reductionists reiterate that drug exceptionalism still gives our criminal legal system license to use drugs as a pretense to target and punish marginalized people, including low-income people and communities of color. And it allows the state to decide whose reasons for drug use are acceptable and whose reasons are illegitimate. Exempting only certain drugs for punishment still means that law enforcement officers can still use other drug-related charges or low-level charges to criminalize and punish people. This is why harm reductionists unanimously support all drug and paraphernalia decriminalization – that is, making possession a civil offense so it is treated like a parking ticket that does not lead to arrest or criminal charges on your record.

When Portugal decriminalized drugs in 2001 and Oregon did so in 2020, drug-related arrests dramatically dropped so that people who used any drugs, "hard" or "soft," were able to avoid punishment. Instead, people in Portugal were given the opportunity to meet with a dissuasion commission, i.e., a panel comprised of a combination of psychologists, social workers, physicians, or other health professionals, to talk about their drug use and whether they would like to access services, housing, or treatment. In Oregon, people are given a ticket for $100 that could be waived if they call a hotline to learn about what supports they could access if they need help to stay safe or stop using drugs, but also other services that could help. These policies were both passed while their governments also invested unprecedented funds into building out their harm reduction and treatment infrastructure, as well as funding other essential services like outreach, housing assistance, and employment support. We should look to these examples as policies that can help a broader range of people who use drugs to get support, rather than punishment.

Resisting Drug Exceptionalism

Drug exceptionalism is a social and cultural phenomenon. The problem with drug exceptionalism is that few of the lines we draw between drugs are grounded in brain chemistry or research on their effects. The distinctions we make are often entirely unrelated to the actual health risks posed by these drugs. Instead, our history has shown us that drug exceptionalism has been driven by racism, xenophobia, and social control – because people were stigmatized first for their differences, so that the drugs they were associated with began to carry that stigma as well. In all these cases, the idea of the prototypical user is often deeply intertwined with the opinions we have about the drug itself. And sometimes the views about the drug change if we notice that different people are using them.

What these changes should teach us is that all substances come with relative benefits and relative harms, regardless of whether they are culturally acceptable at a given moment or not. Just wait; it could all change. Harm reductionists remind us that all drugs carry risks; there truly are no exceptions. A drug's legality or social status is not a valid reason to exceptionalize it, and any person who chooses to use any drug or drug type should be armed with objective information about benefits and risks, whether they are using the newest cure-all medication or the most demonized drug in the headlines. Decisions about which drugs to exceptionalize and which to legalize are rarely based on objective metrics of safety. There was a time in my life when smoking cigarettes was normalized and even cool, while marijuana was seen as a counterculture drug used by dropouts, artists, and musicians. But today it is a drug that is widely accepted as being used by working professionals, grandparents, and patients with epilepsy or cancer.

Harm reductionists believe that adults have the right to alter their consciousness with drugs regardless of whether that drug is culturally acceptable at the moment. They also believe that people who use drugs should have access to the education, tools, and resources to make informed decisions about what they put into their bodies so that they can stay as safe as possible while experiencing the effects they seek. Harm reductionists recognize that users of all drugs seek different benefits and effects, and most people could benefit from support while trying to navigate the risks and reduce the potential harms of drug use. Harm reductionists are also clear-eyed that although all drugs carry risk, consumers of any substance have the right to use drugs of known quality and potency. Consumers of all drugs should all be informed and have access to a full continuum of services for support. This can happen only if we close the harm reduction gap.

Harm reductionists accept the reality that there will always be people who use psychoactive drugs in every community. This includes all of us, whether the drugs we use are deemed legal or illegal, whether they are prescribed or taken to self-medicate, whether they are for fun or to function, and whether they are perceived as "good" or "bad." Harm reductionists resist drug exceptionalism since it still perpetuates drug-related stigma and could still mean some are subject to criminalization.

Harm reductionists do not judge the desire to alter one's consciousness and, in fact, see it as normal and morally neutral human behavior. While consuming drugs is one way to change our perceptions and moods, there are many other behaviors people engage in that can affect how we think and feel, such as exercise, dance, creative arts, meditation, shopping, prayer, sex, and gambling.

Harm reductionists understand that our motivations are diverse, and our experiences can vary a great deal. Some people use drugs to alter their consciousness and shift perspective. Others want to get high and feel good. There are those who seek to enhance their performance and get an edge. Sometimes people want to self-soothe, dissociate, or go numb. Drugs can help elevate or stabilize mood, and they can quell pain. People around the world use drugs to socialize, let loose, and have fun. Drugs can enhance spiritual experiences and provide valuable insights. But harm reductionists do not believe that any one reason is more worthy or valid than any other. Some of us use drugs occasionally, some of us use frequently, and others have experimented in the past, or will one day in the future. Our motivations and frequency of drug use can also vary greatly from drug to drug. Most do not experience life-altering negative consequences and instead simply get the benefits they seek. Harm reductionists would like this to be the reality for all people who use drugs.

Drugs play a part of the lives of millions of people around the world every single day. And although many depictions of drug use in film and media often sensationalize or stigmatize certain forms of drug use to stoke fear or outrage, the reality for many people is that their drug use is a mundane and unremarkable part of their lives. Harm reductionists do not view drug use as a moral failing, or as a sign that drug users are lacking in character because of what they choose to put in their bodies. They do not view people who use drugs as being deficient or in need of rescuing. Most harm reductionists do not proclaim that people who use drugs have a spiritual or medical disease because of what they choose to put into their bodies. Harm reductionists also do not view drug use as a sign of so-called criminality or deviance, either.

People can live safe and fulfilling lives in a world with drugs, if armed with the proper tools and education. In fact, humans have been using various drugs for millennia and, in most cases, have long since developed strategies to help keep one another safe. Harm reductionists believe that we simply must promote those practices and expand their applications to help more people. While many of these strategies may seem like common sense, not all of us have been taught how to implement them in our lives. Some of us have learned through trial and error, and some of us could benefit from help or support as we try to put them into practice and decide which strategies work best for us. However, although regulated drugs and those deemed medications come with warning labels and recommended use, those who use banned drugs may have few reputable sources to turn to and are left to figure out these things on their own. And they deserve access to a safe supply of drugs too.

Harm reductionists recognize that we have always lived in a world with drugs, and drugs themselves are not going anywhere, despite efforts to ban, restrict, or stigmatize certain substances in this broad category. And, by living through the aftermath of policies passed to rid the world of certain drugs, we've learned that attempted crackdowns on the underground drug supply and drug trade only make us all less safe. Today, we see this happening in real time in the United States and around the world, as politicians and law enforcement try to convince us that a drug-free world is desirable and possible if we only spend more money and resources banning certain drugs and putting enough people behind bars. These misguided efforts create global instability and tensions, damage our environment, facilitate the development of a more potent and unpredictable drug supply, and force people who use and/or sell certain drugs farther into the margins. All the while, these resources could have been spent on regulatory regimes to oversee drug production and quality control, to fund rigorous scientific research on drug effects and harms, to expand social safety nets with treatment and harm reduction on demand, and to provide public education about drugs.

We should stop thinking about whether drugs are good or bad (or moral or immoral), and start considering the potential benefits and harms of drug *policies*. Good drug policies promote public education and safety around drugs, ensure that drug supplies are regulated for safety, and provide steady access to harm reduction services and treatments for those who want to get support or help; while bad policies do the opposite, making drug use more dangerous, punishing people for altering their consciousnesses, and ultimately driving countless people into the shadows to avoid detection and stigma. We don't have bad drugs in this country – we just have bad policies.

Harm reductionists question the foundation of our drug laws and believe that we must start from scratch if we want to take a new approach to drugs. The scheduling system was never developed on a careful evaluation of drug effects, and the decision to place it under the authority of a law enforcement entity rather than a health authority revealed that health was not a priority – it was meant to punish. A system that was developed 50 years ago or longer can be dismantled and reconstructed. It is never too late.

Notes

1 Although one may have some adulterants or be of unknown potency due to the underground manufacturing, while the other may not.
2 Substance Abuse and Mental Health Services Administration. *Key Substance Use and Mental Health Indicators in the United States: Results from the 2021 National Survey on Drug Use and Health* (HHS Publication No. PEP22-07-01-005, NSDUH Series H-57). Center for Behavioral Health Statistics and Quality, Substance Abuse and Mental Health Services Administration, 2022.

Index

Printed in the United States
by Baker & Taylor Publisher Services